An Apocalyptic History of the Early Fatimid Empire

EDINBURGH STUDIES IN ISLAMIC APOCALYPTICISM AND ESCHATOLOGY

This series features studies devoted to end-time expectations in Islam and the intellectual, social and political contexts in which they occur and become virulent, from the beginning of Islam until the twenty-first century. Concerning the apocalyptic aspect, the series is dedicated to investigating apocalypticism in Muslim thought and history: notions of the catalytic events ushering in the end of history, mahdism and other forms of (political and non-political) millenarianism. Eschatologically, studies in this series will examine traditions of imagining and reasoning about the hereafter: judgment, salvation, and reward and punishment in paradise and hell.

Series Editors
Professor David Cook (Rice University) and Professor Christian Lange (Utrecht University)

Editorial Advisory Board
Professor Abbas Amanat, Professor Fred Donner, Professor Jean-Pierre Filiu, Professor Yohanan Friedman, Professor Mercedes García-Arenal, Professor Mohammed Khalil, Professor Daniel De Smet and Professor Roberto Tottoli

Titles in the series

Eschatology in Classical Islamic Mysticism From the 9th to the 12th Centuries
Michael Ebstein

The World of Image in Islamic Philosophy: Ibn Sina, Suhrawardi, Shahrazuri and Beyond
L. W. C. van Lit

An Apocalyptic History of the Early Fatimid Empire
Jamel A. Velji

edinburghuniversitypress.com/series/ESIAE

An Apocalyptic History of the Early Fatimid Empire

Jamel A. Velji

EDINBURGH
University Press

Edinburgh University Press is one of the leading university presses in the UK. We publish academic books and journals in our selected subject areas across the humanities and social sciences, combining cutting-edge scholarship with high editorial and production values to produce academic works of lasting importance. For more information visit our website: edinburghuniversitypress.com

Edinburgh University Press Ltd
The Tun – Holyrood Road
12 (2f) Jackson's Entry
Edinburgh EH8 8PJ

Typeset in Cambria by
Servis Filmsetting Ltd, Stockport, Cheshire

A CIP record for this book is available from the British Library

ISBN 978 0 7486 9088 6 (hardback)
ISBN 978 0 7486 9089 3 (webready PDF)
ISBN 978 0 7486 9090 9 (epub)

Contents

Acknowledgements vii

Introducing Ismaili Apocalypses 1

1 From *ẓāhir* to *bāṭin*: An Introduction to Fatimid Hermeneutics 14

2 Oaths, Taxes and Tithes: Organising an Imminent Utopia 22

3 *Taʾwīl* of an Apocalyptic Transcript I: *The Book of Unveiling* 42

4 *Taʾwīl* of an Apocalyptic Transcript II: *The Book of Righteousness and True Guidance* 61

5 To Temper an Imminent Eschatology: The Contributions of al-Mahdī and Qāḍī l-Nuʿmān 75

6 A Spiritual Progression to a New Eschatological Centre: The *Taʾwīl al-daʿāʾim* on the Hajj 97

7 Actualising the End: The Nizari Declaration of the Resurrection 109

8 From Movement to Text: The *Haft-bāb* 123

Acknowledgements

It is a great delight to acknowledge the generosity of those who helped this project come to fruition.

Michael Sells, David Dawson and Anne McGuire initially cultivated my interest in the study of religion as an undergraduate at Haverford, and it was under the careful and inspiring guidance of Michael Sells that I wrote my undergraduate thesis on the Nizari declaration of the *qiyāma*. At McGill's Institute of Islamic Studies I had the pleasure of working with Eric Ormsby and A. Üner Turgay on matters apocalyptic and Islamic. At the University of California at Santa Barbara I benefitted from the outstanding guidance of Richard Hecht, a model mentor who gave me the tools to call myself a religionist. As I train my own students I continue to draw on his wisdom and that of my other UCSB committee members: Stephen Humphreys, Racha El-Omari, and Christine Thomas. Ahmad Ahmad, Rudy Busto, Mark Juergensmeyer, Stefania Tutino, and Thomas Carlson were always generous with their advice and their time, as was Sally Lombrozo, who somehow ensured that all of us were right on track.

I had the great fortune of spending a very fruitful year at the University of Toronto working with Todd Lawson. Professor Lawson encouraged my interest in Shia apocalypticism, suggesting that I take a closer look at the *Kitāb al-kashf*. My work with him over the course of that year was formative for my thinking and I am grateful that he was able to serve as an external member of my dissertation committee.

At the Institute of Ismaili Studies in London, I had the pleasure of discussing an iteration of my project with the many scholars there: Professors Farhad Daftary, Delia Cortese, Nader El-Bizri, Aziz Esmail, Azim Nanji, Rashida and Faquir Hunzai, Omar Alí-de-Unzaga and Professor Eric Ormsby. Professor Michael Brett from SOAS was also incredibly generous with his keen insights. At a wonderful conference on Islamic eschatology in Germany, Professor Hermann Landolt provided exceptional organisational advice. Professors Fred Donner and Carel Bertram patiently listened to a description of the project and also offered their valuable suggestions. Professors Jonathan Bloom and Sheila Blair helped me to sharpen the focus of this project. Professor Ali Asani kindly invited me to present my work in progress to his class on Ismaili history and thought at Harvard University. The Goldberg family, Rebecca Mackenzie, and Benjamin Martinez were instrumental with this book's cover design. Professor Ismail Poonawala kindly read through the entire manuscript and offered excellent feedback.

Along with Racha El-Omari, Andrew Lane and Himmet Taskomur deserve special thanks for their Arabic language training, which was crucial in helping me to decipher the complexities of Ismaili texts. Alnoor Dhanani meticulously reviewed the translations in this book. It was a great pleasure to work with him on this project.

During my return to Haverford College as a faculty member, I benefitted tremendously from the advice of my departmental colleagues: David Dawson, Tracey Hucks, Terrence Johnson, Anne McGuire, Ken and Naomi Koltun-Fromm, and Travis Zadeh. James Gulick provided very helpful support for research and teaching, and Rob Haley located many difficult to obtain sources. Members of the Provost's Office helped to facilitate research and teaching at the College, especially Arpi Harnett, Julie Sheehan, Susan Penn, Lisa Griffin, Wendy Sternberg, Rob Fairman, Judy Young, and Fran Blase.

One of the benefits of working in the Tri-College consortium is the opportunity for intellectual exchange across campuses. The department of Religion at Swarthmore College has become a familiar place, and I am grateful to have benefitted from the advice of members of that outstanding department, in particular Tariq al-Jamil, Stephen Hopkins, and Ellen Ross. Our annual colloquium also facilitated the visits of Shahzad Bashir and Bruce Lincoln, two scholars whose work has had a tremendous influence on my own.

I am tremendously grateful to Cristina Fuller for her keen editorial eye and dedication in seeing this project to fruition; to Valerie Joy Turner for her exceptional edits and for taking on this project in the midst of so many others; to Nicola Ramsey and other members of the editorial staff at Edinburgh University Press; and to the series editors, Christian Lange and David Cook. Christian in particular deserves special thanks for reading through the entire manuscript in great detail and providing such detailed feedback with characteristic precision and generosity.

I am delighted to embark upon a new academic adventure at Claremont McKenna College, and am grateful to my colleagues in the Department of Religious Studies here, Esther Chung-Kim, Stephen Davis, Gaston Espinosa, Gary Gilbert, Cynthia Humes and Dan Michon, for their incisive questions and comments on this project. They and many other members of the CMC and wider Claremont community have been very welcoming and supportive.

Financial support for this project was provided by the US Department of Education (Javits and FLAS Fellowships); the Social Science and Humanities Research Council of Canada; the UCSB Interdisciplinary Humanities Center; the Institute of Ismaili Studies, London; the Josephine de Kármán Fellowship Trust; the Provost's Office at Haverford College, and the Dean's Office at Claremont McKenna College. I am grateful for their support.

I am grateful for the guidance and friendship of Elizabeth Alexandrin and Michael Jerryson who helped me think through various aspects of this project; Randy Ko for providing a consistent supply of delicious coffee; Anthony Distinti for his always wise council; to Omid Ghaemmaghami for stimulating conversations related to Shiism and its study; and to Benji, Barbara, Adam and Susan Green for adopting us as family on the East Coast.

I thank Jeremy Steinberg, Lindsey Palmer, and Alison Marqusee for providing valuable comments on portions of an earlier draft of this book and I thank my former students at Haverford and UCSB for so many wonderful conversations.

My family has provided boundless support throughout this endeavour. Special thanks are due to my parents, Anvar and Pari Velji, who have done so much for me, and have modelled what hard work and service to humanity are all about. My brother, Badier Velji, deserves thanks for perennial enthusiasm. My wife Chloe Martinez possesses superhuman tolerance for my tendency to be caught up in my work and somehow also continues to be nothing but encouraging, funny and boundlessly optimistic. I thank her and our daughter Amina (and now her new sister Saafia) for their support.

For my family and my teachers

Introducing Ismaili Apocalypses

This is a book about apocalypticism, a mode of religiosity so powerful and generative that it has been implicated in a variety of major events across geographies and time periods. Apocalypticism played a significant role in the rise of major religious traditions such as Christianity[1] and Islam.[2] It is inexorably intertwined with the 'founding' of the Americas[3] and more recently has been channelled destructively in horrific acts of violence, including the Holocaust.[4] As a religionist, I am fascinated by the nature of apocalypticism – its mythic framework and how it is deployed to effect social transformations. This long-standing interest has led me to investigate a host of related questions. How, for instance, are apocalyptic predictions made and then reinterpreted? Who makes these predictions and where does their authority come from? How do apocalyptic orators describe heaven and hell or the damned and the saved? Why do people believe them? How does time function in apocalyptic contexts? And perhaps most importantly for this study, how does apocalypticism, despite its spectacular failure rate, not only endure, but operate to continuously reorder societies across geographies and cultures?

The rich global history of apocalypticism has been well documented.[5] Yet in the Islamic context – where apocalypticism figures quite prominently – only a handful of studies exist on the subject.[6]

These works – many of which are outstanding – reflect the disciplinary conventions of Islamic studies and tend to focus on specific intellectual, philological or historical trends rather than addressing wider social and theoretical questions concerning the nature of apocalypticism more broadly. This book is an attempt to address some of these wider questions using sources from an empire that was, like so many other movements in Islamic history, brought to power on the heels of an apocalyptic revolution. It examines how rulers of the Fatimid Empire (909–1171) used apocalyptic imagery to establish and maintain a substantial empire in North Africa.

Fatimid revolutionary activity capitalised on the question of Shia leadership after the disappearance of the twelfth *imām* in 874. From this political vacuum emerged a secret society claiming that the Shia *mahdī*[7] was at hand. Representatives of this *mahdī* paid special attention to converting politically marginalised communities, particularly in present-day Tunisia and Morocco; those who converted to Ismailism were told that they were the divine's chosen instruments, entrusted with restoring the leadership of the Muslim community to its rightful custodians, the Shia *imāms*.[8] Like many other apocalyptic movements, the Fatimids employed esoteric interpretation of scripture (*ta'wīl*), a religious hierarchy and apocalyptic expectation to consolidate power and build legitimacy. They succeeded in establishing a substantial empire, in the process founding the city of Cairo in 969. While scholars have acknowledged that apocalypticism served as a motivating force for revolution and the establishment of the state,[9] there remains little scholarship on what this apocalypticism actually looked like. First, what were some of the structures of this apocalypticism that helped convince people to join this movement? And second, what were the rhetorical methods that the Fatimids used to reinterpret the imminence of the end of time while simultaneously building a successful empire?

These questions – concerning the anatomy of apocalyptic propaganda, its persuasive force and the hermeneutics of its reinterpretation – are questions that have cross cultural and contemporary relevance. To briefly cite three examples: messianic or apocalyptic rhetoric appeared in the 2008 American presidential election of Barack Obama, in which supporters labelled him the messiah and his detractors called him the Antichrist (or the representative of the Antichrist). In 2011, Harold Camping recruited thousands of supporters across the country based on his calculations concerning the imminent end of time (twice); and globally we have recently witnessed predictions of the Mayan apocalypse. These predictions have come and gone – the world is still here – but apocalypticism endures: through a study of the Fatimids I wish to posit why this might be the case.

Addressing these questions from the Fatimid perspective has a number of advantages: the Fatimid vision of Islam represents an interpretation of Islam that is not widely known outside of the world of specialists in Islamic studies; there are various Muslim communities today, numbering in the millions, who lay claim to a Fatimid lineage and for whom the Fatimid tradition is very much alive in shaping communal memory; and while much scholarly work on apocalypticism has been conducted outside the Islamic tradition, there are only a handful of studies focusing on apocalypticism within the Islamic tradition. Thus this cross disciplinary engagement not only enriches religious studies with material from the Islamic tradition, it also infuses the study of Islam with perspectives and methods from other fields – heeding a call that many Islamicists have been making for decades.[10]

There is another more pragmatic reason for studying the Fatimids: we possess a wealth of extant materials from this period – from material culture such as numismatic evidence,[11] to art and architecture,[12] to texts such as historical records and theological works.[13] In addressing our tripartite issues of apocalyptic imminence, reinterpretation and relationship with authority, Fatimid theological texts are quite rich in evidence. It is these texts therefore that will serve as our chief subjects of study. As we will soon discover most of these texts are works of *ta'wīl* (symbolic or esoteric interpretation) that bring us into the world of the unseen, the world that only the initiated or elect can perceive. And while this hermeneutical method was certainly not unique to Fatimid exegesis – we see *ta'wīl* in Sufi and Twelver Shia works as well, for instance – Fatimid exegesis is remarkable for its creativity, its ability to synthesise and integrate an eclectic range of interpretive modalities into its form.[14] This book examines three works of *ta'wīl* in detail: the *Kitāb al-rushd wa-l-hidāya* (Book of righteousness and true guidance), attributed to Ibn Ḥawshab (d. 914), the *Kitāb al-kashf* (Book of unveiling) attributed to his son Jaʿfar b. Manṣūr al-Yaman (d. c. 957), and the *Ta'wīl al-daʿā'im* (Esoteric interpretation of the pillars of Islam) by Qāḍī l-Nuʿmān (d. 974). Each of these works was penned by an influential member of the Fatimid hierarchy. The first two texts concern the anticipation of the *mahdī* as it relates to the Fatimid revolution and provide us with insights into the interplay between the dissemination of hidden knowledge and preparation for the *mahdī*'s advent, while the latter illustrates some of the hermeneutics of this reinterpretation.

The *Kitāb al-kashf*, for instance, reinterprets the Quranic narrative through *ta'wīl* to construct new meaning, framing the eschatological figure's imminent arrival as the definition of utopia itself.[15] The dualities undergirding the Quranic narrative[16] become refashioned here as well. They become refracted through the prism of *walāya*, a term connoting spiritual inheritance, divine friendship and love for the *imām*.[17] Those who do not possess *walāya* for the proper religious authority – here the Fatimid *mahdī* – can never obtain salvation. The refashioning of the Quranic narrative through *ta'wīl* makes the preservation of secret knowledge – as well as absolute obedience to the *mahdī*'s cause – true Islam. For those who believe in this true cause the revolution signals nothing other than an imminent and permanent restoration of true leadership of the community to its rightful custodians, the Shia *imāms*, as well as the vindication and eternal salvation of the oppressed throughout history.

As the Fatimids translated expectations of the *mahdī* into a successful empire, this imminence had to be reinterpreted. *Ta'wīl* once again served as a vehicle for expressing narratives linking theology and history. Here I examine the *Ta'wīl al-daʿā'im*, the esoteric analogue to a book of Fatimid laws penned by one of the most important ideological architects of the Fatimid Empire, Qāḍī l-Nuʿmān. The *Ta'wīl al- daʿā'im* is remarkable for a number of reasons, not the least of which is that it illustrates how the *ta'wīl* of regularly performed rituals such as Friday prayers and fasting during the month of Ramadan tell a deeper story of the messianic figure's new place in sacred history.

Other Fatimid authors, those contemporary to al-Nuʿmān and those who came after him, spent much time writing about the eschatological figure of the *mahdī*, indicating that the apocalyptic and messianic impulse was very much alive and in some cases difficult to contain. Indeed messianic claims and counter claims punctuated early Fatimid history, finding powerful expressions in events such as the rebellion of Abū Yazīd, a Khārajī who invaded the capitol city of al-Mahdiyya in 332/943, and in the founding of the Druze tradition in 1017 during the reign of al-Ḥākim. While this book does not trace the rich apocalyptic history of these or other Fatimid-era movements, it does examine in detail another major apocalyptic event in Ismaili history: the Nizari declaration of the *qiyāma* or resurrection. In a dramatic event that took place on 8 August 1164, the leader of the Nizari Ismaili community publicly declared the *qiyāma*, signalling the end of the world. Through an examination of ritual and textual evidence from the period, I argue that the *qiyāma* was a potent manifestation of apocalypticism that served to powerfully reify a major shift in the leadership of the Nizari community.

The application of the terms 'apocalyptic' or 'apocalypticism' to a modality of religiosity operating outside the Christian context will no doubt cause some readers pause. This is understandable, as the interdisciplinary study of apocalypticism remains constrained by the concept's continued tethering to its theological and disciplinary origins. To cite but one example: the editors of the invaluable three-volume *Encyclopaedia of Apocalypticism* state that apocalypticism is a recent term which 'refers to the complex of ideas associated with the New Testament Apocalypse,' especially the imminent end of the world and its associated events. They state that the term is multivalent – it 'is an analogous term, and it admits of different emphases.' The editors write: 'In these volumes we have not attempted to impose a strict definition, but rather to include a broad range of materials that may be regarded as apocalyptic in various senses.'[18] While the editors allow for definitional latitude – indeed, the volume contains essays on everything from contemporary secular apocalypticism to apocalypticism in the classical Islamic context – the paradigmatic apocalypse still appears to be the textual and theological Book of Revelation. This paradigmatic apocalyptic construct has also influenced scholarship on apocalypses in the Islamic tradition.[19]

Following the work of religionist Bruce Lincoln, I consider apocalypticism not as a theological category but as a type of myth, a mode of authoritative discourse by which actors may construct society through the evocation of certain sentiments.[20] Using data from Christian traditions, Stephen O'Leary has shown that time, evil and authority constitute the three 'essential topoi of apocalyptic discourse.'[21] Examining apocalypticism as a mythic construct whose rhetorical force is mediated by certain topoi allows us to consider diachronically the evolving structures of Fatimid apocalypticism with a concomitant concern for the persuasive aims of this discourse. To capture the apocalyptic narratives embedded in these works, I focus on reading my sources with a modified conception of O'Leary's topoi in mind, particularly on discussions of temporality; descriptions of the identity and advent of the eschatological figure; and correlations between the construction of communal boundaries with depictions of heaven and hell. In casting such a wide taxonomical net for apocalyptic phenomena, I frequently use a number of terms interchangeably throughout this work – in particular apocalypse, apocalypticism and mahdism.

This rhetoric-based analysis of apocalyptic data has a number of advantages. First, it allows us to consider the various media through which apocalyptic sentiments are conveyed: whether that is through numismatic materials, rituals, theological texts or sermons. This more composite view of apocalypticism allows us to gain a fuller picture of not only how the phenomenon was expressed but also how it evolved. Second, this approach allows us to interface our findings with wider conversations occurring in the field of religious studies. Much work has been done on the nature of apocalyptic prophecy and the hermeneutics of reinterpretation outside the Islamic context.[22] It is hoped that this book will encourage new comparative trajectories between various iterations of Islamic apocalyptic movements as well as between these movements and those outside the tradition. Third, these comparative trajectories allow us to contribute this data to our understanding of major theoretical questions in the field of religious studies. Here my study of Fatimid and Nizari materials advances our knowledge of the ways in which apocalyptic discourse may help to reorder the premises of authority within a society – a theme that is developed throughout this study. Reflecting upon my Fatimid and Nizari data as a means through which I may make wider claims about the category of apocalypticism and its constituent elements mirrors the methodological approach articulated by historians of religion such as Jonathan Z. Smith and Thomas Tweed concerning the category of religion itself.[23] Both Smith and Tweed stress the responsibility religionists have in reflecting upon how their own data may help to shape our understanding of the wider category of religion. Hence, here I use Fatimid and Nizari materials to broaden our understanding of the category of apocalypticism.

The production of any piece of scholarly work involves a set of choices that inevitably results in 'necessary violence'[24] to one's subject of study. My choice to situate primary source material within a wider set of questions related to the study of religion while retaining some of the disciplinary conventions of Ismaili studies – particularly an emphasis on philology and intellectual history – results in work that continues to privilege a historical version of an official theology. In this case, it is the history of a particular myth: a history of early Fatimid apocalyptic deployment. Second and once again resulting from disciplinary legacy, this study also perpetuates the reification of the categories 'Ismailism' or 'Fatimid'. In reality this was a dynamic identity whose boundaries were often quite diffuse. In fact some of these same apocalyptic tropes were shared by other early Shia communities. A major question for a future study would involve examining how some of these same tropes may have been interpreted differently by other Shia groups.[25] Fourth, while this study does illuminate certain aspects of Fatimid apocalypticism, it cannot make claims about what is distinctive about the phenomenon. A fuller study of the discrete elements of Fatimid apocalypticism would involve an examination of a wider sample of materials from the period along with an elucidation of similarities and differences between these materials and materials from other apocalyptically charged movements in Islamic history.

Finally a note about sources. Fatimid *ta'wīl* poses a particular set of challenges for those who study it. *Ta'wīl* – an esoteric mode of scriptural interpretation that can only be performed by certain individuals – represents a modality of religiosity that is at once mystical and political, poetic and ephemeral. As we see it is not uncommon for authors of *ta'wīl* to produce scriptural interpretations that have a multiplicity of symbolic referents for the same term or verse of the Quran.[26] This multiplicity points to the potency of *ta'wīl* as a mode of mystical exegesis, a point that Henry Corbin has made in a number of his works.[27] Scholars have also recently pointed out the importance of *ta'wil*'s correlate, secrecy, as a means of communal boundary making.[28] While scholarly discussions of *ta'wīl* as a mode of exegesis are in their infancy, an examination of the ways in which various authors address, through *ta'wīl*, iterations of the apocalyptic construct allows us greater insight into the inner workings of this particular mode of exegesis. To allow the non-specialist reader access to this highly complex world, I have chosen to include translations of large portions of previously untranslated texts.

This book is divided into eight chapters. The first chapter provides the reader with a brief introduction to early Shia hermeneutics and the theology of the Fatimids. Chapter 2 discusses the myriad ways in which Fatimid mahdist expectation was tied to the crafting of utopia, particularly through rituals of oath-taking and tithing. Chapters 3 and 4 provide a detailed textual analysis of the *Kitāb al-kashf* and the *Kitāb al-rushd*. I read these texts not only as examples of *ta'wīl* and early Fatimid apocalyptic rhetoric, but also as a means of elucidating connections between apocalypticism and early Fatimid authority. Ultimately I argue that these authors' *ta'wīl* of Quranic visions of the end of time helped to provide potent symbolic currency for the rise of the Fatimid caliph-imams.

Like all apocalyptically charged religious movements, expectations tied to the imminent end had to be reinterpreted when the apocalypse failed to arrive. Chapter 5 examines a key document related to the hermeneutics of reinterpretation: the caliph al-Mahdī's letter to his Yemeni community that outlines his relationship to the eschatological *mahdī*. I then explore, through an extensive discussion of Qāḍī l-Nuʿmān's *Taʾwīl al-daʿāʾim*, the interplay between *taʾwīl* and Fatimid reinterpretations of the arrival of this eschatological figure. There I show how al-Nuʿmān's *taʾwīl* of various rituals, which so often related to the eschatological figure, helped to decouple mahdist expectation from a linear temporality while maintaining apocalypticism's overall theological importance in narratives of Fatimid sacred history. Chapter 6 focuses in detail on al-Nuʿmān's *taʾwīl* of the hajj, and argues that his symbolic interpretation helped to devise a spiritual itinerary to a new eschatological centre.

If the Fatimid case reflects apocalypticism's ability to bring an empire to power, then the Nizari declaration of the end of time reflects apocalypticism's ability to chart a new trajectory for a religious tradition. Chapter 7 moves us forward in time two-and-a-half centuries and westward more than 1,000 miles, from North Africa to the fortress of Alamut about sixty miles from present-day Tehran, to another major apocalyptic event in Ismaili history: the declaration of the *qiyāma* or resurrection made by Ḥasan *ʿalā dhikrihi al-salām* on 8 August 1164. An analysis of the context from which Ḥasan's declaration emerges shows us that his declaration cannot be dismissed as an aberrant manifestation of Islamic antinomianism. Rather we see here how apocalypticism emerges as an elegant solution to two particular logistical problems facing the Nizari community: a prolonged stalemate against the Seljuks and the prolonged physical absence of the *imām*. Through an examination of the *Haft-bāb*, a text recounting that event, chapter 8 shows how Ḥasan's declaration, commensurate with Quranic and Ismaili expectations concerning divine disclosure at the end of time, inaugurated a new phase of history in which all becomes apparent. This divine disclosure included new soteriological practices that required seekers to recognise Ḥasan and his progeny in their true spiritual form. This declaration became a vital means for communal restructuring, inaugurating a newly dynamic and distinctively Persianate phase of Ismailism. The concluding chapter of this book explores in more detail the theoretical features of Fatimid and Nizari apocalypticism using our case studies to reflect more broadly on the relationship between apocalypticism and authority.

Notes

1. For an introduction to Jewish and Early Christian apocalyptic texts, see work by D. S. Russell, in particular his *Divine Disclosure* (Minneapolis, MN: Fortress Press, 2007 [1992]). See also work by John J. Collins, in particular *The Apocalyptic Imagination: An Introduction to Jewish Apocalyptic Literature*, 2nd edn (Grand Rapids, MI: Wm. B. Eerdmans Publishing Co., 1998). The social context of early Christian apocalypticism is discussed by scholars such as Richard Horsely and Scott Hanson in *Bandits, Prophets, and Messiahs: Popular Movements in the Time of Jesus* (Minneapolis, MN: Seabury, 1985); and by Dale Allison in his *Jesus of Nazareth: Millenarian Prophet* (Minneapolis, MN: Augsburg Press, 1998).
2. For a discussion of the apocalyptic ethos of the Quran, see Michael A. Sells, *Approaching the Qur'ān* (Ashland, OR: Whitecloud Press, 1999 [2007]); Todd Lawson, 'Duality, Opposition and Typology in the Qur'an: The Apocalyptic Substrate', *Journal of Qur'anic Studies* 10 (2008), pp. 23–49; Toshihiku Izutsu, *Ethico-Religious Concepts in the Qur'ān* (Montreal: McGill-Queen's University Press, 2002 [1966]). For a discussion of the social framework of early Islamic apocalypticism, see Fred M. Donner, *Muhammad and the Believers* (Cambridge, MA: Harvard University Press, 2010); and Stephen J. Shoemaker, *The Death of a Prophet* (Philadelphia: University of Pennsylvania Press, 2012).
3. For a discussion of Christopher Columbus's apocalyptic theology see *The Book of Prophecies, Edited by Christopher Columbus*, ed. Roberto Rusconi, trans. Blair Sullivan (Berkeley: University of California Press, 1997); Leonard I. Sweet, 'Christopher Columbus and the Millennial Vision of the New World', *Catholic Historical Review*, vol. 72, no. 3 (July 1986), pp. 369–82; and Carol Delaney, *Columbus and the Quest for Jersualem* (New York: Free Press, 2012). For a history of apocalyptic prophecy in the United

States, see Paul Boyer, *When Time Shall be No More* (Cambridge, MA and London: Belknap Press, 1992).

4. See, for instance, David Redles, *Hitler's Millennial Reich* (New York: New York University Press, 2005). On apocalypticism and violence more generally, see Catherine Wessinger, *How the Millennium Comes Violently* (New York: Seven Bridges Press, 2000); Mark Juergensmeyer, *Terror in the Mind of God* (Berkeley and Los Angeles: University of California Press, 2000 [2003]); and various essays in the *Oxford Handbook of Religion and Violence* (New York: Oxford University Press, 2013), including Michael A. Sells, 'Armageddon in Christian, Sunni and Shia Traditions', pp. 467–95, and my 'Apocalyptic Religion and Violence', pp. 250–9 in the same volume.
5. Two recent overviews include John R. Hall, *Apocalypse* (Malden, MA: Polity Press, 2009); and Richard Landes, *Heaven on Earth* (New York: Oxford University Press, 2011). See also Bernard McGinn, John J. Collins, and Stephen J. Stein (eds), *Encyclopedia of Apocalypticism* (New York: Continuum, 1998); Jerry L. Walls (ed.), *Oxford Handbook of Millennialism* (New York: Oxford University Press, 2010).
6. See, for instance, David Cook, *Studies in Muslim Apocalyptic* (Princeton, NJ: Darwin Press, 2002); Mercedes García-Arenal (ed.), *Mahdism et millénarisme en Islam, Revue des Mondes musulmanes et de la Méditerranée* (Aix-en-Provence: Éditions Édisud, 2000), and *Messianism and Puritanical Reform: Mahdis of the Muslim West* (Leiden: Brill, 2006); Jane Olaf-Blitchfield, *Early Mahdism: Politics and Religion in the Formative Period of Islam* (Leiden: Brill, 1985); Abdulaziz Sachedina, *Islamic Messianism: The Idea of the Mahdi in Twelver Shiism* (Albany: State University of New York Press, 1981); Shahzad Bashir, *Fazlallah Astarabadi and the Hurufis* (New York: Oneworld, 2005), and *Messianic Hopes and Mystical Visions* (Columbia: University of South Carolina Press, 2003); and Jean-Pierre Filiu, *Apocalypse in Islam*, trans. M. B. DeBevoise (Berkeley: University of California Press, 2011).
7. Wilfred Madelung, 'al-Mahdī', *Encyclopaedia of Islam*, second edition, ed. P. Bearman et al. (Leiden: Brill, 1960–2005). See also Bashir, *Messianic Hopes*, pp. 1–28.
8. Michael Brett, *The Rise of the Fatimids* (Leiden: Brill, 2001), pp. 85–6.
9. Brett, *Rise*; Farhad Daftary, *The Ismāʿīlīs*, 2nd edn (Cambridge: Cambridge University Press, 2007 [1990]); Heinz Halm, *The Empire of the Mahdī: The Rise of the Fatimids*, trans. Michael Bonner (Leiden: Brill, 1996).

10. See, for instance, Richard Martin (ed.), *Approaches to Islam in Religious Studies* (Tucson: University of Arizona Press, 1985); Carl W. Ernst and Richard C. Martin, *Rethinking Islamic Studies: From Orientalism to Cosmopolitanism* (Columbia: University of South Carolina Press, 2010), pp. 1–19; Carl W. Ernst, *Following Muhammad* (Chapel Hill: University of North Carolina Press, 2003), p. 56.
11. Norman D. Nicol, *A Corpus of Fāṭimid Coins* (Trieste: G. Bernardi, 2006).
12. Irene A. Bierman, *Writing Signs: The Fatimid Public Text* (Berkeley: University of California Press, 1998); Jonathan M. Bloom, *Arts of the City Victorious* (New Haven, CT and London: Yale University Press in association with the Institute of Ismaili Studies, 2007).
13. Farhad Daftary, *Ismaili Literature: A Bibliography of Sources and Studies* (London: I. B. Tauris, 2004); Paul E. Walker, *Exploring an Islamic Empire: Fatimid History and Its Sources* (London: I. B. Tauris, 2002).
14. See, for instance, David Hollenberg, 'Disrobing Judges with Veiled Truths: An Early Ismāʿīlī Torah Interpretation (*taʾwīl*) in Service of the Fāṭimid Mission', *Religion* 33 (2003), pp. 127–45; his 'Interpretation after the End of Days: The Fāṭimid-Ismāʿīlī tāʾwīl (interpretation) of Jaʿfar ibn Manṣūr al-Yaman (d. ca. 960)' (PhD diss., University of Pennsylvania, 2006); and Paul E. Walker, *Early Philosophical Shiism* (New York: Cambridge University Press, 1993), pp. 145–56.
15. Jaʿfar b. Manṣūr al-Yaman, *Kitāb al-kashf*, ed. Muṣṭafā Ghālib (Beirut: Dār al-Andalus, 1984).
16. Lawson, 'Duality'.
17. Maria Massi Dakake, *The Charismatic Community: Shiʿite Identity in Early Islam* (Albany: State University of New York Press, 2007), pp. 16–31.
18. Collins, McGinn and Stein (eds), *Encyclopedia of Apocalypticism*, p. viii.
19. See, for instance, Cook, *Studies*, p. 9.
20. Bruce Lincoln, *Discourse and the Construction of Society* (New York: Oxford University Press, 1989), p. 25.
21. O'Leary continues, '. . . and that this discourse functions as a symbolic theodicy, a mythical and rhetorical solution intended to "solve" the problem of evil through its discursive construction of temporality.' Stephen D. O'Leary, *Arguing the Apocalypse* (New York: Oxford University Press, 1994), p. 20.
22. See, for instance, the classic by Leon Festinger, Henry Riecken, and Stanley Schacter, *When Prophecy Fails* (Minneapolis: University of

Minnesota Press, 1956); and subsequent scholarship refuting or modifying Festinger's thesis, including the essays in Jon R. Stone (ed.), *Expecting Armageddon: Essential Readings in Failed Prophecy* (New York: Routledge, 2000); and Diana Tumminia, *When Prophecy Never Fails: Myth and Reality in a Flying-Saucer Group* (New York: Oxford University Press, 2005).

23. Jonathan Z. Smith, 'Religion, Religions, Religious', in *Critical Terms for Religious Studies* (Chicago: University of Chicago Press, 1998); Thomas Tweed, *Crossing and Dwelling* (Cambridge, MA: Harvard University Press, 2006), p. 53.
24. Shahzad Bashir, comments made during visit to Haverford and Swarthmore Colleges, 1 November 2012.
25. An excellent introduction to this literature is Meir M. Bar-Asher's *Scripture and Exegesis in Early Imāmī Shiism* (Leiden: Brill, 1999).
26. Ismail K. Poonawala, 'Ismāʿīlī *ta'wīl* of the Qur'ān', in *Approaches to the History of the Interpretation of the Qur'ān*, ed. Andrew Rippin (New York: Oxford University Press, 1988).
27. See, for instance, Henry Corbin, *Trilogie ismaélienne* (Paris: Verdier, 1994); and his 'Sabian Temple and Ismailism', in *Temple and Contemplation*, trans. Philip Sherrard and Liadain Sherrard (London: Kegan Paul International in association with Islamic Publications, 1983), pp. 132–82.
28. Maria Dakake, 'Hiding in Plain Sight: The Practical and Doctrinal Significance of Secrecy in Shiʿite Islam', *Journal of the American Academy of Religion* 74.2 (2006): pp. 324–55; see also her *Charismatic Community*; Michael Ebstein, 'Secrecy in Ismāʿīlī Tradition and in the Mystical Thought of Ibn al-ʿArabī', *Journal Asiatique* 298.2 (2010): pp. 303–43.

1

From *ẓāhir* to *bāṭin*: An Introduction to Fatimid Hermeneutics

Key to understanding the ways in which Fatimid apocalypticism was deployed in the construction and maintenance of empire is a discussion of some of the differences between Sunni and Shia hermeneutical methods. One of the major distinctions is that the early Shia emphasised the distinctions between the literal (*ẓāhir*) and hidden (*bāṭin*) meanings of the Quranic text. The Quran itself acknowledges that some of its verses are clear and others are equivocal:

> *He it is Who has revealed the Book to you; some of its verses are decisive* (muḥkamāt), *they are the basis of the Book, and others are equivocal* (mutashābihāt)*; then as for those in whose hearts there is perversity they follow the part of it which is equivocal, seeking to mislead and seeking to give it (their own) interpretation* (taʾwīl). *But none knows its interpretation except God, and those who are firmly rooted in knowledge* (al rāsikhūn fī l-ʿilm) *say: We believe in it, it is all from our Lord; and none do mind except those having understanding* (3:7).[1]

Many Sunni interpreters place a period after 'God'; the verse then reads, '*But none knows its interpretation except God. And those who are firmly rooted in knowledge* (al-rāsikhūn fī l-ʿilm) *say: We believe in it, it is all from our Lord; and none do mind except those having understanding.*' The meaning of these equivocal verses is, then, inaccessible to humans. The Shia, on the other hand, do not place any punctuation after 'God' so that the verse reads, '*But none knows its interpretation except God and those who are firmly rooted in knowledge*,' the *rāsikhūn fī l-ʿilm*, who, according to Shia thought, are the Prophet Muḥammad and the *imāms*.[2]

Multivalent Quranic interpretation became a staple of Shia hermeneutics. Fused to the presence of these equivocal verses was the necessity that those 'firmly rooted in knowledge' interpret them. While the development of Shia *taʾwīl* and *tafsīr* (exegesis) lies far beyond this discussion, it should be noted that in the Shia system, the meanings of equivocal verses are known only to God and His elect.

The early Ismaili system further developed this fundamental distinction between hidden and apparent meanings. The process of *taʾwīl*, derived from the root *a/w/l*, means to return to the origin, not simply the esoteric interpretation of the text, but the *ḥaqīqa*, or eternal truth, embedded within that *bāṭin*. 'The complement of *taʾwīl* is *tanzīl*, that is the part of revelation that defines the formal aspects of religious life, the vessels within which the truths are contained.'[3] *Tanzīl* is then the literal revelation within which the *bāṭin* and the *ḥaqīqa* are found.

The process of making meaning – the manufacturing of symbolic structures, their investment with meaning and their dissemination – was theoretically the *imāms*' exclusive purview. To submit to *taʾwīl* was not only an acknowledgement of the presence of this symbolic realm but was also the most intimate expression of devotion one could have for the exegete. Through this intimate devotion to the exegesis of one's personal religion comes a communal acknowledgment, in turn, of the necessity of the presence of the exegete. The act of *taʾwīl* is an acceptance, an act of submission, an Islam which simultaneously submits to the intimate relationship between *murīd* ('committed one') and *murshid* ('guide') and which submits to a communal structure that invests this exegete with extraordinary power and sacredness.

The early Fatimids developed a structure of history that was cyclical in nature. Each cycle is inaugurated by a prophet, called a speaker (*nāṭiq*), who brings a new scriptural message, a new religious law.

> The first six Speakers were Adam, Noah, Abraham, Moses, Jesus, and Muḥammad. Each one was succeeded by a Legatee (*waṣī*), also called a Silent one (*ṣāmit*), who revealed the esoteric truths concealed in the messages. They were Seth, Shem, Ishmael, Aaron, Simon Peter, and ʿAlī. Each cycle was completed by seven imams, the last of whom would rise in rank to become the Speaker of the next cycle and bring a new scripture and law abrogating the previous one . . . [The *mahdī* Muḥammad b. Ismāʿīl] . . . would abrogate the law of Islam. His divine message would not entail a new law, however, but would consist in the full revelation of previously secret esoteric truths. As the eschatological Qāʾim and Mahdī, he would rule and consummate the world.[4]

Ẓāhir and *bāṭin*, prophecy and history, are interwoven in this system: each law-giving prophet dispensed a revelation to his people which also contained within it truths that were hidden for the elect. The people invested with the meaning and dissemination of these truths were the *waṣī*s or the *ṣāmit*s and their followers. The seventh *imām* at the end of each cycle was the prophet of the next cycle who abrogated the religious law and revealed a new law. The last *nāṭiq* would not bring a new law but would reveal all previously hidden esoteric truths. Early Fatimids believed that this *mahdī* was Muḥammad b. Ismāʿīl, a son of the sixth *imām* Jaʿfar al-Ṣādiq (d. 765); propaganda conducted for the Fatimids was based upon the imminent arrival of this *mahdī*.[5] It is this *nāṭiq*, this *qāʾim* or *mahdī*, whom the *Kitāb al-kashf* predicts will come soon.[6]

The concept of *walāya* too is a fundamental component of Shiism. Possessing an almost dizzying array of meanings in the history of Islam (in law, Sufism and political thought for example) this term is 'an Arabic verbal noun derived from the root *wly*, [and] carries the basic meanings of "friendship, assistance," and "authority, power."'[7] Derivatives of the word appear more than 200 times in the Quran.[8] Landolt writes,

> God's unique position as the most powerful friend and helper (*walī naṣīr*) is one of the major themes of Qurʾanic preaching, and several

> verses make it clear that those who 'turn away' (e.g., 9:74) and/or 'are led astray by him' (e.g., 18:17) have no *walī* (42:8) or *mawlā* (47:11), that is, no one to turn to for help or guidance.[9]

In Shiism, *walāya* is 'devotion to "ʿAlī and the imams from the house of the Prophet," that is, descendants of ʿAlī who are considered imams.'[10] Our text reflects just how important *walāya* is; indeed, as Landolt maintains, around the time of the early 900s – if not earlier –

> *walāyah*, as adherence to the imams and as the recognition of their mission as the true 'holders of the [divine] Command' (*ūlī al-amr*) and the exclusive possessors of the true meaning of the Qurʾan and the 'knowledge of the hidden' (*ʿilm al-ghayb*), remains the key to salvation, without which no pious act of obedience to God (*ṭāʿah*) is truly valid.[11]

Landolt then writes that: '[I]t is for these reasons that *walāyah*, and not the profession of monotheism (*tawḥīd*) as in Sunnī Islam, appears as the principal "pillar of Islam" in the classical collections of Shīʿī traditions, both those of the Ithnā ʿAsharīyah, or Twelvers . . . and those of the Fatimid Ismāʿīlīyah.'[12]

Taʾwīl, the anagogic unfurling of hidden symbolic meaning, is inexorably linked to *walāya*, devotion to the *imāms*, who are the exclusively authorised exegetes of the sacred text. As such they are the exclusive doors to salvation. *Taʾwīl* is incomplete without *walāya*, just as the revelation of Islam is incomplete without Muḥammad. The Fatimids possessed a hierarchy called the *daʿwa*, 'the call,' responsible for secretly disseminating this *taʾwīl*.[13] It is important to note that the dissemination of hidden knowledge was mediated by a hierarchy – *dāʿī*s ('summoners'), *ḥujja*s ('proofs'), *bāb*s ('gates') and other initiatory personnel were involved in the transmission of these messages. In many cases, *dāʿī*s themselves were authorised to produce *taʾwīl*.

The dynamic between secrecy and its disclosure was also a fundamental facet of Ismaili theology.

> By the 890s, in elaborating their distinctive religious system, the Ismailis emphasised a fundamental distinction between the exoteric

> (*zahir*) and the esoteric (*batin*) dimensions of the sacred scriptures and the religious commandments and prohibitions. Accordingly, they held that the revealed scriptures, including especially the Qur'an, and the laws laid down in them had their apparent or literal meaning, the *zahir*, which had to be distinguished from the inner meaning or true spiritual reality (*haqiqa*) hidden in the *batin* . . . The hidden truths could be made apparent through *ta'wil*, esoteric exegesis, the process of educing the *batin* from the *zahir* . . . The Ismaili *ta'wil* was distinguished from *tanzil*, the actual revelation of scriptures through angelic intermediaries, and from *tafsir*, explanation of the apparent or philological meaning of the sacred texts. In the era of Islam, the Prophet Muhammad had been charged with delivering the Islamic revelation, *tanzil*, while ʿAli was responsible for its *ta'wil*. ʿAli, designated as the *sahib al-ta'wil*, or 'master of *ta'wil*,' was thus the repository of the Prophet's undivulged knowledge and the original possessor of Islam's true interpretation after the Prophet, a function retained by the ʿAlid imams after ʿAli himself.[14]

Ismaili hermeneutic was predicated upon the distinction between the apparent (*ẓāhir*) and the hidden (*bāṭin*). The truth (*ḥaqīqa*) embedded within the *bāṭin* was, in the era of Islam, entrusted to ʿAlī and his *imāms*. This entire hermeneutical system presupposes both an interpreter close to the divine and a plurality of spiritual structures that lay behind what we can only see opaquely in this realm without proper divine guidance. *Ta'wīl*, then, becomes an 'anagogical hermeneutic,'[15] an exercise not only of elucidating inner meaning but also of simultaneous spiritual ascent, a movement of the soul toward the reality of the unseen. To submit to *ta'wīl* was not only an acknowledgment of the presence of this symbolic realm, but was the most intimate expression of devotion one could have for the exegete. This act of submission (*islām*) both reified the individual relationship between *murīd* and *murshid* while making the locus of communal authority the exegete and his appointed agents.[16] The Fatimids' hermeneutical system helped translate their revolutionary aspirations into a successful empire.

On the ground, the empire was the product of clandestine revolutionary activity that began around the latter half of the ninth century. This activity was organised around the imminent arrival of the *mahdī*, Muḥammad b. Ismāʿīl, the eldest son of Jaʿfar al-Ṣādiq, the sixth Shia *imām*. The organisers of this movement propagated the belief that Muḥammad b. Ismāʿīl was in *ghayba*, occultation, and would return to usher in a utopian era of history that would restore Islam to its rightful custodians, the Shia *imāms*.[17] These supporters of Muḥammad b. Ismāʿīl, or the Ismailis, eventually developed a formal hierarchy to disseminate their teachings, known as the *daʿwa*, or call. Historians tell us that this *daʿwa* became centrally organised by the 870s, and was headquartered at Salamiyya, Syria.[18] By the 890s the *daʿwa* spread to other areas including Rayy in Iran, around Kufa, Iraq, the Persian Gulf and Yemen. Each of these *daʿwas* was headed by a *dāʿī*, or caller, whose mission it was to secretly attract new recruits to the true religion.[19]

Halm rightly observes that the 'explosive force' of the mission was grounded not only in an imminent expectation of the messianic figure – a characteristic shared by other Shia groups – but also in the role of this figure as inaugurator of utopia.[20]

> The Mahdi (or Qāʾim) ... will openly reveal the 'true religion,' which until now has been concealed behind all previous religions, and known to the small circle of the initiated, to the entire world. With this all previous religions will become superfluous, since the unveiled Truth will have no further need of symbols and coverings. Even Islamic law, which now is still valid, will be abolished, as it will have fulfilled its purpose, which is to conceal the True Religion. The abolition of the law (*rafʿa al-sharīʿa*) is the Mahdi's true message: he will renew the original Edenic religion of Adam, the pure worship of the One God, without rites, commandments, or prohibitions.[21]

Halm describes this utopia as a return to origins – the pure religion of Adam that has until now been concealed to the majority of people and known only to the elect throughout history. It is through *taʾwīl* that the Fatimid mission becomes organised and disseminated, the medium through which a permanent soteriology and terrestrial mission intersect. Through *ta'wīl* the elect know that the *mahdī* will come soon and will reveal the nature of true religion for all to see, dramatically and permanently vindicating true believers throughout history. We now turn to what this *ta'wīl* of the end looked like, and how it reflected an imminent utopia.

Notes

1. *The Qur'an*, trans. M. H. Shakir (Elmhurst, NY: Tahrike Tarsile Qur'an, 1989).
2. Mahmoud Ayoub, 'The Speaking Qur'ān and the Silent Qur'ān: A Study of Imāmī Shīʿī *tafsīr*', in *Approaches to the History of the Interpretation of the Qur'ān*, ed. Andrew Rippin (New York: Oxford University Press, 1988), 186–7.
3. Azim Nanji, 'Shīʿī Ismāʿīlī Interpretations of the Qur'an', in *Proceedings from the International Congress for the Study of the Qur'ān*, 2nd edn (Canberra: Australian National University, 1980), pp. 39–40.
4. Wilferd Madelung, 'Ismaʿilism: The Old and the New *Daʿwa*', in *Columbia Lectures on Iranian Studies 4: Religious Trends in Early Islamic Iran*, ed. Ehsan Yarshaten (New York: Persian Heritage Foundation, 1988), p. 94.
5. See the masterful reconstructions of the Fatimid revolution by Halm and Brett.
6. Brett, *Rise*, p. 123.
7. Hermann Landolt, '*Walāyah*', in *The Encyclopedia of Religion*, ed. Mircea Eliade (New York: Macmillan, 1987), p. 316.
8. Landolt, p. 316.
9. Landolt, p. 316.
10. Landolt, p. 319.
11. Landolt, p. 319. Note the parallels here between *walāya* in the Shīʿī tradition and in the Islamic mystical tradition. In the latter, there tend to be numerous *walīs*, or 'helpers, saints' who are endowed with *walāya*, 'the special charismatic quality of a Ṣūfi, that which enables him to be the subject of miracles, or more precisely, charismata (*karāmāt*)'. Landolt, p. 321.
12. Landolt, p. 320.
13. For the organisation of this hierarchy, see, for instance, Farhad Daftary, 'The Ismaili *Daʿwa* Outside the Fatimid *dawla*', in *L'Égypte Fatimide: Son*

Art et Son Histoire, ed. Marianne Barrucand (Paris: Presses de l'Université de Paris-Sorbonne, 1999), pp. 29–43.

14. Farhad Daftary, *Intellectual Traditions in Islam* (London and New York: I. B. Tauris in association with the Institute of Ismaili Studies, 2000), p. 89.
15. Henry Corbin, *History of Islamic Philosophy*, trans. Liadain Sherrard and Philip Sherrard (London: Kegan Paul International in association with Islamic Publications, 1993), p. 38.
16. Jamel A. Velji, 'Apocalyptic Rhetoric and the Construction of Authority in Medieval Isma'ilism', in *Roads to Paradise: Eschatology and Concepts of the Hereafter in Islam*, ed. Sebastian Günther and Todd Lawson (Leiden: Brill, forthcoming). This chapter outlines a relationship between Fatimid and Nizari authority and apocalypticism – a theme revisited and further developed in this book.
17. Halm, *Empire*, pp. 20–2.
18. Farhad Daftary, *A Short History of the Ismailis* (Edinburgh: Edinburgh University Press, 1998), p. 39.
19. A detailed account of the spread of the *da'wa* can be found in Halm, *Empire*, pp. 5–42.
20. Halm, *Empire*, p. 21.
21. Halm, *Empire*, p. 21.

2

Oaths, Taxes and Tithes: Organising an Imminent Utopia

As a terrestrial reflection of the interpretive process, the organisational structure of the Fatimid movement vividly illustrates how the invocation of various moments of the pristine past helped to inaugurate, on earth, a utopian future. Fatimid organisational structures and the hermeneutics that supported them reflect the fusion of a sense of imminent eschatology to a sense of utopian expectation; a fusion that appears frequently in other apocalyptic contexts as well. Historians of religion and scholars of Biblical materials have in fact long ago observed the parallels between primordial time and the end of time – often utopian time – in apocalyptic myths and writings.[1] These scholars have observed that apocalypticism frequently envisions a utopian future devoid of terrestrial corruption or decay, parallel to our primordial existence.

This chapter examines some of these social structures and their roles in helping to reconstitute society around the imminent advent of the *mahdī*. First, I address in detail the Fatimid oath of allegiance as expressed through a selection of early texts recounting such initiatory accounts and pay special attention to the ways in which pledging the oath enabled the initiate to enter into an elite and sacred lineage. The accounts of these oaths are supported by ample reference to Quranic descriptions of those on the right side of sacred history. Like any oath, the initiate's pledge is in actuality an obligation of exchange: here, a pledge to uphold *walāya* and to act in accordance with the tenets of true belief in exchange for spiritual enlightenment and protection through the unveiling of hidden knowledge. The promise of inclusion in a terrestrial and spiritual utopia under the guidance of the *mahdī* then becomes attainable only through an initiatory process that both locates the initiate in a sacred lineage and obligates the believer to work on the *mahdī*'s behalf.

Recurring throughout early Fatimid materials is a central emphasis placed on believers' pledging the oath of allegiance. Heinz Halm, in his study of these oaths, writes:

> From the authentic literature of the Isma'ilis we know that initiates were pledged to observe the secrecy of the 'inner meaning' (*bāṭin*), and that they were sworn to such secrecy prior to their initiation by taking an oath, called a *mīthāq* or *ʿahd*; apart from these two nouns, our sources also often contain the verbal phrase *akhadha ʿalayhi* 'he pledged him', and the initiate is accordingly called *al-maʾkhūdhu ʿalayhi*.[2]

He then describes the initiatory account in the *Kitāb al-ʿālim wa-l-ghulām* (Book of the teacher and pupil),[3] one of the earliest authentic texts to provide such an account. Halm writes:

> This initiation romance describes in an idealised way how a young man is taken into the confidence of an itinerant *dāʿī*, who eventually initiates him. The climax of the text is a description of the preparations leading to the revelation of the secrets. Here, too, the *ʿahd* forms the beginning of the instruction. The master says to the young man: 'For religion there is a key which grants or forbids access to it, like the difference between whoring and marriage.'
>
> The pupil: 'The key of which you speak must be a great thing with God, if it actually distinguishes between what is allowed and what is forbidden, between truth and falsehood! What is it?'
>
> The master: 'It is God's *ʿahd*, which confirms his truths and contains our duties towards him. It is Paradise for his followers

> (*awliyā'*), God's rope on earth and a guarantee of safety (*amān*) among his servants. I will say it to you and pledge you to it!'[4]

The initiation correlates with the unveiling of hidden mysteries. After reciting the end of the *ʿahd*, the initiate,

> . . . praised and glorified God and thanked him for what he had allotted to him, and became aware that he now belonged to the party of God (*ḥizb Allāh*) and to the party of the saints (*awliyā'*), because he had accepted their *ʿahd* (*bi-qabūli ʿahdihim*); then he ended his praise. The teacher, however, began to explain and clarify, and his explanations and clarifications regarding the foundations of external things (*al-ẓāhira*)[5] and their initial creation started with God's having created all things and called them into existence from nothing.[6]

Oath-taking becomes a precondition for access to the mysteries of religion. These mysteries include not only a detailed account of creation, but also explain how the ranks of the *daʿwa* are inexorably linked to the creative process. After pledging the oath the seeker is made aware of his status as now belonging to the party of the elect. The initiator's clarification and exposition of the hidden nature of the external world and other mysteries reifies the initiate's new communal identity through a shared vision of the symbolic realm. Note that the oath is described as paradise for believers, as it grants access to the unveiling of the hidden mysteries of reality (*ta'wīl*). This secret knowledge is exclusive, as it is only shared by those who subscribe to the *bāṭin* and the *walāya* of the *imāms* and his authorised agents, who demarcate the true party of God (*ḥizb Allāh*) from others in history. Witness how another initiation account in a different Fatimid text articulates in more detail the sacred genealogy that the initiate is now joining:

> Following that he summoned me to the faith and he gave permission for our colleagues whom he had summoned before me to enter into his presence. Thus, they joined in the *daʿwa*. When it was time for the oath, he said, 'Know, may God have mercy on you, that this oath is a sunna from God in respect to His people and His servants.

God took it from His prophets, and each prophet took it from his own community. The proof of this is from the Book of God, since He says, *When We took a covenant from the prophets, from you, from Noah and Abraham and Moses and Jesus, the son of Mary, and We took from them a solemn pledge* [33:7]; and His saying, *When We took the pledge of the tribe of Israel not to worship any except God* [2:83]; and His statement, *When We took the pledge of the tribe of Israel and We sent among them twelve leaders* [5:12]; and His saying, *From those who said that they were Christians, we took their pledge* [5:14]; and His saying, *When We took your pledge not to shed each other's blood* [2:84]; and His statement to the Apostle of God, *Those who swear allegiance to you, swear allegiance to God Himself, His hand above theirs; whoever violates it violates himself and whoever remains true to what he promised to God shall be due a great reward* [48:10].' Thereafter he reviewed everything in the Qur'an mentioning the covenant and fidelity to it. He said, 'There is no religion except on the basis of a covenant. Of whomever God has not taken a covenant, has no one to guard him nor any religion to restrain him. Prior to this *you were a dissolute people* [48:12].' He said, 'Truly God has said, *God has purchased from the believers their souls and their wealth in exchange for paradise when they will fight on behalf of God, killing and being killed, a promise He made truly in the Torah, the Gospels and the Qur'an. And who is truer to his covenant than God? Rejoice therefore in your pledge of allegiance which you have pledged to Him. That is a wondrous triumph* [9:111].' And He said, *God was pleased with the believers when they swore allegiance to you under the tree* (to the end of the verse) [48:18]. Then he said, 'Today you have pledged allegiance to God and you are truly His servants and you have acknowledged Muḥammad and pledged allegiance to him.' He continued, 'God has explained that He was not satisfied with the worship of those who came first except upon their pledging allegiance to Muḥammad, His Prophet. How could He then approve your worship without a pledge?'

I said: 'By God, O by God, I have never heard of this and yet I have read all that reached us concerning the teachings of the sects

> and the many doctrines of both heretics and believers, but I had never heard of this. Surely, it is quite obviously true, and its proof and veracity are certainly evident. We used to think and maintain that God extracted the descendants of Adam from his back and took from them the covenant.'
>
> He said: 'This is wrong and no proof will support it, nor would an intelligent person consider it to be valid, since God, the Most High, says, *Be mindful of the favour God showed you and of His pledge with which He bound you when you said: we hear and we obey* [5:7]. How could it be that He reminded them of something they could not remember, and then they gave Him this understandable reply. No, it is as we see it; it was those from before you.'
>
> I said: 'There is no religion in the absence of a covenant.'
>
> He said: 'That is correct. Have you not heard God's words, *none shall have the power of intercession except those who have taken a covenant with the Most Merciful* [19:87], and, *They said, the fire will touch us only for a limited number of days; say, have you taken a covenant with God – God will never go back on His covenant – or do you assert of God what you have no knowledge of?* [2:80]. Thus, the covenant is a precondition for worship and an intercession for him with God. Whoever violates it has a painful chastisement. The covenant is the means. God, the Most High, said, *O you who believe, fear God and seek the means to approach Him* [5:35].'[7]

This lengthy account illustrates some of the manifold ways in which both awareness of the true meaning of the covenant and pledging becomes the primary means through which divine felicity is obtained. Pledging the covenant foists the initiate into a community governed by *walāya* of those who were chosen by the divine to take the covenant – now and throughout history. The initiate takes the same covenant as Noah, Abraham, Moses, and Jesus, for instance, and their communities; this covenant is the mechanism by which the Children of Israel affirm divine unity; and it is the same covenant pledged by Christians and the Prophet's true followers. Remarkably, this covenant also becomes clearly demarcated from the primordial covenant in its Quranic form sworn by all of humanity in 7:172. In the latter, all of humanity, in the form of Adam's precreated descendants, is commanded to testify that God reigns over them, so that on the Day of Resurrection humanity would not be unaware of divine judgment. Here, that interpretation of the covenant is rejected in favour of an interpretation that is explicitly initiatory in nature, one that affirms active awareness of the obligation and requires of its initiates specific actions.

In an illustration of the variegated nature of *ta'wīl*, one of the earliest Fatimid texts that we have, the *Kitāb al-kashf*, retains the relationship between the pledging of oaths and the construction of sacred history while likening its oath-taking to another event in primordial history: the *amāna*, or trust. The *Kitāb al-kashf* actually begins with the Quranic verse discussing this event in sacred history:

> *Indeed, We offered the Trust* (amāna) *to the heavens, the earth and the mountains, and they declined to bear it and feared it; [but] man undertook to bear it. Indeed, he was unjust and ignorant* [33:72].

> I, O brother, compel you by God's oath (*ʿahd*) and His covenant (*mīthāq*), and I bind [you] with what God has forever compelled His prophets and messengers – namely, to a firm oath and a binding covenant. And I forbid to you what God has forbidden His prophets and messengers and His gates and His proofs. Likewise your father who gave you drink and your brother who has been fed with you from the same source [are bound by this oath]. Just as carrion, blood and the flesh of the pig [are forbidden, it is forbidden] that you divulge it. No one is to recite it other than you, and do not utter it to anyone; [it is] *the natural disposition* (fiṭra) *with which God has made human beings* [30:30]. Do not write it for anyone except for he who is worthy of the truth, who is a believer and who is truthful. Should you transgress and do other than what I command of you and should you divulge it, then God, His messenger, and His *waṣī* [ʿAlī] will free you from their promise to guide you, God will overpower you, and the sword of truth [of the *qāʾim*] will pierce you (*yanfudhu fīka*) with His judgment, even if this is detested by polytheists (*mūshrikūn*). This report

> has come [to us] on the authority of the *awliyā'*, and the *awliyā'* [have come to us] on the authority of the *awsīya'*, and the *awsiyā'* [have come to us] on the authority of the *du'ā* and the *du'ā* [have come to us] on the authority of the *nuqabā'*, and the *nuqabā'* [have come to us] on the authority of the *nujabā'* and the *nujabā'* [have come to us] on the authority of the *abwāb*, and the *abwāb* [have come to us] on the authority of the *ḥujaj*, who said 'tell the people of *walāya*, keep our secret and obey our commands and do not reject our doctrine. We will make you the best of creation. For before you, among earlier communities, there were those who fulfilled the trust (*amāna*), kept the secret, and carried out what they had been commanded. For those who were bearers of His trust, God made [for] them messengers and gates to His *awliyā'*.'[8]

The primordial concept of *amāna*, or divine trust, is tacitly collapsed and refashioned into the same oath governing knowledge that the narrator entrusts to the initiate (and by extension the reader). This is the same oath sworn by prophets and messengers throughout history. *Amāna*, possessing a sense of a covenant grounded in some kind of obedience and/or responsibility,[9] is here explicitly transformed into something secret, something that must be zealously guarded, and something only for the elect. *Amāna* is entrusted only to those who take the *'ahd* or *mīthāq*.

Initiation not only requires the seeker to uphold *amāna*, but also provides the initiate with the knowledge to realise his or her innate predisposition, *the nature* (fiṭra) *made by God in which He has made men.* The entire verse, 30:30, reads, *Then set your face upright for religion in the right state – the nature* (fiṭra) *made by God in which He has made men; there is no altering of God's creation; that is the right religion, but most people do not know.*[10] The *fiṭra* is humankind's original, innate disposition, the 'faculty of knowing God, with which He has created mankind.'[11] This is true Islam, 'the right religion,' which, according to 30:30, most people do not know. Our author thus reformulates the original Quranic narrative, transforming the primordial conception of trust bestowed upon all of humankind into a secret knowledge of true religion entrusted to the elect who have pledged allegiance to the true cause throughout history.

The preservation of secret knowledge is paramount here; indeed, it becomes equated to nothing other than true religion. Through this selection we learn that: 1) this book, and the knowledge contained within it, is secret; 2) divulging its secrets will automatically result in not only the nullification of the oath's protective powers, but of active punishment by the eschatological figure; and 3) that this report was mediated by members of an official hierarchy, and carries with it the sacred imprimatur of this hierarchy. At the apex of this hierarchy are the *ḥujjas* – which are possibly the *imāms* here[12] – who tell their friends to keep the secret of their teachings; if they do, they will become like past communities who also kept the secret and were favoured by the divine.[13]

It is also remarkable to note here how the key Quranic theme of divine disclosure – its emphasis on disseminating the message of Islam throughout all of history via the dispatching of prophets to various communities – is entirely inverted in this text. Here it is not divine disclosure that is important, but the preservation of divine secrets, secrets transmitted from God to be tightly guarded by His prophets, His *imāms*, and others in His chosen circle. The knowledge of this secret is now inherited by the reader, under the seal of an oath that has bound elect communities for generations. The possession of these secrets – and their preservation – becomes the highest form of religiosity here. Those who come to know these secrets – and then revert to other forms of belief or who reveal these secrets – become analogous to those who knew the true divine message of the Quran but refused to believe in it.[14]

To be sure, our author writes 'For whoever divulges the secret, indeed he rejected the truth after having known it. There is no power save that of God the High, the Great.' He then reproduces the following selection of the Quran:

> *Indeed those who disbelieve, it is all the same for them whether you warn them or do not warn them; they will not believe* [2:6]. Jaʿfar

> al-Ṣādiq, upon him be peace, said that by this God meant the adversaries (*al-aḍḍād*) and those who follow them. And He says to them: *God has set a seal upon their hearts and upon their hearing, and upon their vision is a veil. And upon them is a great punishment* [2:7].[15]

Those who disclose the 'the secret' are temporally collapsed into those who would not listen to the divine commands during Muḥammad's time. Through the process of *ta'wīl,* those who disclose the secret of this text are likened to disbelievers in Muḥammad's time who are, in turn, equated to those who disbelieve in the *imāms*. These people are those 'who have a seal upon their hearts and hearing,' and those who can expect 'a great punishment.' Our author then states that they are transformed into animals in the depths of hell, evicted on this earth from the ranks of the *daʿwa*, the only true means of salvation, since they violated the divine compact.

Seeing Fatimid oath-taking as part of a theology of secrecy, Michael Ebstein translates the same passage from the *Kitāb al-kashf,* and highlights the importance of the oath in conversion. He writes that after taking the oath,

> the initiate joins a new family: in place of the relationship he once had with his biological parents and siblings, he now enjoys new family ties with a spiritual father (i.e., the *daʿwa* representative who has initiated him into the Ismāʿīlī faith) and brother (i.e., his coreligionist).[16]

Ebstein also observes the pact's nexus to primordial events, showing, importantly, how

> [t]his interpretation is deterministic by its very nature: it was already in primordial times that Shīʿite believers – by virtue of their belief in the Imāms – were distinguished and separated from the remainder of mankind ... The concealment of the Ismāʿīlī faith in this passage is linked to the primordial relationship between God, His Prophets, His friends and the true believers; the purpose of this concealment is to safeguard the sacredness of the Ismāʿīlī faith – a faith that from time immemorial belongs only to the elite of mankind, i.e. the Ismāʿīlī believers.[17]

These secrets will be revealed at the end of time for all to see. Ebstein's observations underscore two important aspects of oaths: their ability to powerfully reformulate communal boundaries, as well as their connections to primordial events.

I now turn briefly to a recent study on Homeric oaths to illustrate how oaths more generally fuse the primordial moment with the formulation of communal boundaries. In her book on Homeric oaths, Margo Kitts, citing Roy Rappaport's work on ritual theory, considers oath-taking as a formalised ritual.

> Rather than establish interior states, says Rappaport, formalized rituals instantiate conventions that specify canonical ideals for individual behavior, implicating the performers in commitments that are wider than self-interest. The theory turns on a ritual's 'metaperformative' power. Metaperformative rituals not only compel recognition of the authority of the conventions they represent, they actually bring those conventions into existence through performance . . . As acts, they have a conventional force. Of special reference for oath-making rituals are factive illocutions, which establish the matters of which they speak. For instance, 'I dub thee knight,' uttered by the right person in the right circumstances and not in jest, confers knighthood upon someone who may or may not be up to the tasks of knighthood; the conventional force of the ritual commits him to it anyway. Oaths, too, by being performed, clearly establish the matters of which they speak . . .[18]

The performative nature of the oath establishes communally recognised responsibilities for the oath-taker while also obviating any internal doubt he or she might have about his or her role. In considering the oath as a ritual act, it is particularly interesting to note that the perceived invariability of such acts:

> . . . mirrors the creative dynamic found in those many creation stories that conceive of a pre-existing inchoate substance *informed* and, as it were, *temporalized* by a dynamic word – that is, an empowered liturgical utterance that creates order and directed movement out of

> an originary formless and aimless matter (such as in Genesis 1:2) . . . In other words, the liturgical invariability performs the same role as does the magical voice that creates order out of chaos.
>
> More complexly, liturgical orders also are said to inform and temporalize the ritual's participants, by infusing the preritualized 'inchoate substance' of the participant (a preritualized identity conceived as formless and atemporal from the perspective of ritual canon) with liturgy's canonical shape and vitality, and by committing the performer to the ritual's terms thereafter.[19]

Kitts's work, then, helps us to make sense of the highly charged valences oaths carry in many of our early Fatimid materials – the 'key to religion,' the difference between fornication and marriage, the fact that 'there can be no religion without an oath.' In our texts, the Fatimid oath of allegiance and the ritual of taking it appear with only minor variations, illustrating the importance of invariability as part of its ritual force. Further, this invariability acquires force through the reproduction of a Quranic history that envisions those who have taken the oath of allegiance as the only protagonists throughout history. The ritualised interaction between initiate and *dāʿī* here parallels the divine colloquy between God and His representatives on earth. The pledging of the oath becomes a process of creation through the instantiation and temporalisation of the seeker's identity as mediated through the invocation of various moments of the pristine past in which oaths are taken, all the while committing the initiate to uphold that which is obligated by the oath.[20]

While there has indeed been scholarly work done on various aspects of Islamic oaths,[21] the Fatimid case is interesting because we have evidence that links oath-taking rituals to support for the *mahdī* and thus the belief in the approaching end of time. The *Kitāb al-rushd*, for instance, explicitly mentions the fusion of oath and apocalypse. Our author begins his discussion of the oath by stating that it is a key to all knowledge.

> Know, may God have mercy upon you, that God has made a key to all knowledge: it is His oath (*ʿahd*) and His covenant (*mīthāq*), which He

> has made the greatest of His causes. He has reiterated this throughout His book, and in the treasuries of His religion and His wisdom; through it He accepts obedience to Him.[22]

This oath – here the *ʿahd* and His *mīthāq* – is the (only) way in which God accepts obedience. The account continues by stating that the prophets and their followers were bound by the taking of oaths.

> He had enjoined an oath upon Adam, as He has said *We had already taken an oath from Adam before but he forgot* [20:115], and He said to Muḥammad, *And when we took from the Prophets their covenant* (mīthāq) . . .[23] That was an honour that He conferred upon them, arising from the honour of the oath and its exalted position. He said, *My oath does not include the evildoers* [2:124]. He has made its fulfilment an obligation, as He has said *Fulfil any oath you make in God's name . . .*[24] And He says, *Indeed, those who pledge allegiance to you pledge allegiance to God. The hand of God is upon their hands . . .*[25] So He makes clear by this that whoever pledges allegiance to His prophet has pledged allegiance to Him, and whoever takes an oath to him, God too has bound Himself to his oath.
>
> God has honoured the oath by attaching Himself to it, and He will give a great reward for fulfilling it, as He has said, *Those who fulfil the oath to God and do not break the covenant . . . they will have reward of [this] abode – Gardens of perpetual residence . . .*[26] So He has praised the oath, and has made an ample reward for one who fulfils it, and a painful punishment for one who breaks it, as He has said, *But those who break the oath to God after their covenant to him . . . to the words, and they will have a dreadful home* [13:25]. He has said *And we did not find most of them honouring [their] oaths,*[27] and He has said, *So they prostrated, except for Iblis, he was one of the jinn and departed from the command of his Lord* [18:50]. God thus relegates one who does not take an oath to Him to the station of Iblis, who incurred God's anger, and so God cursed him. He has said, *Indeed, the worst of living creatures in the sight of God are those who have disbelieved, and they will not believe* [8:55].[28]

The oath-taker becomes one of those who now have access to true knowledge. They become elided with the elect in Quranic history, included among the ranks of the prophets and others who have fulfilled the divine obligation. As in our other examples, pledging and fulfilling the oath becomes the criteria for divine favour and is explicitly linked with admission to either heaven or hell.

Perhaps the most vivid direct evidence linking oath-taking, terrestrial mission, and apocalyptic imagery comes at the end of the text, with our author's *taʾwīl* of a dramatic passage of the Quran, 74:38–47 – a passage in which the inhabitants of heaven ask why the people of hell are there.

> *The Companions of the Right will ask, 'What drove you to the Scorching Fire?' And they [the people of hell] will answer, 'We were not among those who prayed; nor did we feed the poor; we used to indulge in idle talk with those who engaged in it; and we used to deny the Day of Judgment until the Certainty came upon us'* (74:42–7).

Our author states, *'And we used to deny the Day of Judgment until the Certainty came upon us,* means that we denied the *mahdī* (*nukadhdhibu al-mahdī*).' Our author then adds to this verse:

> And the believers will reply 'We did not deny the *mahdī*; rather, we continuously gave him our loyalty and we are among the people of his oath (*ʿahd*) and of his protection (*dhimma*). By this [support] we merited the gardens but you merited the torment of hellfire by your denial of the Companions of the Right and the companions of the *dāʿī*.'[29]

The nexus between the oath and its proper fulfilment is illustrated here through a reformulation of ethical imperatives centred on support for the *mahdī* and his cause.

Taxes, *Dār al-hijras* and 'The Islands'

Taxes and tithes, too, illustrate ways in which religious obligations reaffirmed the *daʿwa*'s sense of election as a new creation with the *mahdī* at its helm. According to one account of the organisation of the *da'wa* in Iraq, that transmitted by Ibn Rizām and reproduced by Halm:

> ... the recruiters not only had to disseminate the doctrine in their parishes, but they also had to levy the taxes that the believers owed to the Mahdi. Our informant tells of a series of contributions which Ḥamdān Qarmaṭ and ʿAbdān imposed upon the new converts: to begin with, a contribution of one silver dirham *pro capite* [sic], called 'the creation' (*al-fiṭra*), then a contribution of a gold dinar, called the exile (*al-hijra*), supposedly due each time one entered a state of great ritual impurity ... after that 'the livelihood' (*al-bulgha*), a contribution of seven gold dinars, receipt of which was acknowledged by the dāʿī with a meal of sweets supposed to have originated literally in Paradise, and to have been sent down by the Mahdi himself. The dāʿī is said, moreover, to have levied a fifth (*khums*) on all property and earnings, in accordance with the Quranic verse 8:41, which assigns a fifth of all booty to God, his Prophet, and the heirs of the Prophet – in other words, to the Mahdi.[30]

The payment of required contributions graphically reifies the construction and maintenance of new communal identity under the guidance of the *mahdī*, elegantly complementing the work of oaths in instantiating a new religious identity for the initiate. The payment of the *fiṭra* evokes the primordial moment as well as the initiate's creation under the guidance of the *da'wa* and the *mahdī*. Paying the *hijra* becomes a symbolic acknowledgment of transgression of communal bounds as defined by the hierarchy; its payment allows the readmission of the initiate into the communal fold. Paying the *khums* acknowledges the *mahdī*'s rightful inheritance of the Prophet's legacy and legitimacy to lead the community, while paying the *bulgha* reaffirms the *mahdī*'s direct connection to paradise. The account continues:

> Finally, ʿAbdān imposed 'the friendship' (*al-ulfa*) on them; 'that meant that they collected everything they had in one single place, and in this way they all became equal, and no one surpassed his comrade and brother through possessions of any kind ... It signified

> to them that they had no need of possessions at all, since the entire earth was to belong to them alone, and to no one else . . .'[31]

Further, according to Halm, Ibn Rizām:

> . . . emphasizes that all contributions were raised in the name of the awaited Mahdi Muḥammad b. Ismāʿīl; the dāʿīs 'said that he was the Imam and the Mahdi, who would appear at the end of the ages, and who would establish justice; the tribute is due to him, and the recruiter takes it from people for him; all the goods which people collected would be kept for him until he should appear.'[32]

The communal pooling of property – a common feature of millenarian movements across religious traditions even today – here is meant to erase hierarchies of this world that are based upon the acquisition of material goods, and reconstruct communal boundaries around utopian expectations. Property only acquires value in two ways. First, as a foreshadowing or terrestrial mirror of utopia, where the elect will inherit the earth and property will become superfluous; and second, as anticipatory utility for the *mahdī* upon his arrival.

The appellation of the movement of the time was also a reflection of the intersection of utopian vision with terrestrial mission. Daftary explains:

> The Ismailis now referred to their religio-political campaign and movement simply as *al-daʿwa* (the mission) or *al-daʿwa al-hādiya* (the rightly guiding mission), in addition to using expressions such as *daʿwat al-ḥaqq* (summons to the truth) or *dīn al-ḥaqq* (religion of the truth); they also referred to themselves as *ahl al-ḥaqq* (people of the truth). The united Ismailis, as noted, then rallied around the doctrine of the Mahdiship of Muḥammad b. Ismāʿīl.[33]

Further, he writes,

> . . . in order to prepare for the emergence of the Mahdi, in 277/890 Ḥamdān built a fortified *dār al-hijra*, or abode of migration, near Kūfa for the Qarmaṭīs, where they also gathered supplies of weapons and other provisions. This abode was to serve for the Qarmaṭīs

> as the nucleus of a new society, as Medina had served the Prophet Muḥammad in the aftermath of his emigration from Mecca. It would also serve as a base of operations for launching assaults against the Abbasids. Similar *dār al-hijra*s were later founded for other early Ismaili communities in Yaman, Baḥrayn, North Africa and elsewhere.[34]

Through the invocation of mythic origins, here Muḥammad's flight to Medina, Ismaili strongholds become loci for the *mahdī*'s new society. It is important to point out that the term *hijra* was used in a number of other mahdist movements in Islamic history to refer to the emigration to or of a *mahdī* figure.[35] The symbolic potency of this seminal event has been employed by various mahdist and non-mahdist groups for a number of reasons – not the least of which is that it represented, during Muḥammad's lifetime, the fulfilment of divine predictions concerning the triumph of Muḥammad's mission. This fulfilment, too, had apocalyptic overtones, as observed by Donner, among others:

> It seems just as likely, however, that the early Believers were convinced that, by establishing their community in Medina, they were ushering in the beginning of a new era of righteousness, and hence that they were actually witnessing the first events of the End itself. It is possible, then, to conjecture that they thought that the events leading to the Last Judgment were actually beginning to unfold before their very eyes.[36]

It is no coincidence that time itself originates in the Islamic calendar with the Prophet's *hijra* from Mecca to Medina. The Fatimid establishment of *dār al-hijra*s was thus a realisation of powerful expectations concerning the arrival of permanent righteousness through a descendent of Muḥammad who would complete the work of the final prophet at the end of time.[37] Further, the proliferation of these abodes was related in some cases to the establishment of the *jazāʾir*, or islands. The Fatimids divided the entire world into twelve islands, each of which was headed by a high-ranking member of the *daʿwa*. These islands were ultimately expected to be administrative centres for a new global order governed by the true religion.[38]

Thus, ideologically, Fatimid revolutionary activity was a reflection of utopian aspirations. Utopia was to be brought about by the revolutionary mission which, reflecting its various appellations, embodied the truth; this truth was reified through practices of communal organisation such as tithes and the divesting of individual property, and was to be spread across the world through administrative centres. Initiates to this cause were bound by a covenant to the *mahdī* that placed them among the most elect upholders of divine righteousness throughout Quranic history. Upon taking the oath, they became the most elect of creation through a return to a moment of the pristine past, regenerated through the *daʿwa* via initiatory practices that mirrored moments in which the divine directly obligated His elect to pledge the most sacred oath. In exchange for protection and the disclosure of esoteric knowledge, initiates were pledged to secrecy and support for the *mahdī*. Indeed, oath-taking in the *Kitāb al-rushd* explicitly links support for the *mahdī* with admission to heaven. In the next chapter I address in more detail the ways in which eschatological and apocalyptic imagery such as heaven and hell served as potent symbolic currency for the rise of the Fatimids.

Notes

1. Hermann Gunkel, *Creation and Chaos in the Primeval Era and the Eschaton*, trans. K. William Whitney Jr. (Grand Rapids, MI: Wm. B. Eerdmans, 2006 [1895]); see also Mircea Eliade, *The Quest: History and Meaning in Religion* (Chicago: University of Chicago Press, 1969), esp. pp. 88–111; G. van der Leeuw, 'Primordial Time and Final Time', in *Man and Time: Papers from the Eranos Yearbooks*, Bollingen Series 30, vol. 3, ed. Joseph Campbell (Princeton, NJ: Princeton University Press, 1957).
2. Heinz Halm, 'The Ismaʿili oath of allegiance (*ʿahd*) and the "sessions of wisdom" (*majālis al-ḥikma*) in Fatimid times', in *Mediaeval Ismaʿili History and Thought*, ed. Farhad Daftary (New York: Cambridge University Press, 1996), p. 92.
3. Jaʿfar b. Manṣūr al-Yaman, *Kitāb al-ʿālim wa-l-ghulām*, translated as *The Master and the Disciple: An Early Islamic Spiritual Dialogue*, ed. and trans. James W. Morris (London: I. B. Tauris, 2002).
4. Halm, 'The Ismaʿili oath', p. 92.

5. Here the foundations of external things, *al-asbāb al-ẓāhira*, indicate the building blocks of the created world; see also Jaʿfar b. Manṣūr, *Kitāb al-ʿālim*, trans. Morris, p. 178, n. 38.
6. Halm, 'The Ismaʿili oath', p. 92.
7. Wilferd Madelung and Paul E. Walker, ed. and trans., *The Advent of the Fatimids: A Contemporary Shiʿi Witness* (New York: I. B. Tauris, 2000), pp. 95–7.
8. *Kitāb al-kashf*, ed. Ghālib, pp. 23–4.
9. Edward William Lane, *An Arabic-English Lexicon* (Cambridge: Islamic Texts Society, 1984), s.v. '*amānah*'.
10. Shakir translation.
11. Lane, s.v. '*fiṭra*'.
12. Daftary, *The Ismāʿīlīs*, 2nd edn, p. 118.
13. For more on this determinism and its relation to the primordial pact, see in particular Mohammad Ali Amir-Moezzi, *The Divine Guide in Early Shiʿism: The Sources of Esotericism in Islam*. Translated by David Streight (Albany: State University of New York Press, 1994), pp. 29ff. and Dakake, *Charismatic Community*, pp. 141–55.
14. *Kitāb al-kashf*, ed. Ghālib, p. 147.
15. *Kitāb al-kashf*, ed. Ghālib, p. 25.
16. Ebstein, p. 318.
17. Ebstein, pp. 318–19.
18. Margo Kitts, *Sanctified Violence in Homeric Society* (New York: Cambridge University Press, 2005), p. 28.
19. Kitts, pp. 39–40 (emphasis original).
20. See also the interesting discussion on the function of oaths by Georgio Agamben, who writes that the oath draws together an ethical and political imperative that attests to humanity's responsibilities as logos-centred beings. He writes:

> The oath is . . . understood as the anthropogenic operator by means of which the living being, who has discovered itself speaking, has been responsible for his words, and, devoting himself to the *logos*, to constitute himself as the 'living being who has language'. In order for something like an oath to be able to take place, it is necessary, in fact, to be able above all to distinguish, and to articulate together in some way, life and language, actions and words–and this is precisely what the animal, for which language is still an integral part of

its vital practice, cannot do . . . And just as *mana* expresses, according to Lévi-Strauss, the fundamental inadequation between signifier and signified, which constitutes 'the disability of every finite thought,' so also does the oath express the demand, decisive in every sense for the speaking animal, to put its nature at stake in language and to bind together in an ethical and political connection words, things and actions. *The Sacrament of Language*, trans. Adam Kotsko (Redwood City, CA: Stanford University Press, 2010), p. 69 (emphasis original).

21. See, for instance, Roy Mottahedeh, *Loyalty and Leadership in an Early Islamic Society* (Princeton, NJ: Princeton University Press, 1980), 2nd edn (London, New York: I. B. Tauris, 2001); and Andrew Marsham, *Rituals of Islamic Monarchy* (Edinburgh: Edinburgh University Press, 2009).
22. Ibn Ḥawshab Manṣūr al-Yaman, *Kitāb al-rushd wa-l-hidāya*, edited by Muḥammad Kāmil Ḥusayn, in W. Ivanow (ed.), *Collectanea*: Vol. 1 (Leiden: Brill, 1948), p. 211.
23. 'until the end of the verse', which reads, *and from you and from Noah and from Abraham and Moses and Jesus, the son of Mary; and we took from them a solemn covenant* (mīthāq) (33:7).
24. 'until the end of the verse', which reads, *and do not break oaths after you have sworn them, for you have made God your surety: God knows everything you do* (16:91).
25. 'until the end of the verse', which reads, *So he who breaks his word only breaks it to the detriment of himself. And he who fulfills the oath he has pledged–He will give him a great reward* (48:10).
26. 'until the end of the verse', which reads, *they will enter them with whoever were righteous among their fathers, their spouses and their descendants. Angels will enter upon them from every gate, [saying], 'Peace be upon you for what you patiently endured. How excellent is the world of [this] abode' God extends provision for whom He wills and restricts [it]. And they rejoice in the worldly life, while the worldly life is not, compared to the Hereafter, except [brief] enjoyment* (13:20ff.).
27. 'until the end of the verse', which reads, *but We found most of them defiantly disobedient* (7:102).
28. Ibn Ḥawshab, *Kitāb al-rushd*, ed. M. Kāmil Ḥusayn, pp. 211–12.
29. Ibn Ḥawshab, *Kitāb al-rushd*, ed. M. Kāmil Ḥusayn, p. 213.
30. Halm, *Empire*, pp. 48–9.
31. Halm, *Empire*, pp. 49–50.

32. Halm, *Empire*, p. 50.
33. Daftary, *Short History*, pp. 39–40.
34. Daftary, *Short History*, pp. 41–2.
35. For material on the Sudanese Mahdi's *hijra*, see John O. Voll, 'The Mahdī's Concept and Use of "Hijrah"', *Islamic Studies* 26:1 (1987), pp. 31–42; and Nels Johnson, 'Religious Paradigms of the Sudanese Mahdīyah', *Ethnohistory* vol. 25, no. 2 (Spring 1978), pp. 159–78. For the importance of the *hijra* in the case of Ibn Tūmart, see Allen Fromherz, *The Almohads, the Rise of an Islamic Empire* (London and New York: I. B. Tauris, 2010), esp. pp. 117ff.; and García-Arenal, *Messianism*, esp. pp. 173ff.
36. Donner, p. 81. Donner also suggests that the term *hijra* in the early Islamic context 'may have served as the decisive marker of full membership into the community of Believers, much as baptism does for Christians' (p. 86); further study of the use of this term in the Fatimid sources is warranted to establish if its use there denoted a communally binding meaning.
37. For a detailed discussion of the ways in which Qāḍī l-Nuʿmān portrayed the Fatimid mission as being parallel to that of the Prophet, see James E. Lindsay, 'Prophetic Parallels in Abu ʿAbd Allah al-Shiʿi's Mission among the Kutama Berbers, 893–910', *International Journal of Middle East Studies* 24 (1992): pp. 39–56.
38. For a detailed discussion of the location of the *jazāʾir* and the organisational structure of the *daʿwa*, see Daftary, *The Ismāʿīlīs*, 2nd edn, pp. 217–21. See also Qāḍī l-Nuʿmān, *Taʾwīl al-daʿāʾim*, vol. 1, p. 182.

3

Ta'wīl of an Apocalyptic Transcript I: *The Book of Unveiling*

An analysis of some of the social structures that reflected belief in an imminent utopia reveals the fundamental interplay between secrecy, *walāya*, and obligation among believers to work on behalf of the *mahdī*. This cause was after all articulated as true religion – a return to various moments of the pristine past and a regeneration of true believers under the guidance of the *mahdī* and his authorised agents through the *da'wa*. The *da'wa*, the *dār al-hijra*s and the wider organisation of the islands or *jazā'ir* were highly symbolic – reminiscent of the Prophet's own mission – and anticipatory, insofar as these centres logistically operated as visions of a terrestrial utopia.

Texts from this period too anticipate an imminent apocalypse – or at least an expectation that an eschatological figure would arrive imminently to vanquish the enemies of the Shia. Historian Michael Brett carefully outlines how these texts anticipated the advent of the *mahdī*, and illustrates the ways in which these expectations might have been tied to the emergence of the Fatimids.[1] But what was the nature of the apocalyptic visions embedded within these texts? And what were some of the arguments put forth for belief in the Fatimid *mahdī*?

The next two chapters examine the apocalyptic topographies of two such texts: the *Kitāb al-kashf* and the *Kitāb al-rushd wa-l-*

hidāya. Both texts are complex works of Fatimid esoteric interpretation (*ta'wīl*) that provide us with further details concerning the ways in which authors used specific verses of the Quran to argue for the coming of the *mahdī*. While these texts do not exclusively discuss apocalypticism, the theme of the *mahdī* reappears throughout, making them particularly rich sources for outlining some of the features of this symbolism. In addition to enhancing our understanding of how these authors used apocalyptic or eschatological imagery of the Quran to argue for the advent of the *mahdī*, this analysis provides us with further insights into the inner workings of Fatimid *ta'wīl* as a mode of Quranic exegesis more generally. Further, many of these apocalyptic or eschatological verses of the Quran were used in the *ta'wīl* of these two texts. This not only illustrates an abundant concern with the imminent end of time but it also shows us how Quranic apocalypticism and its Fatimid interpretive product operated as powerful rhetorical constructs to effect changes in conceptions of salvation. In both Fatimid texts for instance, we witness a theme in which the *mahdī* is symbolically equated to various aspects of the Quranic resurrection. Carrying forward a trope discussed in the last chapter, belief in the *mahdī* and working for his cause would inevitably result in salvation.

An appreciation of the nature and nuance of these texts' apocalyptic symbolism requires a brief introduction to the Quran's apocalyptic élan. As Michael Sells and others have observed, the primary subject of the early Meccan suras was the idea of a divine reckoning,[2] and during the time in which many of these suras were revealed, the term *dīn* ('reckoning'), was synonymous with religion: 'the acceptance of the reckoning' was religion itself.[3] Acceptance of the reckoning also implied the acceptance of an ethical code articulated by the Quran – the code that set forth the criteria by which God measures one's actions at the end of time. Toshihiko Izutsu argues that a basic moral dichotomy permeates not just the early Meccan suras, but the entire Quranic text. Throughout the Quran, individuals are grouped into certain moral categories commensurate with their belief in the reckoning. He writes that human qualities themselves are sharply divided

> . . . into two radically opposed categories, which – in view of the fact that they are too concrete and semantically too pregnant to be called 'good' and 'bad', or 'right' and 'wrong' – we might simply call the class of positive moral properties and the class of negative moral properties, respectively. The final yardstick by which this division is carried out is the belief in the one and only God, the Creator of all beings.[4]

These principles, he writes, are 'very broadly speaking, based on the conception of eschatology.'[5] In other words, the Quranic ethics – 'the ethics of the present world'[6] – are determined by the Quranic sense of belief in the reckoning. Sura 107, an early Meccan sura, demonstrates the correlation between proper moral conduct and divine judgment.

> In the Name of God the Compassionate the Caring
> Do you see him who calls the reckoning a lie?
> He is the one who casts the orphan away
> who fails to urge the feeding of one in need
> Cursed are those who perform the prayer
> unmindful of how they pray
> who make of themselves a display
> but hold back the small kindness.[7]

Those who call the reckoning a lie are not simply nonbelievers in the reckoning. They also fail to uphold God's expectations for proper moral conduct in this age. Those who deny the reckoning are the same people who cast away the orphan, who do not feed the poor, who perform the prayer unmindfully, who show off and who are unable to be kind. An entire moral universe is created around belief in the reckoning; those who do not believe in the reckoning are those who squarely inhabit the realm of those who fail to uphold divine expectation.

The duality of the Quran, mediated by the final judgment, not only produces 'positive moral properties' and their opposites, it also allows for the construction of typologies – those who paradigmatically embody the divine message, representing the ultimate good, and those who paradigmatically embody divine disobedience.[8] Sura 98:5–11 elegantly reflects this clustering:

And all they were commanded
was to worship God sincerely
affirm oneness, perform the prayer
and give a share of what they have
That is the religion of the sure
Those who deny the faith –
from the people of the book
or the idolaters –[9]
are in Jahannam's fire
eternal there
They are the worst of creation
Those who keep the faith
and perform the prayer
they are the best of creation
As recompense for them with their lord –
gardens of Eden
waters flowing underground
eternal there forever
God be pleased in them
and they in God
That is for those who hold their lord in awe[10]

This sura was revealed later in Muḥammad's mission, when Jewish and Christian communities as well as Arab polytheists did not convert as easily as the Prophet thought they would.[11] Dualistic symbolism equates the historical reality of their resistance to convert with moral failure, here failure to uphold the tenets of the Quran. But the Quranic text also places this historical moment into a mythical framework, forging an atemporal narrative in which these individuals become the typological embodiments of divine ignorance – they become 'the worst of creation.' Through their fusion with ossified, eternal categories of damnation, these people are at once labelled as outcasts from the believers and as examples, for future generations, of people who cannot adhere to the divine message. They are forever preserved in the Quranic narrative as not only inhabitants of hell but as the actual personifications of hell, the very embodiment of moral failings and eternal damnation. These individuals are placed in direct contrast with those who uphold the divine message, those who are 'the best of creation.' This duality is the material substrate for the crafting of election and damnation – a powerful force for the mediation of ethical boundaries – and plays a particularly important role in the crafting of the Shia as a distinct religious community, as scholars such as Maria Dakake have pointed out.[12]

Complementing our discussion of the ways in which oath-taking, taxes and tithing helped to galvanise support for the *mahdī* and his cause is an examination of the ways in which the persuasive force of the Quran's apocalyptic narrative was harnessed and re-signified by the authors of the *Kitāb al-kashf* and the *Kitāb al-rushd*. Both texts re-signify this narrative by arguing for a new ethical system that placed at its centre support for the *mahdī* and his cause. The *Kitāb al-kashf* (Book of unveiling)[13] has not yet been translated into any European language. The text is organised into six chapters and takes the form of an esoteric Quranic commentary, meant to be read only by those who have pledged allegiance to the Fatimid cause. While the text is attributed to Jaʿfar b. Manṣūr al-Yaman (d. 957), a member of the Yemeni Ismaili hierarchy, Madelung shows that this work predated him and was probably not written by Jaʿfar himself (though he could have edited and compiled it and might even have taken it to the Fatimid court at Cairo).[14] The dating of this text implies that it was most likely written toward the latter half of the ninth century, when members of the Fatimid hierarchy were organising their secret revolution to overthrow the Abbasids. According to this text, this *mahdī* or *qāʾim* is a descendent of ʿAlī, the Prophet's cousin and son-in law; his arrival seems to be imminent and is often equated to the resurrection itself.

The remainder of this chapter explores in detail the hermeneutics of unveiling in *Kitāb al-kashf* and focuses in particular on the ways in which it argued for the *mahdī*'s coming by re-signifying the

Quran's apocalyptic imagery. I use the term 're-signify' to denote a dual hermeneutical process: the process of uncovering hidden meanings within the Quranic text through the specification of symbolic referents – a hallmark of *ta'wīl* – and the simultaneous process of crafting new meaning through the narration of these specified referents. I show that re-signifying the end of time as the *mahdī*, who becomes the locus of salvation, allows our author to also re-signify the categories and contents of the Quran's dualities. Frequently in the text these dualities are mediated through the prism of *walāya* to the *mahdī*. This re-signification of humanity's *telos*, and of the mission to remain on the right side of history, must have provided powerful rhetorical appeal for the *mahdī*'s cause. The discussion below first illustrates in detail how the *Kitāb al-kashf* re-signifies the Quranic Day of Resurrection. It then shows how *walāya* serves to both reinforce obedience to the *mahdī* and to specify those who are on the right and wrong sides of history.

One of the major means of eschatological re-signification in the *Kitāb al-kashf* is the author's *ta'wīl* of Quranic descriptions of the end of time. In the *Kitāb al-kashf* the Day of Resurrection is repeatedly re-signified as the *mahdī* and his coming. In one selection, for instance, our author offers his *ta'wīl* of portions of Sura 78, which addresses the resurrection in its entirety. After reproducing 78:17, which reads *Indeed the Day of Judgment* [*or sorting out*] *is an appointed time* (*inna yawm al-faṣli kāna mīqātan*), our author writes 'the day of sorting out is the *mahdī*, may he be blessed' (*yawm al-faṣli huwa al-mahdī*). Our author continues: 'through whom God sorts between truth and falsehood, believer and denier. He is the appointed time of God's command and its fulfilment, and [he is] the seventh of seven *nāṭiqs*.' Our author continues his *ta'wīl* of the sura, *the day the horn is blown* is in actuality the day he [the *mahdī*] will make public the normally secret *da'wa*, and invite the people to him so that his role will be apparent to all. '*When heaven is opened and will become gateways*' [78:19] means the esoteric hidden knowledge of the *imāms* will be unveiled, so that there will be places for the gateways (*abwāb*), among them every questioner (*sā'il*) and seeker (*ṭālib*) who will have been taught by the *imām*. '*When the mountains will have vanished and be but a mirage*' [78:20]. Our author equates the mirage to the *ḥujjas* whose temporal authority will vanish; they will become lowly and subservient to the newly manifested *mahdī*.[15]

The Quran's eschatological narrative of ontological reversal becomes a script for the arrival of the *mahdī*.[16] At the end of time, the mountains – which seem like permanent fixtures of the natural realm – will be flattened, here made like a mirage. Similarly the *ḥujjas*, proofs of the *imām*'s existence in his physical absence, will become like a mirage yielding their authority to the newly manifested pivot of the universe, the *mahdī*. This ontological reversal also involves the disclosure of all hidden truths. The blowing of the horn signals the public emergence of the normally secret *daʿwa* and its ranks. The opening of the heavens is re-signified as the disclosure of the hidden knowledge of the *imāms*, knowledge that seems to encompass both the ranks of the *daʿwa* and the details of its membership. At the end of time it will be apparent that the *imām* secretly knew and taught each of these members of the *daʿwa* structure through his *abwāb*, members of the *daʿwa* whose rank is just under that of the *imām*.[17] Upon the *mahdī*'s arrival, all divine truths will be unveiled for everyone to witness – in this narrative, the divine truths are the judgment of the *imām*, his knowledge, and the ranks and membership details of the *daʿwa*. In the text, visions of mahdist anticipation and vindication for true believers are frequently tethered to descriptions of apocalyptic punishments for those who do not fulfil their obligations to the true cause; belief in the *mahdī* becomes a defining feature of this cause.

An example of the description of punishments reserved for those who fail to uphold the true cause can be found in our author's interpretation of Quran 2:8–9, which states, *Some of the people say 'we believe in God and the last day* (al-yawm al-ākhir) *but they are not believers. They think to deceive God and those who believe, but they deceive only themselves and perceive [it] not.*' Our author writes,

> He [God] means by this the Shia who fall short in the knowledge of the truth, for they say *'we believe in the last day.'* But the last day is

> the *mahdī*, the master of the age, blessings be upon him (*al-yawm al-ākhir al-mahdī ṣāḥib al-zamān*).

Our author then likens the Shia who refuse belief in the *mahdī* – unbelievers of the Last Day – to those unbelievers throughout history, invoking Quran 2:12: *Unquestionably, it is they who are the corruptors, but they perceive [it] not.*[18]

Here our author accomplishes three tasks simultaneously: first, he elides a symbol of the end time – here the Last Day – with the historical *mahdī*. Second, he defines 'they' in the phrase *'they think to deceive Allah'* as the Shia who profess belief in this *mahdī* but do not truly believe in him. And finally, he recasts those disbelieving Shia into the place of typological oblivion, equal to all corruptors throughout history. Symbolic elision through the rhetorical structure of *ta'wīl* on these two levels – typology and eschatology – not only redefines the ultimate reality (*al-yawm al-ākhir*) as a person but recasts those people who do not believe in him as equivalent to the worst of the corrupt. In re-signifying the Quranic end of time as belief and support for the *mahdī*, the *Kitāb al-kashf* also re-signifies the contents and contours of the Quran's apocalyptically mediated dualities, specifying those who will obtain salvation and those who will not. The concept of *walāya* becomes instrumental in delineating and describing those who are saved and those who are damned throughout the text.

Reflecting Landolt's findings that '*walāyah* as a socioreligious concept seems indeed exclusive: one turns either to the right or to the wrong side, and the two sides are always engaged in battle,'[19] the *Kitāb al-kashf* employs typologies of belief to argue that those who disbelieve in the *walāya* of the Shia *imām* ʿAlī, his progeny, and the *mahdī* are antagonists of God. In his *ta'wīl* of 47:1, which states, *those who disbelieve and avert [people] from the way of God – He will waste their deeds,* our author writes:

> the clear path (*sabīl al-wāḍiḥ*) is the commander of the faithful, blessings be upon him. He is the right path (*ṣirāṭ al-mustaqīm*). Whoever disbelieves in his *walāya*, and encounters God in that [state of disbelief], God will nullify his work, misguide his effort, and make him dust

> scattered. God will make them fall prostrate in the fire. [God] will certainly compensate any person among them on the Day of Judgment, but even if his deeds were as large as immovable mountains, if God does not consider his support of the *walāya* of the *amīr al-mu'minīn* to be worthy, He will not let his deeds be of benefit to him.[20]

Re-signification of the path of God as the commander of the faithful – explicitly identified as ʿAlī in other places in the *Kitāb al-kashf* – is supported here by an eschatological narrative that explicitly rewards the 'types' of individuals who believe in the *walāya* of ʿAlī. At other places in the text, based in part on the reading of Quran 25:31 that is reproduced in the *Kitāb al-kashf*, the narrative of sacred history itself is constructed around these typologies: *And likewise We made for each Prophet an enemy from among the evildoers* (25:31). In the case of this text, sacred history is simply a progression of the battles between groups of people who support the *imāms* throughout history, and those who do not.[21]

There seems to exist 'correct' *walāya* and a kind of counter-*walāya*,[22] or *walāya* to the wrong side – the *walāya* to false *imāms*. Our author re-signifies Quran 2:1–3 in the following manner.

> [2:1 *Alif Lam Mim.*
> 2:2: *This is the book about which there is no doubt, guidance for those who are mindful [of God].*
> 2:3: *Who believe in the unseen, and establish prayer, and spend out of what We have provided for them.*]
> *Alif lam mim. This is the book about which there is no doubt* [2:1–2]. He said *alif, lam, mim* is Muḥammad, may God's blessings be upon him; God commenced speaking to him. *The clear book* is the commander of the faithful, ʿAlī b. Abī Ṭālib, may God's blessings be upon him, *about which there is no doubt,* He says there is no hesitation about this. *A guidance for those who are mindful* He [says] this is the *imām* of the faithful, [the faithful] who cling fast to the *walāya* of ʿAlī . . . and guard themselves from the *walāya* of enchantment and false idols (*jibti wa-l-ṭāghūt*)[23] and the *imāms* who lead astray (*a'immat al-ḍalāl*). *Who believe in the unseen* [2:3], in the unseen which they

> know is part of the knowledge of the *imāma. And establish prayer, and spend out of what We have provided for them* [2:3]. The prayer is Ḥusayn, and the *imāms* are from his progeny.[24]

Alif Lam Mim, the disconnected letters that begin this sura, are re-signified as Muḥammad, whose speech, according to this theology, needs interpretation. This unclear speech is tacitly juxtaposed to the notion of the clear book, ʿAlī, the commander of the faithful presumably in his position as *waṣī*, or legatee, the interpreter and disseminator of Muḥammad's message. The Book which is now equated to ʿAlī, is *a guidance for those who are mindful,* the guidance being the *imām* of the believers and the mindful being those who 'cling fast to the *walāya* of ʿAlī and guard themselves from the *walāya* of enchantment and false idols and the *imāms* who lead astray.' Thus there exists not only a kind of counter-*walāya* but also counter-*imāms*. *Walāya* to the right side is inexorably intertwined with the station and knowledge of the *imām*, a knowledge that is part of the realm of the unseen. The exegete possesses this hidden knowledge that is transmitted through *walāya* to the elect through the unveiling of a series of symbolic meanings in the Quran.

The repeated emphasis of following the correct divinely appointed leaders throughout history is a recurring and major theme throughout the *Kitāb al-kashf.*

> God said *have you not considered those who exchanged the favour of God for disbelief?* [14:28]. The favour of God is the *walāya* of the commander of the faithful, and their [the communities'] exchange is their disavowal of His *walāya* . . . God the Exalted has said, *You were the people who perished* [48:12]. As for the Banū Umayya, [the Umayyads], their allotted term is until the day of *qiyāma*. The *qiyāma* (day of resurrection) is the manifestation of the *nāṭiq*. His rising, may God's blessings be upon him, is *hell, where they will burn, a wretched abode* [14:29], and *they have attributed to God equals to mislead from His way* [14:30], that is, the false *imāms* whom they have set beside God and whom they obey. [This obedience is] like the obedience the friends of God have for the *imām*, the commander of the faithful, may God bless him . . .[25]

People not only take false *imāms*, but *They love them as they should love God* (2:165), love that should be reserved for the true *imāms* whom God has selected. The results of following the incorrect *imāms*, whether false Shia *imāms* or false leaders of the community, will be vividly displayed for all to see on the day of resurrection, which we have seen is the manifestation of the *mahdī*.

> O Muḥammad! If only you could see those who have wronged the commander of the believers, meaning ʿAlī, upon him be peace, *when they see the punishment* on the day of the rising of the *qāʾim [they will be certain] that all power belongs to God and that God punishes severely* [2:165]. God will then say to the enemies of the commander of the faithful *When those who have been followed disown their followers, when they all see the suffering, when all bonds between them are severed* [2:166], namely of *walāya* with those who had followed him, *the followers will say, 'If only we had one last chance, we would disown them as they now disown us* [2:167] . . . *In this way, God will make them see their deeds as a source of bitter regret: they shall not leave the Fire.*[26]

The *Kitāb al-kashf*'s re-signification of these eschatological passages recasts true believers as supporters of ʿAlī, and by extension the *qāʾim*, reshaping the Quranic narrative so that God speaks directly to His enemies, who are now defined as the enemies of the commander of the faithful. This passage once again illustrates the centrality of *walāya* as the means for obtaining terrestrial salvation and eternal felicity.

The importance of following the correct *imām* is repeatedly emphasised throughout the *Kitāb al-kashf*. At one point, those who do not follow the correct *imāms* are considered evildoers. Our author interprets 10:17–18 as follows:

> *So who is more unjust than he who invents a lie about God or denies His signs? Indeed, the evildoers will not succeed. And they worship other than God, that which neither harms them nor benefits them, and they say 'these are our intercessors with God.' Say 'Do you inform God of something He does not know in the heavens or on the earth?' Exalted is He and high above what they associate with Him.*

> Meaning, *so who is more unjust than he who invents a lie about God* by that he ascribes to the religion (*dīn*) of God an *imām* whom God has not ascribed. *Or denies His signs,* meaning or denies the *imāms* of the religion of God, whom God has chosen. *Indeed, the evildoers will not succeed,* meaning, he will not be saved from the torment of God, and nor will he gain God's reward – and this is success. Those who commit evil in fabricating the lie about God and the *imāms* of His religion, they will not succeed.[27]

In the original Quranic narrative, the 'unjust' are equated to those who lie about God, or those who deny His signs (*āyāt*). In the re-signified narrative, those who invent a lie about God either believe in a false *imām* or deny the institution of *imāma* altogether. Further, the *imāms* themselves are equated to God's religion, and are His signs. The people who disbelieve in these divinely appointed agents are defined as evildoers, and will not be saved from God's torment. These deniers will also not succeed in the temporal realm, as indicated by the word *falāḥ*, meaning to acquire what one deserves in terms of material prosperity or happiness.[28] Thus belief in the divinely appointed *imāms*, the 'signs of God,' ensures not only eschatological success (*thawāb*) but material success (*falāḥ*) as well.

If selections of the Quran's apocalyptic élan can become, through *ta'wīl*, synonymous with the *mahdī* and his advent, then apocalyptic punishments promised to disbelievers in the divine message reserved for the afterlife now become synonymous with the temporal punishments reserved for disbelievers, those who disbelieve in the *mahdī*, the succession of ʿAlī, and the *mahdī*'s descent from divinely appointed *imāms*. This punishment is frequently described as occurring with the sword (*bi-l-sayf*) of the *qā'im*, and inevitably involves permanent, temporal victory over disbelief and disbelievers.

> *Nay! When the earth has been levelled – pounded and crushed – And your Lord has come and the angels, rank upon rank* [89:21–2]. By the earth he means the *ḥujja*, God's blessings be upon him, and his manifestation and his rising and his dissemination of his true identity after he was received. *And your Lord has come* means the *qā'im*,

> God's blessings be upon him, the master of the age. As for the angels, they are his friends (*awliyāʾ*) and his helpers (*anṣār*), and the people of his *daʿwa*.[29]

The earth is the *ḥujja*, the proof of the coming of the *qāʾim*, who subsequently becomes subservient to the ultimate authority of the *qāʾim* after the latter's arrival. Here this *qāʾim* is explicitly identified as 'your Lord,' the master of the age. In an eschatological scenario reminiscent of the Christian rapture depicted in Matt. 24:30–31 and 1 Thess. 4:15–17, the *qāʾim*, the lord, becomes manifest with the angels, who are explicitly identified as his helpers, friends and people in his *daʿwa*. The secrecy of the *daʿwa* is no more, the wait for the coming of the eschatological figure is no longer, and the triumph of true Islam will reign permanently.

The author of the *Kitāb al-kashf* then continues his *taʾwīl* of this sura:

> . . . *when Hell is that Day brought near* [89:23]. Here, hell means the *nāṭiq*, who will become manifest with the sword; he will impose his verdict upon them by killing [them] – this is Hell. *[O]n that Day man will take heed, but what good will that be to him then?* [89:23], meaning by that the reprehensible man Abū Bakr, may God curse him. On this day he will remember [the role] that he had played in opposing the commander of the faithful, he means by this [the role] Abū Bakr [had played] and by those who were like him in position and state and those who believed in his lie.[30]

Judgment here occurs on the plane of temporality and in a fascinating hermeneutic move our author identifies the *qāʾim* simultaneously with both 'your Lord' and hell – 'your Lord' for those who believe in him and are part of his *daʿwa* and hell for those who disbelieve in him and who are like Abū Bakr and his followers.

The motif involving the coming of the *qāʾim* – and concomitant, permanent temporal punishment for the disbelievers – recurs throughout this text:

> *On that Day, people will follow the summoner from whom there is no escape* [20:108]. Here, the caller [*dāʿī*] is the *qāʾim* with his sword. There is no untruth concerning his emergence, and there is no repelling his call (*daʿwa*). *[E]very voice will be hushed for the Lord of Mercy; you will hear nothing but* hams . . . [20:108]. *Hams* is the [sound of the] movement of feet [that can be heard] until the commander of the faithful finishes disputing with his enemies about the eschatological return, namely, the eschatological return after which there is no return. This is the meaning of God's words: *What about the one who has been sentenced to punishment? Can you [Prophet] rescue those already in the Fire?* [39:19]. By this He means he is among those who have lost [their] dispute on that day and he merits the *walāya* of the wrongdoers. The sword of the *qāʾim* will have taken him and he will not have anyone to save him from the fire *whose fuel is men and stones, prepared for the disbelievers* [2:24].[31]

The Quranic caller is re-signified as the *qāʾim* with his sword. His 'call,' his advent, is inevitable; it cannot be forestalled. The shuffling of footsteps associated with divine judgment is re-signified as the movement of footsteps of those who will be judged by the *qāʾim* in the final eschatological return.[32] There is no return after this – this return is the final eschatological scenario indicated by the Quran. At this final moment of history, *walāya* itself becomes the ultimate criterion of the *qāʾim*'s final judgment; those who believe in the *walāya* of anyone other than him will be shown their error before being subjected to 'the fire.' Eschatological, eternal punishment here is in no uncertain terms the judgment of the *qāʾim*, which is equivalent to hell for those who disbelieve in him.[33]

How long must the community wait before the advent of the *qāʾim*? Our author cites *taʾwīl* of 72:25 to answer this question; here I reproduce the verses surrounding 72:25 for context:

> *Say, 'I pray to my Lord alone; I set up no partner with Him'* (72:20).
> *Say, 'I have no control over any harm or good that may befall you'* (72:21).
> *Say, 'No one can protect me from God: I have no refuge except in Him* (72:22).

> *I only deliver [what I receive] from God – only His messages.' Whoever disobeys God and His Messenger will have Hell's fire as his permanent home* (72:23): *when they are confronted by what they have been warned about, they will realise who has the weaker protector and the smaller number* (72:24).
> *Say, 'I do not know whether what you have been warned about is near, or whether a distant time has been appointed for it by my Lord'* (72:25).

In elaborating upon the statement of the *imām*, who is 'the wise,' our author writes:

> And the wise, upon him be peace, in commenting on the saying of God, the High the Exalted . . . *I do not know if what you are promised is near or if my Lord will grant it for a [long] period* means by this the rising of the *qā'im* with his sword . . .[34]

The sura continues: *[He is] Knower of the unseen, and He does not disclose His* [knowledge of the] *unseen to anyone* (72:26).

Our author then continues his discussion with the *ta'wīl* of 21:110. The intertextuality of the Quran's apocalyptic narrative and the *Kitāb al-kashf*'s commentary upon it becomes more apparent in the light of the surrounding verses; here I reproduce 21:105–11.

> *We wrote in the Psalms, as We did in [earlier] scripture: 'My righteous servants will inherit the earth'* (21:105). *There truly is a message in this for the servants of God!* (21:106). *It was only as a mercy that We sent you [Prophet] to all people* (21:107). *Say, 'What is revealed to me is that your god is one God – will you submit to Him?'* (21:108) *But if they turn away, say, 'I have proclaimed the message fairly to you all. I do not know whether the judgment you are promised is near or far* (21:109), *but He knows what you reveal and conceal* (21:110). *I do not know: this [time] may well be a test for you, and enjoyment for a while'* (21:111).

Our author writes:

> *He knows what you reveal and conceal.* This verse is about those who disobeyed the commander of the faithful, blessings be upon

> him, and those who betrayed him, and what united them – namely, enmity against him and against those whom God raised to his station.[35]

Knowledge of what is revealed and concealed is the knowledge of whoever disagrees or disobeys – openly or secretly – with the commander of the faithful and his divinely appointed station. The arrival of the *qā᾿im* will make this knowledge openly manifest and this will be the time in which the righteous shall inherit the earth. But the time of the *qā᾿im*'s arrival – like the arrival of the Day of Judgment – is unknown. This ambiguity allows mahdist expectation to remain imprecise while the text simultaneously infuses temporality with a sense of eschatological imminence.

We might now ask how our author re-signifies paradise. Part of the *ta᾿wīl* of these famous verses – *O reassured soul, return to your Lord well pleased / and pleasing / enter among my righteous servants / and enter my paradise* (89:27–30) – yields an answer. Our author writes that the reassured soul is the soul of the believer. Righteous servants are, in fact,

> the *imāms* and the *nāṭiqs*, blessings be upon them. He who does not take up obedience to them is not a true believer, but he who takes up obedience to them and recognises them in their eras has merited divine contentment and pleasure. Here paradise is the *ḥujja*, upon him be peace, because every *imām* can only be reached through his *ḥujja*, and the *ḥujjas* are the gates of the *imāms*.[36]

Our author goes on to say that in some esoteric (*bāṭin*) commentaries, the Lord in this verse refers to the commander of the faithful who is 'the lord of the bond of faith (*ʿuqdat al-īmān*) and its master, upon him be peace.'[37]

Righteous servants who inhabit paradise here become the *imāms* and law-giving prophets throughout history; paradise itself becomes the *ḥujja*; and the Lord is re-signified as the commander of the faithful. But if paradise is re-signified as the *ḥujja*, what or who exactly is this *ḥujja*?

Brett argues that the *ḥujja* in the *Kitāb al-kashf* 'applies to the Imam'; he also states that Abū ʿAbdallāh uses this term for the *mahdī*.[38] Daftary writes that the term *ḥujja* appears to be the *imām*'s representative and again according to Daftary, the *Kitāb al-kashf* allows for more than one of these representatives.

> The original Shīʿī application of the term *ḥujja*, going back to the time of Imam al-Ṣādiq, was retained by the pre-Fāṭimid Ismāʿīlīs who held that in every era (*ʿaṣr*) there is a *ḥujja* of God, whether he be a prophet (*nabī*), a messenger-prophet (*rasūl*), or an imam. They also used *ḥujja* in reference to a dignitary in their religious hierarchy (*ḥudūd al-dīn*), notably one through whom the inaccessible hidden Mahdī could become accessible to his adherents. As a rank in the early *daʿwa* organization, the *ḥujja* came directly after the imam and had a special significance during the *dawr al-satr* . . . during his concealment the Qāʾim Muḥammad b. Ismāʿīl would have to be represented by his *ḥujja* . . . The early Ismāʿīlīs used the term *ḥujja* in a third sense, namely as the designated successor of the *nāṭiq* (or the imam), whilst they were both alive . . . It is interesting to note that the *Kitāb al-kashf* allows for several *ḥujjas* by specifying that only the 'greatest *ḥujja*' (*al-ḥujja al-kubrā*) succeeds to the imamate after the imam of his time.[39]

It seems that the *ḥujja* discussed here could be the awaited *imām* himself or the proof of the *imām*; in either case, however, the *ḥujja* represents access to paradise, and may even symbolise paradise itself.

The *Kitāb al-kashf*, then, shows us how the symbolic suffusion of the Quran's apocalyptic and eschatological imagery can so powerfully result in a *taʾwīl* that reifies the divinely appointed nature of the Fatimid hierarchy. This re-signified vision of the end of time creates a soteriological structure that centres around belief and support for the *mahdī* and his cause, while at the same time, through *walāya*, typologically identifies those who will benefit from divine favour and those who will not. This re-signification also creates a sense of mahdist expectation, an expectation that we see in the next text we examine, the *Kitāb al-rushd wa-l-hidāya*.

Notes

1. Brett, 'The Mīm, the ʿAyn, and the Making of Ismāʿīlīsm', *Bulletin of the School of Oriental and African Studies* 57 (1994): pp. 25–39. See also Brett, *Rise*, pp. 111–32.
2. Sells, *Approaching*, p. 35.
3. Sells, *Approaching*, p. 95.
4. Izutsu, p. 105.
5. Izutsu, p. 108.
6. Izutsu, p. 108.
7. Sells, *Approaching*, p. 124.
8. See Lawson, 'Duality', pp. 36–41, for an insightful discussion on the relationship between duality and typology. He writes (p. 40) in reference to the apocalyptic nature of the Quran: 'it seems clear that while duality and opposition provide a skeleton, typological figuration puts the flesh on that skeleton, and that when this happens the apocalyptic or revelatory reality is truly born. The apocalypse enters history once again with the experience and preaching of Muḥammad, who is both the symbol and exemplar of all previous prophetic types.'
9. Sells, *Approaching*, p. 104.
10. Sells, *Approaching*, p. 106.
11. Sells, *Approaching*, p. 105.
12. Dakake, *Charismatic Community*.
13. Daftary, *The Ismāʿīlīs*, 2nd edn, p. 98.
14. See the discussion of this in Madelung, 'Das Imamat in der frühen ismailitischen Lehre', *Der Islam* 37 (1961), pp. 52–8, as cited in Jaʿfar b. Manṣūr al-Yaman, *Kitāb al-ʿālim*, trans. Morris, p. 57, n. 57. There, Morris writes: 'There is no reason why Jaʿfar should not have been the "editor" or compiler of this work . . .' See also Halm, *Empire*, p. 79.
15. *Kitāb al-kashf*, ed. Ghālib, pp. 147–8.
16. Brett has argued that the *Kitāb al-Kashf* 'looks like the textbook of the revolution that brought the dynasty to power' through his reading of the terms *ḥujja* and *imām* as parallel with the historical proclamation of al-Mahdī as God's *ḥujja*. See Brett, *Rise*, p. 124.
17. Daftary, *The Ismāʿīlīs*, 2nd edn, pp. 216–17.
18. *Kitāb al-kashf*, ed. Ghālib, p. 26.
19. Landolt, p. 317.

20. *Kitāb al-kashf*, ed. Ghālib, p. 37.
21. Velji, 'Apocalyptic Rhetoric'.
22. For an outstanding discussion of *walāya* and counter-*walāya* in the thought of the Fāṭimid *dāʿī* al-Muʾayyad, see Elizabeth Alexandrin, 'The Sphere of Walāya: Ismāʿīlī Taʾwīl in Practice according to al-Muʾayyad (d. ca. 1078 C.E.)', PhD diss. (McGill University, 2006), pp. 275–92.
23. See, for instance, Q. 4:51.
24. *Kitāb al-kashf*, ed. Ghālib, p. 38.
25. *Kitāb al-kashf*, ed. Ghālib, pp. 38–9.
26. *Kitāb al-kashf*, ed. Ghālib, p. 40.
27. *Kitāb al-kashf*, ed. Ghālib, p. 150.
28. Lane, s.v. '*falaḥ*'.
29. *Kitāb al-kashf*, ed. Ghālib, p. 70.
30. *Kitāb al-kashf*, ed. Ghālib, p. 71.
31. *Kitāb al-kashf*, ed. Ghālib, pp. 80–1.
32. *Rajʿa* is 'The returning to the present state of existence after death', Lane, s.v. '*Rajʿah*'.
33. Another vision of the eschatological battle described in the *kashf* has been discussed by Shin Nomoto in his masterful dissertation on Abū Ḥātim al-Rāzī. There he writes that the Qāʾim will '. . . conquer Makkah and Madīnah with the support of the Archangel Gabriel (Jabrāʾīl) at the end of time, and with his advent God's religion will be perfected'. 'Early Ismāʿīlī Thought on Prophecy According to the Kitāb al-Islāh by Abū Ḥātim al-Rāzī (d. ca. 322/934–5)', PhD diss. (McGill University, 1999), p. 120. See also *Kitāb al-kashf*, pp. 48–50.
34. *Kitāb al-kashf*, ed. Ghālib, p. 90.
35. *Kitāb al-kashf*, ed. Ghālib, p. 90.
36. *Kitāb al-kashf*, ed. Ghālib, p. 72.
37. *Kitāb al-kashf*, ed. Ghālib, p. 72.
38. Brett, *Rise*, p. 125.
39. Daftary, *The Ismāʿīlīs*, 2nd edn, p. 118.

4

Ta'wīl of an Apocalyptic Transcript II: *The Book of Righteousness and True Guidance*

Another text written before the Fatimids officially ascended to power, the *Kitāb al-rushd wa-l-hidāya* (Book of righteousness and true guidance), concerns the imminent reappearance of the Mahdī. Wladimir Ivanow wrote that 'the work is full of the intense spirit of expectations of the *Mahdī* the promised messiah in the person of the last and seventh *Nāṭiq*.'[1] My discussion of the text illustrates some of the modalities of *ta'wīl* that help convey this intense mahdist spirit. Among these modalities, numerological correspondences figure prominently in creating a sense of mahdist expectation by correlating certain chapters of the Quran to the awaited *mahdī*.

The author of the text also uses numerical correspondences to re-signify various Quranic terms, which when properly deciphered, point to key figures in the Fatimid hierarchy. The hermeneutics of numerological correspondence are coupled with a theme that we witnessed in the last chapter: the re-signification of the end of time and its attributes as the *mahdī* and his arrival; this work thus creates, as in the *Kitāb al-kashf*, a powerful appeal to join and work for the true cause.

Numerical correspondences occur throughout the *Kitāb al-rushd* – a feature we find commonly in writings from this period and beyond.[2] Here the most prominent numerical correspondence is the correlation between certain chapters of the Quran that correspond to Muḥammad and the following chapters that correspond to the *mahdī*. This correspondence results in a reading of the text that oscillates, symbolically, between the past and the awaited future, between Muḥammad and the awaited eschatological figure. For instance, our author writes that Sura 24 begins a new heptad of chapters; the sura after that, Surat al-Furqān (25), directly mentions Muḥammad. Our author counts six more suras after this, and states that the seventh, in this example Sura 32, refers to the *mahdī*. This reading of the Quran is then fused to the hermeneutic feature we witnessed earlier in the *Kitāb al-kashf*: the *ta'wīl* of various Quranic descriptions of the end of time, which now refer to the *mahdī* and his advent. These two interpretive mechanisms and others that we see throughout the text unveil symbolic references to the Fatimid *mahdī*, his hierarchy and the elect community that will be rewarded at the end of time.

The text begins with a discussion of various numerological correspondences between the Quran and the Fatimid hierarchy.

> The Quran begins with *bismillāh al-raḥmān al-raḥīm;*[3] *'bismillāh'* is [comprised of] seven letters. Twelve letters arise from this. The twelve letters that follow are *al-raḥmān al-raḥīm*. The sura is *sūrat al-ḥamd*, which has seven verses. The seven [letters], which are the *bismillāh*, signify the seven *nāṭiqs*. The twelve letters that arise from these signify that for each *nāṭiq* there are twelve *naqībs*. Thus the twelve letters, which are *al-raḥmān al-raḥīm*, that arise from them [i.e., the seven, the *bismillāh*], [together] become nineteen [letters]. This signifies that from the *nāṭiqs* – after each *nāṭiq* – seven *imāms* and twelve *ḥujjas* arise, which makes nineteen.[4]

The *bismillāh* invocation, the *basmala*, refers to Fatimid conceptions of sacred history that include the seven speaker-prophets and each of their twelve *naqībs* or persons in charge of each *jazīra* (island). Each of these speaker-prophets also gives rise to seven *imāms*, each of whom gives rise, in turn to twelve *ḥujjas*. It should be noted here that the term *ḥujja* may also be synonymous for the position of *naqīb*.[5] Regardless, the very reading of the *basmala* is transformed into an invocation of the signification of Fatimid sacred history and its associated hierarchy.

The text also states that the deeper realities of the disconnected letters of the Quran, the dots on some of the letters, and the order of the Quran itself, for instance, all have a pattern: they may point to the various persons associated with the Fatimid hierarchy (*da'wa*), to their ontological position in the hierarchy, or to the order of these figures' appearance on the plane of history. The framing of history, too, acquires meaning through numerical correspondence. Our author writes:

> The period of time (*waqt*) between Muḥammad and the *mahdī* is 'the sixth time' (*al-waqt al-sādis*). Muḥammad is the sixth *nāṭiq*, the Quran was revealed to him, and the number of its chapters refers to the six periods (*al-awqāt al-sitta*) between the seven *nāṭiqs*, seven *imāms*, and twelve *ḥujjas*.[6]

The total number of chapters of the Quran, 114, is a product of six periods multiplied by seven (the *nāṭiqs* or the *imāms*) added to twelve (the *ḥujjas*); thus 6 × 19 = 114. In addition to pointing to the seven *nāṭiqs* and the authorised figures who come between them, this pattern also indicates that between each of the seven *nāṭiqs* there are seven completer (*mutimm*) *imāms*, the *imāms* between each *nāṭiq*.[7]

Our author further explains that the Quran can be divided into sevens to indicate Muḥammad and the arrival of the *mahdī*. He writes, for instance, that 'In every seventh sura, when there is a mention of a new obligation or command, [this] signifies the *nāṭiq* who is to come after Muḥammad.'[8] He writes:

> The number [pattern] resumes after Surat al-'Anfāl [Sura 8]. The next sura after it is Surat al-Barā'a [Sura 9] that begins with *A release by God and His Messenger* – and he is Muḥammad, may God's blessings and peace be upon him. Then after Surat al-Barā'a there are six suras and the seventh is Surat al-Naḥl [Sura 16], [which begins with], *God's judgment is coming, so do not ask to bring it on sooner.* This signifies the completion of the seven *mutammims* in number,

> and also signifies the [advent of the] seventh *nāṭiq*; He says that *God's judgment is coming, so do not ask to bring it on sooner.* That is the time of his manifestation (*wa huwa waqt ẓuhūrihi*).[9]

The pattern continues throughout the text: a group of suras begins a group of seven, with our author stating that the next sura refers directly to Muḥammad. Sura 24, for instance, begins a new heptad; the sura after that, al-Furqān (Sura 25), makes direct mention of Muḥammad. Our author counts six more suras after this, and makes explicit that the seventh, in this example Sura 32, refers once again to the 'completion of the seven *mutammims* in number, and likewise the seventh of the *nāṭiq*s by mention of the resurrection' [*al-qiyāma*].[10] This pattern allows the author to equate the rich and variegated dimensions of the Quranic resurrection to the *mahdī* and his advent. Through this hermeneutic, the time of the manifestation of the seventh *nāṭiq* is correlated with descriptions of the Day of Meeting (40:15), the ever-approaching Day (40:18), the Day of Mutual Neglect (Sura 64), and the Deafening Blast (80:33), for instance.

The re-signification and repetition of the *mahdī* as various aspects of the Quran's apocalyptic and eschatological scaffolding serves to preserve the rhetorical force of these passages while reorienting their meaning around the imminent advent of the *mahdī*. For instance, our author reproduces this selection from Sura 72 (in italics below), which states:

> Whoever disobeys God and His Messenger will have hell's fire as his permanent home: *when they are confronted by what they have been promised, they will realize who has the weaker protector and the smaller number. Say, 'I do not know whether that which you have been promised is near, or whether a distant time has been appointed for it by my Lord.'* He is the One who knows what is hidden (72:23–6).

He then writes: *that which you have been promised,* is the time of the manifestation of the seventh of the *nāṭiq*s, and it is [or he is] the Hour [*wa-huwa al-sāʿa*]. And He has said, *What will make you perceive? Perhaps the Hour is near* [42:17]. Our author then writes that the 'Surat al-Jinn points to the seven *mutammims* in number and points, by what it contains, to the seventh of the *nāṭiqs*.'[11] The Hour thus becomes the approaching advent of the *mahdī* figure, the locus of ultimate salvation, the standard for proper belief. To be sure, verse 42:18 of the Quran reads, *those who do not believe in it seek to hasten it, but the believers stand in awe of it. They know it to be the Truth; those who argue about the Hour are far, far astray*. The contours of right belief are constructed around proper appreciation for the veracity, potency, and ultimacy of the promised Hour – here support for the *mahdī* and his cause. It is interesting to note too, that the exact time of the *mahdī*'s advent remains unfixed, preserving the Quran's own sense of eschatological ambiguity.

In addition to equating the *mahdī* and his advent to the 'deafening blast' inaugurating the resurrection (80:33), to the 'overwhelming day' of the end of time (Sura 88), and to the *fire of God, stoked for blazing rising up over their hearts*[12] (Sura 104), our author states that the advent of the *mahdī* is the completion of *tawḥīd* (unity) and of religion itself. In his discussion of the chapter of Sincerity (112), he writes:

> *Say, He is God, one*[13] and it is, just as it is said, the completion of *tawḥīd* – the time of the manifestation of the seventh of the *nāṭiqs*, and indicates the completion of the seven *mutammims* in number. It [also] indicates the seventh of the *nāṭiqs* by the perfection of *tawḥīd* and the perfection of religion [*dīn*], and is the time of his manifestation.[14]

Our author has, then, divided the Quran according to a numerical scheme that correlates certain chapter numbers to the sixth *nāṭiq* (Muḥammad) and each of the following chapters to the potentially imminent advent of the seventh *nāṭiq* (the *mahdī*), and the seven final *imāms*. This correlation constructs a metanarrative of the Quran that operates between the time of Muḥammad and the time of the awaited *mahdī*, who acquires various attributes of the Quranic resurrection – the overwhelming day, the deafening blast, the Hour, the Fire, the completion of *tawḥīd*. The repeated references to him and the time of his manifestation as various elements of the resurrection seem to suggest that history's consummation is expected fairly soon. Yet the exact date of his arrival remains unfixed. In direct reference to when this Hour will arrive, our author writes:

> *They ask you [Prophet] about the Hour, 'When will it arrive?' Say, 'My Lord alone has knowledge of it: He alone will reveal when its time will come, a time that it momentous* [literally, 'weighs heavy'] *in both the heavens and the earth. All too suddenly it will come upon you'* [7:187]. And He says, *People will ask you [Prophet] about the Hour. Say, 'God alone has knowledge of it.' How could you [Prophet] know? The Hour may well be near* [33:63]. And He says *They ask you [Prophet] about the Hour, saying 'When will it arrive?', but how can you [tell] them that?* . . . until the end of the sura, [which reads], *Its time is known only to your Lord; you are only sent to warn those who fear it. On the Day they see it, it will seem they lingered [in this life] an evening [at most] or its morning* [79:42–6].

Our author writes:

> The Hour is the manifestation of the *mahdī*, the *nāṭiq*, the seventh of the *nāṭiq*s. God has concealed the time of his manifestation from His prophet and the people, and has emphasised this issue upon His prophet in His book because it was a custom [*sunna*] for the *nāṭiq*s before him – that He would not make apparent to them the time in which He was going to send any one of them. And His saying *weighs heavy* refers to the *imām*s and the *ḥujja*s who do not know the time of the manifestation of the *mahdī*. *All too suddenly it will come upon you.*[15]

The indeterminacy of the end of time is reinterpreted here as indeterminacy concerning the dispatching of the speaker-prophets, the last of whom is the *mahdī*. Our author seems to suggest that this indeterminancy, perhaps along with the momentous nature of the *mahdī*'s arrival, weighs on the *imām*s and *ḥujja*s, who, by divine design, do not know the precise date when the *mahdī* will arrive.

Similar to the other texts of *ta'wīl* we examine here, the end of time is not the exclusive subject of the *Kitāb al-rushd*. The text, often elegantly, discusses the relationship between the Fatimid hierarchy and the terrestrial realm.[16]

Repeatedly throughout this and other early Fatimid texts, we witness the theme of coming alive. This is often accomplished through the acquisition of religious knowledge (*ʿilm*), which, in turn, is repeatedly likened to life-giving water that descends from the sky. A fine example is our author's *ta'wīl* of 7:57. The entire verse states:

> [*It is God who sends the winds, bearing good news of His coming grace, and when they have gathered up the heavy clouds, We drive them to a dead land where We cause rain to fall, bringing out all kinds of crops, just as We shall bring out the dead; perhaps [then] you will be reminded.*]
>
> By the good news of the winds He meant the movement of heavy clouds. The heavy clouds are the *dāʿīs* and the dead land is the land whose people are following knowledge of the *ẓāhir* [the apparent]; in it there is no life [i.e. the *dāʿīs*] which calls [the people of] the land to the truth. His saying *We cause rain to fall,* the rain [lit. water sent down] is knowledge of religion, *bringing out all kinds of crops;* those who enter into the *daʿwa* consist of believers from every place while the *ahl al-bayt* in that land are, because of their knowledge, the crops. [*J*]*ust as We shall bring out the dead:* its meaning is He will bring forth the ignorant from the death of ignorance, *perhaps [then] you may be reminded,* that is, you [will] see the growth of the trees by means of water in the *ẓāhir* and by it you will reflect on the explanation of believers as those who have knowledge of religion and [those who have] emerged out of ignorance, just as fruits and plants emerge out of the earth. The good news is the *waṣī* [whose rank is directly below that of a prophet, entrusted with the responsibility for disseminating the *bāṭin* to the elect], for it is he who sends out the *dāʿīs* by whose hands there is life. God has said, *the clouds that are compelled between heaven and earth* [2:164], namely the *imām* and the *ḥujja* is the one who compels, one who demands obedience. While the religious scholar (*ʿālim*) calls to the knowledge of the *ẓāhir imām,*[17] the knowledge of the *ḥujja* is [knowledge of the]

> *bāṭin* [esoteric]. Thus the descent of rain from the clouds is a symbol for the knowledge which is heard from the *dāʿīs*, and the growth of plants is similar to the growth of the believer through knowledge of religion.[18]

The *dāʿīs* are likened to clouds heavy with rain. These *dāʿīs* disseminate life-giving knowledge – the *ʿilm* of religion – just as the clouds send life-giving rain. Those receptive to this knowledge grow spiritually as crops grow from land that might seem barren. Note how the frequent Quranic argument linking seasonal regeneration to belief in the resurrection (Q. 22:5, 30:50, 41:39, 71:17–18, for instance) is transformed into the true believer's movement from the *ẓāhir* to the *bāṭin* – the end of ignorance and concomitant acquisition of true knowledge under the purview of the Fatimid hierarchy. The *imām/ḥujja* compel obedience, the *waṣīs* dispense the *dāʿīs* and the *dāʿīs* dispense this life-giving knowledge to those who are ignorant, allowing true religion to flourish.

It is not only aspects of the natural order that acquire symbolic referents; aspects of creation do as well. One such example occurs in our author's *ta'wīl* of Quran 9:36, which reads: *God decrees that there are twelve months – ordained in God's Book on the Day when He created the heavens and earth – four months of which are sacred.*

Our author writes:

> *God decrees that there are twelve months* means the *nuqabā'* and the *ḥujjas*. *[O]n the Day when He created the heavens and the earth* is the day He sent the *nāṭiqs* and established the *nāṭiqs* for the sake of the *waṣīs*, *four months of which are sacred,* among the *nuqabā'* are four whose ranks are higher.[19] Then He says *That is the correct religion, so do not wrong yourselves in these months,* meaning that is the correct religion which pleases Him and which He has established for them. *And do not wrong yourselves* by denying them, for whoever refuses to acknowledge the friends of God and turns to others has indeed wronged himself. The ranks of God are the stations of the messengers and the *waṣiyya* and the *imāma* and the *ḥujjas* and what they have established of the obligations of God and His *sunna*.

> Whoever transgresses the command of God concerning them has wronged himself.[20]

In the Quranic verse, a correlation exists between the creation of the twelve months, the creation of the heavens and the earth, and the setting apart or making sacred of the four months. God, in His fashioning of creation, seems to also order temporality through the creation of twelve months. Note how our author's *ta'wīl* of this verse refashions the subject of the months to indicate the twelve *nuqabā'* or *ḥujjas* – the leaders of each of the twelve islands. The temporal moment of the creation of the twelve leaders of the islands is located not in the present, but is, through this *ta'wīl*, located within the creative process itself. Just as time is ordered into twelve months, so is the Fatimid hierarchy, and reflecting that hierarchy, four of these *nuqabā'* are exalted over others. Our author equates true religion with an acknowledgment of the divinely ordained positions of all these agents. These are the friends of God; those who do not follow them will inevitably go astray. Our author then further clarifies the elect of God's ranks: the stations of the messengers, the *waṣiyya*, the *imāma*, the *ḥujjas* and their ordinances. Like the ordering of time from the moment of creation, they are the exalted among God's ranks.

The text ends with the author's *ta'wīl* of a dramatic passage of the Quran, 74:38–47, when the inhabitants of heaven ask the people of Hell why they are there.

Our author writes:

> Among the believers are those who are in the state of ritual consecration of the pilgrim. God has said, *every soul shall be accountable for what it has earned except for the Companions of the Right* [74:38–9]. Every *dāʿī* is accountable for what he preaches and whom he guides, except for those in the state of ritual consecration of the pilgrim – they are the companions of the *dāʿī* in the gardens.[21]

Ivanow, using another key early Fatimid text, the *Kitāb al-ʿālim wa-l-ghulām* as evidence, identifies the term *muḥrim* – traditionally used as a term for someone who is in a state of ritual purity for the hajj – to mean 'a sense of initiated convert.'[22] If this interpretation is correct, those converts initiated by the *dāʿī* are the 'Companions of the Right'– defined here as true believers. Sura 74:38–47 reads:

> *Every soul is held in pledge for its deeds, but the Companions of the Right will stay in gardens and ask about the guilty. 'What drove you to the scorching Fire?' and they will answer, 'We did not pray; we did not feed the poor. We indulged with others [in mocking the believers]; we denied the Day of Judgment until the certain end came upon us.*

Our author writes:

> *In Gardens and ask about the guilty*, meaning, those sinners are the ones who are guilty of denying the truth and who do not believe in it. The believers – the companions of the *dāʿī* – will say to the deniers of truth, *'What drove you to the scorching Fire?'* meaning, what made you deserve the punishment of hellfire? The deniers of truth will say *'we did not pray,'* meaning, we were not among the callers to the truth, as prayer [*ṣalāt*] in the *bāṭin* is the *daʿwa*. The Companions of the Right, who are the believers, the companions of the *dāʿī* –will say, 'we were not among the *dāʿīs* but we are in the garden.' The deniers of the truth will say *'we did not feed,'* meaning, we are not clearly seen nor are we regarded as believers through [having] wisdom. The believers, the companions of the *dāʿī*, say, we are not among those who are clearly seen or regarded [as believers through having wisdom] either. The deniers of truth will say *'we used to indulge with others'* meaning, we engaged in conversation and speech. The believers will say, we also engaged in conversation and speech. The deniers of truth will say *'we used to deny the Day of Judgment until the certain end came upon us'*; its meaning is that we denied the *mahdī*, the seventh of the *nāṭiqs*. The believers will reply 'We did not deny the *mahdī*; rather, we were loyal to him continuously and we are among the people of his covenant [*ʿahd*] and of his protection [*dhimma*]. As a result we have merited the gardens while you have merited the punishment of hellfire by your denial of the Companions of the Right and the companions of the *dāʿī*. Thus the believer is

> *muḥrim* at the station at which he has attained understanding. This is the *ta'wīl* and *tafsīr* of this verse in the *bāṭin* and the *ẓāhir*.[23]

Once again the matrix of apocalyptic religion is used to radically redefine the parameters of true belief, giving temporal and soteriological structure to the *mahdī*'s cause. This challenging selection indicates that there is a symmetry among the damned and the saved: both were not members of the *da'wa*; both did not articulate their beliefs outwardly and both engaged in idle talk. The barometer of true belief here is continuous support of the *mahdī* – governed by the covenant – which in turn is linked to the idea of attaining true understanding. Just as the Quran presents belief in the reckoning as central to belief in Islam itself, the author of this text presents belief in the *mahdī* as central to true understanding of right religion.

Numismatic Evidence

Numismatic evidence too suggests that the early tenth-century revolutionary Fatimids envisioned their terrestrial successes as a product of their divinely appointed role to bring an imminent and permanent triumph over disbelief at the end of history. While the Fatimids did not make drastic changes to their predecessors' coinage until the period of the caliph-imam al-Muʿizz[24] (r. 952–975), evidence indicates that before this they circulated coins with slight inscriptional changes.[25] These changes were not obvious[26] – one must have had to look very closely to see these changes – but the messages seem clear: with the new dynasty the fulfilment of predictions concerning the advent of the *mahdī* has arrived, along with an imminent triumphalist message of truth over falsehood.

One of the most interesting examples dates from 909; it is a coin issued by Abū ʿAbdallāh al-Shīʿī, the early Fatimid *dāʿī* who ruled over portions of the western Maghrib on behalf of the *mahdī* before the latter's emergence. Its inscription reads: 'The proof [*ḥujja*] of God has arrived and disperses His enemies.'[27] As we have seen with the *Kitāb al-kashf*, the term *ḥujja* could be read multivalently; it is a technical term that may refer to a member of the Fatimid hierarchy right below the *mahdī*, who, in the latter's absence, serves as proof of the *mahdī*'s existence. Or, as Brett argues, it could refer to Abū ʿAbdallāh al-Shīʿī's term for the *mahdī* himself. The coin's date places it between Abū ʿAbdallāh al-Shīʿī's subduing of Ifrīqiya and the *mahdī*'s emergence in 910, making it quite likely that the inscription refers to the divine fulfilment of Fatimid predictions concerning the *mahdī*'s advent.

Quranic inscriptions, too, allude to the triumph of belief over falsehood. Like coins minted before them,[28] the marginalia of Fatimid coins were frequently inscribed with Quran 9:33: *It is He who has sent His Messenger with guidance and the religion of truth, to show that it is above all [other] religions, however much the idolaters may hate this.* The religion of truth was the Fatimid vision of Islam in distinction to other interpretations, and this vision, according to Qāḍī l-Nuʿmān – whom we encounter extensively in the next chapter – is associated with the advent of the eschatological figure.[29] Early Fatimid coins bore other Quranic verses as well: a type of undated coin minted in the name of the first Fatimid caliph, ʿAbdallāh al-Mahdī, for instance, bore a circular marginal inscription on the reverse from 17:81: *And say, 'The truth has come, and falsehood has passed away: falsehood is bound to pass away,'* a verse that is thought to relate to the *mahdī*'s role in revealing true religion.[30] Other coins struck during the time of the first Fatimid caliph are inscribed with Quran 6:115: *And the word of your Lord has been fulfilled in truth and in justice. None can alter His words,*[31] and 30:4–5: *Authority belongs to God before and after, and on that day the believers shall rejoice in the help of God.*[32] Thus numismatic and textual evidence bears witness to the force of apocalyptic religion in helping to galvanise support for the Fatimid *mahdī*, a utopian symbolic currency that the Fatimids – like other apocalyptically charged groups in Islamic history and beyond – then had to temper. How did the dynasty consolidate power while also contending with this issue of an expected (and seemingly imminent) apocalypse?

Notes

1. Ibn Ḥawshab Manṣūr al-Yaman, *Kitāb al-Rushd wa-l-hidāya*, trans. W. Ivanow in *Studies in Early Persian Ismailism* (Leiden: Brill, 1948), p. 30.
2. T. Fahd, 'Ḥurūf', *Encyclopaedia of Islam*, second edition, ed. P. Bearman, et al. (Leiden: Brill, 1960–2005), vol. 5, pp. 595–6. See also Bashir, *Fazlallah Astarabadi*, pp. 64–83, for an outstanding explanation of how the leader of a fifteenth-century Persian mahdist movement engaged in his own interpretation of the science of letters.
3. I have modified the transliteration here to emphasise the numerical patterns.
4. Ibn Ḥawshab, *Kitāb al-rushd*, ed. M. Kāmil Ḥusayn, p. 189.
5. See, for instance, the discussion in Daftary, *The Ismāʿīlīs*, 2nd edn, p. 218.
6. Ibn Ḥawshab, *Kitāb al-rushd*, trans. Ivanow, p. 35 [with slight adjustments]; ed. M. Kāmil Ḥusayn, p. 6.
7. Ibn Ḥawshab, *Kitāb al-rushd*, trans. Ivanow, p. 35, ed. M. Kāmil Ḥusayn, p. 191.
8. Ibn Ḥawshab, *Kitāb al-rushd*, ed. M. Kāmil Ḥusayn, p. 191.
9. Ibn Ḥawshab, *Kitāb al-rushd*, ed. M. Kāmil Ḥusayn, p. 192.
10. Ibn Ḥawshab, *Kitāb al-rushd*, ed. M. Kāmil Ḥusayn, p. 193.
11. Ibn Ḥawshab, *Kitāb al-rushd*, ed. M. Kāmil Ḥusayn, p. 195.
12. Sells, *Approaching*, p. 118.
13. Sells, *Approaching*, p. 136.
14. Ibn Ḥawshab, *Kitāb al-rushd*, ed. M. Kāmil Ḥusayn, p. 196.
15. Ibn Ḥawshab, *Kitāb al-rushd*, ed. M. Kāmil Ḥusayn, pp. 200–1.
16. While the primary focus of the *Kitāb al-rushd* is indeed the construction of an imminent mahdism, a discussion on solely this aspect of Fatimid theology without reference to its mystical or noetic elements would risk obscuring its elegance and complexity. Methodologically, a focus on end-time theology has also been an issue in the study of contemporary millennial groups more broadly. For instance, Gordon Melton writes, 'The belief that prophecy is the organizing or determining principle for millennial groups is common among media representatives, nonmillennial religious rivals, and scholars. In their eagerness to isolate what they see as a decisive or interesting fact, they ignore or pay only passing attention to the larger belief structure of the group and the role that structure plays in the life of believers'. J. Gordon Melton, 'Spiritualization and

Reaffirmation: What Really Happens when Prophecy Fails', in *Expecting Armageddon, Essential Readings in Failed Prophecy*, Jon R. Stone (ed.) (New York: Routledge, 2000), p. 147.

17. This, presumably, refers to the Quran.
18. Ibn Ḥawshab, *Kitāb al-rushd*, ed. M. Kāmil Ḥusayn, pp. 205–6.
19. This is a theme that appears in other early Fatimid texts. Daftary writes, 'Amongst the twelve *ḥujjas* serving the imam, four occupied special positions, comparable to the positions of the four sacred months amongst the twelve months of the year'. *The Ismailis*, 2nd edn, p. 218.
20. Ibn Ḥawshab, *Kitāb al-rushd*, ed. M. Kāmil Ḥusayn, p. 203.
21. Ibn Ḥawshab, *Kitāb al-rushd*, ed. M. Kāmil Ḥusayn, p. 212.
22. 'Perhaps in KAG we find its explanation, in the sense of one "who dons the *iḥrām* of the pilgrim, and, strengthened by the helping hand, is enabled to circumambulate the Ancient House of God." Under the latter, Kaʿba, not the original Islamic sanctuary is meant, but the Imam, the *qibla* of the Ismailis.' Ivanow, *Studies*, pp. 25–6.
23. Ibn Ḥawshab, *Kitāb al-rushd*, ed. M. Kāmil Ḥusayn, pp. 212–13.
24. Sherif Anwar and Jere L. Bacharach, 'Shiʿism and the Early Dinars of the Fāṭimid Imam-caliph al-Muʿizz li-dīn Allāh (341–65/952–75): An Analytic Overview', *Al-Masāq*, vol. 22, no. 3 (December 2010), p. 260.
25. Anwar and Bacharach, p. 264.
26. Nicol, *Fāṭimid Coins*, p. xi.
27. Walker, *Exploring an Islamic Empire*, pp. 95–6; Nicol, p. 1; Alnoor Jehangir Merchant, 'Qurʾanic Inscriptions on Fatimid Coinage', in *Word of God, Art of Man: The Qurʾan and its Creative Expressions*, ed. Fahmida Suleman (New York: Oxford University Press in association with the Institute of Ismaili Studies, 2007), p. 113. See also the discussion in Bloom, pp. 36–7.
28. See, for instance, Jere L. Bacharach, *Islamic History through Coins: An Analysis and Catalogue of Tenth-Century Ikhshidid Coinage* (Cairo and New York: American University in Cairo Press, 2006), p. 17.
29. Bierman, p. 69. See also the discussion in Merchant, esp. p. 111.
30. Merchant, pp. 111–12.
31. Nicol, p. 4
32. Nicol, pp. 5–6.

5

To Temper an Imminent Eschatology: The Contributions of al-Mahdī and Qāḍī l-Nuʿmān

Paul Walker opens his recent work on Fatimid history with an elegant description of the initial public proclamation of Fatimid rule:

> On 20 Rabīʿ II 297/Friday 4 January 910, the mosques of the old Aghlabid governorate in North Africa and Sicily rang with the proclamation of a new ruler, one no longer subservient to an eastern caliphal overlord but completely independent, replacing, in fact, not only all former rulers but the earlier forms of Islamic government back to the golden era of the Prophet himself and of his rightful successor ʿAlī b. Abī Ṭālib. The caliph al-Mahdī's victory was in reality a revolution in the true sense. For his Ismaili followers, it constituted a restoration of correct and righteous government, and of God's ordinance; it represented the assumption of power by His real friends, the family of His prophet and their most loyal supporters. Years of hardship and repression at the hands of usurpers were now over; in this one corner of the far west, a lengthy period of secret struggle in many other regions of the Islamic empire had at last achieved a glorious end.[1]

Walker describes the rise of the Fatimids, according to Ismaili followers, as a successful revolution – a 'glorious end' that is grounded in a return to an idealised past, a time when truth has triumphed over falsehood. One of the most remarkable and unexplored aspects of early Fatimid political theology is how early exegetes of empire so effectively harnessed the utopian dimensions of apocalypticism while distancing its imminence. This chapter explores some of the hermeneutical mechanisms used by two exegetes in particular to locate the Fatimid empire and/or the *imām* as the locus of earthly utopia while postponing the end of time. These questions – of eschatological postponement and simultaneous consolidation of authority – are inspired by and related to theoretical discussions in the sociology of religion concerning the reinterpretation of apocalyptic prophecy.[2] My analysis differs from this body of literature in at least two respects. First, I focus here on the specific mechanisms of reinterpretation and consolidation articulated by my sources; my analysis is thus more textual than sociological. Second, while my method might best be described as textual, the questions of eschatological reinterpretation and consolidation of authority are designed to elicit data that can be used both theoretically and comparatively to advance intra-, inter-religious, and theoretical work on these two questions, work that will, in turn, help to open this more specialised literature to wider audiences.

The first source that I examine here is a letter written by the caliph al-Mahdī to his Yemeni followers. Brett writes:

> The text of this Letter is a mere summary of the original, recollected after many years by Jaʿfar ibn Manṣūr al-Yaman, the son of Ibn Ḥawshab, the Dāʿī of the Yemen, who came to Ifrīqiya long after the death of his father in 302/914–15, and some time after the death of the Mahdi himself in 322/934. As a text, therefore, it belongs once again to the literature of the dynasty in the middle period of the century, when its ancestry was a matter of renewed concern.[3]

He further writes that: 'The text as we have it falls into two halves, and may well represent not just one, but a whole series of letters written in those years in reply to a variety of questions put to the Mahdi on the crucial subject of his ancestry, identity and mission.'[4] The second half of the letter discusses the place of the caliph al-Mahdī in sacred history – more specifically, his identity and his relationship to the awaited *mahdī* at the end of time. Al-Mahdī's role in sacred history is described through his commentary on a tradition attributed to Jaʿfar, the sixth *imām*.

> A man belonging to the *shīʿa* came to Jaʿfar, son of Muḥammad – peace be upon him – and said: 'Son of God's apostle! Of the Umayyads so-and-so and so-and-so ruled, and of the Abbasids, so-and-so ruled. Will there be from your family only one *mahdī*, whose hands will accomplish the resurrection?' Jaʿfar, son of Muḥammad – God's blessings be upon him – said: 'God would have made light of the family of Muḥammad if they produced but one *mahdī!* On the contrary, we give you good tidings of the expected *mahdī* through whom the truth will become powerful; [he is but] the first one who will ascend the pulpit of his grandfather, and who will fight under the banners of the believers to achieve his rights, and through whom tribulation ceases to trouble the people of his party (*shīʿā*) and in whose dynasty the totality of believers will become powerful. With his appearance the glory of the family of Muḥammad will last until the end of the world and from his progeny will go forth [many] leaders (*hudā*), as [divinely] aided *mahdī*s till the hour [of reckoning] arrives. And from our family [will go forth] the rightly-guided (*mahdī*) and the guide (*hādī*) and the one guided by him (*muhtadī bihi*) and he over whose head the sun rises. But if you had asked about the one concerning whom God's apostle – God bless him and his family – said: 'The resurrection will take place when the government of the world is in the hands of a man from my progeny, from the progeny of al-Ḥusayn; it is behind whom Jesus, son of Mary, will say his prayers', [I would tell you that] that will be in the time of the 'earthquake' and when deeds are of no avail. Let, therefore, no one desire him but he who relies on his knowledge, [*ʿilm* as opposed to *ʿamal* 'deeds'] that means that in his days new deeds will be of no avail and repentance will not be accepted. And he is the end of the world.'[5]

Throughout this selection, reinterpretation of original mahdist expectation becomes intertwined with the consolidation of authority in a number of complex ways. First, al-Mahdī cites Jaʿfar al-Ṣādiq, the sixth Shia *imām*, in order to claim that members of the family of the Prophet have, historically, disseminated the 'good news' concerning the advent of an expected *mahdī*. The caliph al-Mahdī writes, further, that the advent of this predicted *mahdī*, who is present, is not tantamount to the advent of the eschatological *mahdī*. Rather, the caliph argues that he is part of an exalted lineage whose members have fulfilled events common in apocalyptic literature, in particular ascending the pulpit of his grandfather and fighting under the black banners to achieve victory for the family of the Prophet.[6] The citing and fulfilment of apocalyptic tradition – a common rhetorical strategy in apocalyptic literature – here not only displaces the expectation of a single unique *mahdī* onto a collection of *mahdī*s, it also reaffirms the caliph's claims to his ʿAlīd credentials and bolsters his credibility to rule over the Shia.

This credibility then becomes an argument for the exclusive authority of the ruling dynasty. The argument is made in part through the caliph's interpretation of the Arabic root h–d–y, a root meaning 'to guide.' The term *mahdī* is the past participle of this root, literally meaning 'he who is rightly guided.' In the work above, the caliph al-Mahdī mitigates the imminent temporal expectation denoted by the term and simultaneously bestows on himself and his family divine proximity by equating all its leaders to *mahdī*s, literally 'those who are rightly guided,' rather than only to the singular eschatological figure. The dynasty then becomes the exclusive source of guidance – the *hudā* (divinely aided *mahdī*s) and the eschatological *mahdī* all come from this divinely guided source.[7]

Finally, it is remarkable to observe the way the very act of temporal displacement – the distancing of a singular mahdist event at the end of history – here is correlated to a modality of apocalyptic fulfilment. Al-Mahdī presents his rule and the advent of the Fatimids as a turning point in history that ushers in a new era of justice and true guidance 'in whose dynasty the totality of believers will become powerful.' The caliph al-Mahdī's assumption of power brings us historically closer to the advent of the eschatological *mahdī*, who will come 'when the government of the world is in the hands of a man from my progeny.'

His presentation of himself and his dynasty as a fulfilment of apocalyptic prophecy here creates an almost inverse relationship between the nature of apocalyptic fulfilment in the immediate moment and its relationship to the Hour, which necessarily becomes more distant.

The apocalyptic construct here, then, simultaneously allows for the caliph al-Mahdī to claim genealogical legitimacy via a tradition of Jaʿfar through eschatological fulfilment while locating the caliph's family as restorers and custodians of true guidance. Apocalyptic expectation is not abandoned; far from it – it is deployed and reinterpreted to bestow legitimacy on the ruling dynasty while assuring that future rulers and their believers will acquire power commensurate with mahdist expectations. When the fruition of the dynasty's power and the concomitant emergence of the eschatological *mahdī* will occur is left ambiguous. In fact, when asked about when the eschatological *mahdī* will come, the Mahdī states that instead of the *mahdī* coming after a heptad of *imāms*, there will be as many *imāms* as God wishes.[8]

The Mahdī's letter illustrates a central feature of apocalyptic discourse and its relationship to authority. Elision of eschatological or apocalyptic symbols onto individuals in the terrestrial realm, mediated by a sense of imminence or expectation, allows for dramatic and lasting changes in authoritative structures. The Mahdī's letter deploys imagery concerning the fulfilment of apocalyptic predictions to legitimate his claims to a Shia lineage by linking him to Jaʿfar and Muḥammad, and by justifying his temporal right to rule. This imagery was used not only to help propel the caliph to power, but also to argue for the dynasty's exclusive right to rule. This iteration of apocalypticism – apocalyptic discourse stripped of its immediacy and coupled to a mahdism that was now displaced from one individual onto a collection of Fatimid rulers – became an important means of legitimating Fatimid power, as well as the Fatimids' place in history.

The second text that I examine here is the *Taʾwīl al-daʿāʾim*, the symbolic analogue to Qāḍī l-Nuʿmān's *Daʿāʾim al-Islām*. Al-Nuʿmān was perhaps the most important ideologue of the Fatimid state.[9] He joined the service of the caliph al-Mahdī in 313/925, and, upon his grandson al-Manṣūr's ascension to the caliphate in 334/946, al-Nuʿmān became supreme judge of all Fatimid territories. In 349/960, he penned the *Daʿāʾim al-Islām*, which was commissioned and reviewed by al-Manṣūr's successor, al-Muʿizz. The *Daʿāʾim* remains an important source of Ismaili law even today.

Al-Nuʿmān held lessons on Ismaili jurisprudence that were open to all after Friday prayers. By 341/953, under the caliph al-Muʿizz, he was entrusted with leading the *majālis al-ḥikma* (sessions of wisdom); these were sessions open only to initiates.[10] In these *majālis*, al-Nuʿmān taught these initiates secret knowledge personally authorised by the caliph-imams; the *Taʾwīl al-daʿāʾim* is a record of these *majālis*,[11] and as such offers us significant insights into the ways in which mahdist expectation was renarrativised through the use of officially sanctioned symbolic interpretation. Though I focus specifically on this work of *taʾwīl*, apocalyptic themes emerge in many other works of al-Nuʿmān, including his official history of the Fatimid dynasty, the *Iftitāḥ al-daʿwa* and the *Sharḥ al-akhbār*, his collection of non-legal traditions.[12] I have decided to focus on the *Taʾwīl al-daʿāʾim*[13] not only because it remains understudied, but also because unlike the *Kitāb al-kashf* and the *Kitāb al-rushd*, it illustrates how *taʾwīl* as a mode of symbolic interpretation can be used to distance utopian expectation while simultaneously reifying the Fatimids' right to rule.[14]

The majority of this chapter addresses the ways in which the *Taʾwīl al-daʿāʾim* infuses regularly practiced ritual structures with symbolic meanings that are linked to linear history. Frequently, *taʾwīl* of these rituals locates the community within the historical period between the advent of the caliph al-Mahdī and the eschatological figure *al-qāʾim*, and helps to resolve questions concerning the relevance of the present given the postponement of the full effulgence of utopia. This hermeneutic also addresses questions of the community's place in history and future eschatological expectations. While the immediacy and symbolic currency of this expectation is displaced onto these ritual structures, the regular performance of these rituals allows for the maintenance and, through the regular performance of the ritual, the action that embodies eschatological expectation. Al-

Nuʿmān's *ta'wīl* is complex and frequently consists of a multiplicity of referents; readers should therefore be forewarned against expecting a simple answer regarding how al-Nuʿmān addresses the paradox of mahdism – a question that has been addressed elsewhere.[15] Here I am interested in exploring the ways in which the *ta'wīl* of regularly performed ritual structures operates to reify Fatimid authority and distance utopian expectation. I focus in particular on al-Nuʿmān's *ta'wīl* of two central ritual structures: the daily prayer cycle and the hajj.

We begin with al-Nuʿmān's discussion of the regular prayer cycle. He writes:

> It is said that the times of prayer are the times of prayer in the *ẓāhir* – times established during the hours of night and day. The prayer times of the *bāṭin* is the true *daʿwa*. It also has established times, and these are the times in which the *walī* of every period establishes his proclamation and [establishes] those whom he appoints for setting up his *daʿwa*.[16]

Further, he writes that each of the five daily prayers has an analogue in the *bāṭin* – 'for each of the five *ṣalāt*s there is a correspondence.'[17] And frequently, each prayer contains multiple symbolic correspondences. Al-Nuʿmān writes that the *ẓuhr* (or noon) prayer, is the first prayer after daylight, and corresponds to Muḥammad

> who was the first to establish the five obligatory prayers and their rules [literally limits] according to his *sharīʿa*. [The *ẓuhr*] prayer consists of four *rakʿas*. It is the first ritual prayer prayed by the Messenger of God. He set up [its time] for the first part of the seventh hour of daylight.[18]

Al-Nuʿmān states that the four *rakʿas* corresponds to the four letters of Muḥammad's name (i.e., m–ḥ–m–d). There is also a correspondence to reciting it in the seventh hour: it is the number of letters of Muḥammad's name as well as the three letters of ʿAlī's name (i.e., ʿ-l–ī).

These seven letters are also symbolic nodes corresponding to the unfolding of sacred history, as they correspond to the seven *nāṭiqs* and the seven *imāms*, those who follow in succession between each of these *nāṭiqs*. The time of the prayer also has symbolic significance: al-Nuʿmān states that before the *ẓuhr* prayer one prays and after it one prays; this corresponds to the fact that the *daʿwa* of Jesus existed before the *daʿwa* of Muḥammad, and after the *daʿwa* of Muḥammad there is the *daʿwa* of ʿAlī and the *imāms* of his progeny.[19]

The *ʿaṣr* prayer is prayed next, in the middle of the afternoon, and also has four *rakʿas*. The prayer is likened to

> the last of the *imāms*, the master of the *qiyāma*, and likewise the number of the letters of his name is four. There will be a *daʿwa* before his manifestation but there will not be a *daʿwa* after his manifestation. The time of the *ẓuhr* prayer and the *ʿaṣr* prayer is one time span: between the two prayers there is only an interval for the worshipper's supererogatory prayer. The likeness of this [*ʿaṣr* prayer] in the *bāṭin* is that the *qāʾim*, the master of the *qiyāma*, is from the *imāms* of Muḥammad, the people of his *sharīʿa*, and is one of his progeny. Both of their times and their tasks are one.[20]

The *ʿaṣr* prayer, and its four *rakʿas*, is likened to the *qāʾim* (the eschatological figure) here; this figure is explicitly identified as an *imām* from Muḥammad's progeny. The time of the *ẓuhr* prayer and the *ʿaṣr* prayer is one time span, which corresponds to the fact that the *qāʾim* will come in the same epoch as Muḥammad.

Al-Nuʿmān frequently correlates the time of ritual performance to the hidden and manifest aspects of religion, where night corresponds to the *bāṭin* and day corresponds to the *ẓāhir*. The *maghrib* prayer, prayed right after sunset, corresponds to the first hidden *daʿwa*, the *daʿwa* of Adam; this is in contrast to the *daʿwa* of Muḥammad and the *qāʾim*, whose *daʿwas* (and times of prayer) are manifest. In addition to correlating the three cycles of prayer to the three letters of Adam's name (i.e., a–d–m), al-Nuʿmān equates these three cycles to 'the *imām*, the *ḥujja*, and the *dāʿī* through whom the *bāṭin daʿwa* operates.' The obligation to pray the *ṣalāt* at night becomes a reflection of the necessity of the *bāṭin* for salvation.

> The analogue of not praying *ṣalāt* before it and the command to pray the *ṣalāt* after it corresponds to the initiate who, before his admission into the *daʿwa* did not perform a *ṣalāt* [in its full sense]. When admitted into the *daʿwa*, his *ṣalāt* becomes a [full] *ṣalāt* because he has performed both the *ẓāhir* of the *ṣalāt* and its *bāṭin*, and has recognised his *imām*. Anyone who has not recognised his *imām* cannot perform a *ṣalāt* [fully]. The Prophet, may God's blessings and peace be upon him and his progeny, said, 'whoever dies without recognising the *imām* of his time dies a death of ignorance.'[21]

The end of the next prayer, the *ʿishāʾ* (evening) prayer, is likened to the greatest four of the twelve *nuqabāʾ*, leaders of the twelve islands of the *daʿwa* entrusted with conveying the *bāṭin*. There is a prayer – and *daʿwa*s – before this prayer and after this prayer (and before this *daʿwa* and after this *daʿwa*).

Al-Nuʿmān's rich interpretation of the *witr* prayer, prayed between the *ʿishāʾ* prayer and the morning prayer, directly addresses the relationship between secrecy and unveiling vis-a-vis Muḥammad, ʿAlī, and the caliph al-Mahdī.

> The *witr* prayer, consisting of three *rakʿas*, corresponds to the *daʿwa* of the Prophet, ʿAlī and al-Mahdī. The first *rakʿa* corresponds to Muḥammad the Prophet of God. The likeness of the second *rakʿa*, which is recited next, is the likeness of ʿAlī. The recitation of the profession of faith [the *tashahhud*] and the salutation [on the Prophet] (*taslīm*) of the prayer follows after [the performance of] both of these [*rakʿas*]. This corresponds to a disruption, which is the emergence of the concealed *daʿwa* – the *daʿwa* of the *bāṭin* – after ʿAlī, by way of the concealment of the *imāms* due to prudent dissimulation (*taqiyya*) from those who have gained power by force. The likeness of the third *rakʿa* of the *witr* prayer is the likeness of al-Mahdī. The likeness of the supplicatory prayer (*qunūt*) which is recited in it [i.e., the third *rakʿa*] after the bowing (*rukū*) is the likeness of the emergence of al-Mahdī's concealed *daʿwa* after the establishment of his *ḥujja*. His [i.e., al-Mahdī's] establishment of him [the *ḥujja*] was at the time of his [i.e., al-Mahdī's] emergence.[22]

The portion of the prayer recited after the second *rakʿa, tashahhud* and *taslīm*, is likened to the suppression of the emergence of the *daʿwa* as a result of the *imāms*' persecution after ʿAlī. The third *rakʿa* is likened to al-Mahdī, and the likeness of the prayer recited after the three *rakʿas* is likened to the manifestation of al-Mahdī's *daʿwa*.

In another passage, al-Nuʿmān further elaborates upon the period between ʿAlī and the caliph al-Mahdī. The *witr* prayer is likened to

> the *daʿwa* of the Prophet, and the *daʿwa* of the *waṣī* [ʿAlī], and the *daʿwa* of al-Mahdī. The night corresponds to the concealment (*satr*) and the secret (*kitmān*); this corresponds to the time span of the concealment of the *imāms* between ʿAlī and al-Mahdī – the extent of this span of time being for the sake of *taqiyya* from their enemies, and to establish the *daʿwa* in the name of the Prophet, the *waṣī*, and al-Mahdī. The Messenger of God had brought good news of him; he mentioned the Mahdī's emergence and what God will reveal about the trial (*miḥna*) through him [i.e., al-Mahdī] and that He will make the Mahdī return the religion to a fresh state under his authority and He will revive the *sunna* of his Prophet through him, proceeding in the manner of its disclosure by those close to ʿAlī, and under the authority of the *imāms* and the progeny of ʿAlī. This is like performing the *witr* prayer throughout the entire night, from its beginning until its end. Whoever performs it [for the entire night] is obligated to follow [the *sunna* of the Prophet] regarding the *witr* prayer and to mention the emergence of the Mahdī and its imminence at its conclusion . . .[23]

Night here is likened to the period of concealment of the *imāms* between ʿAlī and the caliph al-Mahdī, a 'trial' (*miḥna*) for believers.[24] The end of the *witr* prayer is performed at the end of the night, marking the conclusion of the period of concealment of the *imāms* and the emergence of al-Mahdī, he whom the Prophet predicts would return religion to a fresh state and revive the prophetic *sunna* before the end of time. Note here, as in other portions of this text as well as in the Mahdī's letter examined earlier, that predictions concerning the eschatological *mahdī* seem to be fulfilled in part by the arrival of the caliph al-Mahdī.

The *fajr* prayer, performed at daybreak, marks the transition between secrecy and disclosure. He writes that

> the two *rakʿas* of the *fajr* prayer correspond to the *imām* and the *ḥujja* in the state of *satr* [concealment] because they are prayed in the darkness preceding daybreak. Its two *rakʿas* correspond to the Mahdī and his *ḥujja* who stand at the end of the period of the concealment of the *imāms*. They unveil the darkness from all the *imāms*, and they endorse the [performance of both the] *ẓāhir* and the *bāṭin*, just as the *fajr* prayer is performed at a time when light and darkness are mixed together. This is similar to what we have mentioned concerning the *maghrib* prayer – that it too is at a similar time [when light and darkness mix]. Its likeness [i.e., of the *fajr* prayer] is Adam, the first to establish the *ẓāhir* of religion and its *bāṭin*. Similarly the Mahdī and his *ḥujja* are the first among those who emerge [after concealment]. They have both, in this manner, already established the matters of religion in the *ẓāhir* and in its *bāṭin*, following the [period of] the concealment of the *imāms* and the confusion of the community.[25]

Reflecting the transition between night and day – concealment and disclosure – the two *rakʿas* are likened to the *imām*/al-Mahdī and his *ḥujja* who come to power in concealment but who then manifest their ranks openly for all to see. Like Adam at the beginning of time, al-Mahdī and his *ḥujja* establish both the *ẓāhir* and *bāṭin* of religion. Al-Nuʿmān makes clear to his audience that this event has already occurred after the period of concealment and confusion. In another passage he rhetorically places his audience in the *daʿwa* of al-Mahdī, and likens the experience of those praying the *fajr* prayer to the experience of the group of believers, whom he specifies as initiates of the *daʿwa* of al-Mahdī.[26]

Thus, in the way the *taʾwīl* valorises the reality of the *bāṭin* over its opaque signifier in the *ẓāhir*, al-Nuʿmān helps to reorder sacred history by symbolically analogising the times of the day of these prayers and the number of prostrations with their referents in the *bāṭin*. The *taʾwīl* of the times in which the *witr* prayer is performed, for instance, provides an explanation of the historical period and the challenges faced by the community that lived in the time between ʿAlī and the Mahdī. Here we see that it was a trial for the believers, one that was concluded with al-Mahdī's rising and renewal of religion. This theme of al-Mahdī's rising is carried forth with al-Nuʿmān's *taʾwīl* of the *fajr* prayer, which marks the transition between the end of this trial and the open manifestation of the *daʿwa* on the earthly plane. But al-Mahdī's emergence does not signal the perfection of religion or its *telos* as yet: the emergence of the *daʿwa* continues, and the affirmation of the true religion of Muḥammad and ʿAlī will only occur with the advent of the *qāʾim* for all to see, symbolised by the prayer that occurs in the brightness of the afternoon sun.

Similar to the daily prayer cycles, the days of the week, too, have symbolic analogues to sacred history; here they are likened to the speaker-prophets. Sunday is likened to Adam, the first of the speaker-prophets; Monday is likened to Noah, the second speaker-prophet; Tuesday is likened to Abraham, the third; Wednesday is likened to Moses, the fourth; Thursday is likened to Jesus, the fifth; and Friday is likened to Muḥammad, the seal of the prophets. Al-Nuʿmān writes:

> The likeness of Saturday [*yawm al-sabt*, day of the Sabbath] is the likeness of the *qāʾim al-qiyāma* . . . He is the last of the *imāms* and has been counted as one of the speaker-prophets since he is the seal of the *imāms*. He is the most excellent of them just as before him Muḥammad was the most excellent of the prophets. God has made the Sabbath as a likeness for him in the *sharīʿa* of Moses, and He has made it a day in which one does not work, just as there will be no work in the time of the *qāʾim al-qiyāma* [or rising of the *qiyāma*]. This is what God referred to when He said: [*Are they waiting for the very angels to come to them, or your Lord Himself, or maybe some of His signs?*] *But on the Day some of your Lord's signs come, no soul will profit from faith if it had none before, or has not already earned some good through its faith.* [*Say, 'Wait if you wish: we too are waiting.'*] [6:158].[27]

The order and progression of the days of the week symbolise the history of the speaker-prophets, with Saturday in particular acquiring a special eschatological significance. Here Saturday is the likeness of the rising of the *qāʾim*, a day when no further work will be accepted. Further, through inclusion of Quran 6:158, Saturday and its observation of the Sabbath becomes a type of Quranic sign for true belief, similar to the alternation of night and day (e.g., 3:190, 10:6, 23:80) or the sailing of ships on the sea (2:164). In this hermeneutic, each day of the week commemorates a different stage in the progression of sacred history, with religion's most perfect iteration – the coming of the *qāʾim* and cessation of work after the abrogation of the religious law – already observed on Saturday by Moses's community.

In addition to the days of the week and the proscribed prayers symbolising the progression of sacred history, as well as anticipating its *telos*, the deeper meanings of the *ʿīd* rituals, too, tell a narrative of the community's place in sacred history. Al-Nuʿmān writes that each of the three *ʿīd*s has a correspondence: first comes the Friday congregational prayer, *al-jumʿa*; then the *fiṭr*, the breaking of the Ramadan fast, and finally, the *ʿīd al-aḍḥā*, the *ʿīd* celebrated at the conclusion of the hajj. He writes:

> The likeness of the Friday congregational prayer is the invitation (*daʿwa*) to the *imāms*, which is Muḥammad's invitation, because they invite to [Muḥammad's] *daʿwa*. Thus the Friday congregational prayers are the likenesses of the *daʿwas* of the hidden *imāms* consisting of those close to [the time of] ʿAlī the commander of the faithful, until the Mahdī.[28]

Here al-Nuʿmān provides a multiplicity of symbolic meanings for the same ritual. The Friday congregational prayer becomes both Muḥammad's invitation as well as the invitation to the *imāms*, for it is Muḥammad's *daʿwa* to which each of the *imāms* invites. This conflation of Muḥammad's call or invitation with that of the *imāms* thus helps to legitimate the authoritative structure of the *imāms* and the *daʿwa*. This *daʿwa* is delimited in temporal history to a select group of *imāms*: the hidden *imāms* from ʿAlī until al-Mahdī.

Al-Nuʿmān then draws a parallel between fasting and the concealment of the *imāms*.

> Fasting is the symbol for the concealment (*kitmān*) and the cover (*satr*). The end of the fast (*fiṭr*) is the likeness of the Mahdī who, when he emerges makes known the concealed *daʿwa* that [was active] before his emergence. He became known by the *daʿwa*, he elevated it, he removed its cover and its concealment, the likeness of which is the fast. His rising and the manifestation of his *daʿwa* brought delight to the believers, removing the trial (*balāʾ*) [e.g., Q 2:49; 7:141; 8:17; 14:6; 37:106; 44:33] and test (*miḥna*) that they had been under from them, God be praised! This is like the delight of those celebrating the end of fasting at the end of the fast, after [a month of] fasting and their rejoicing at hearing the good news of the end of the fast. This is like the rejoicing of believers in the Mahdī.[29]

The concealment of the *imāms* is likened to fasting – a trial placed upon believers. The use of the Quranic term *balāʾ* evokes the great test of prophets and communities of the past – the period of torment in which Pharaoh killed Jewish sons (7:141); a great battle of Muḥammad (8:17); and Abraham being asked to sacrifice his own son (37:106), for instance. But the advent of the *imām* al-Mahdī inaugurates a new period of history: a period in which the trial of believers is disclosed to them, a period of happiness likened to the breaking of the fast at the end of Ramadan. The period of fasting – equated to the period of secrecy, concealment, and trial between the *imāms* ʿAlī and al-Mahdī – is over with the advent of al-Mahdī. Al-Nuʿmān then writes that in the *bāṭin*, the period of days between the breaking of the Ramadan fast and the *ʿīd al-aḍḥā* 'is the likeness of the spiritual ranks which the *imāms* will establish between al-Mahdī and the *qāʾim* of the *qiyāma*.'[30] In other words, the period spanning the two *ʿīd*s is transformed into the spiritual stations that the *imāms* establish for their believers between al-Mahdī and the *qāʾim*. Al-Nuʿmān then writes that the *ʿīd al-aḍḥā* is symbolically equated to the *qāʾim*,[31] commemorating the arrival of the final eschatological figure.

The spiritual intensity associated with each of the *ʿīd*s corresponds to progressively important moments in sacred history. Friday congregational prayers correspond to Muḥammad's *daʿwa* and the *daʿwa* from ʿAlī to al-Mahdī; celebrations at the end of the Ramadan fast correlate to the emergence and establishment of the *daʿwa* at the hands of al-Mahdī; the approximate three-month period between this *ʿīd* and the *ʿīd al-aḍḥā* becomes a time of spiritual development; and finally, the *ʿīd al-aḍḥā* corresponds to the *qāʾim*. The investing of *ʿīd* celebrations with these symbolic correlates also allows the sacred calendar to unfold according to a metanarrative that, in its ritual structure, rehearses increasingly important moments concerning the end of time: secrecy, unveiling, and the permanent disclosure of all things. Not only does this symbolic analogising allow for these past and expected moments to retain a distinct hierarchy in collective memory, it also allows history – and especially mahdist expectation – to become literally embodied in the performance of rituals.[32] While rituals that correlate with messianic expectation are not unusual in the history of religions – Cargo movements, the Ghost Dance, or the Essene community bear witness to this ubiquity – in our case al-Nuʿmān's symbolic analogising illustrates the process by which this historical expectation is displaced onto ritual structures, which, because of the nature of ritual, become embodied and performed by the collective.

If the daily prayer cycle, the days of the week and the elements of the liturgical calendar have symbolic analogues, then the twelve months, too, have a symbolic correspondence: they are the twelve companions of each speaker-prophet.[33] The ninth month of the calendar, the month of Ramadan, holds special significance for al-Nuʿmān: he explains that the month of Ramadan is the likeness of ʿAlī, Muḥammad's *waṣī* during his lifetime, who inherited leadership of the community after Muḥammad's death. This becomes a hidden matter, associated with the secret *daʿwa*, and its knowledge is protected by *taʾwīl*.[34] Hence the likeness of the days of the month are like the '*imāms* and the *ḥujjas* from his [ʿAlī's] progeny,'[35] a reflection of sacred history that oscillates between disclosure and concealment. After again likening the Ramadan fast to *satr* and *kitmān*, the concealment of the *imāms*, he offers another interpretation of the month that directly addresses the advent of the eschatological figure. He writes:

> The month of Ramadan is also the likeness of the seal of the *imāms*, the master of the *qiyāma*, to whom God gathers the matter of the worshippers, and by whom He will manifest His religion over all others[36] because the month of Ramadan is the ninth month of the year. [Similarly] the pregnant woman delivers the child she is carrying in the ninth month even though the capacities of the fetus are completely developed by the seventh month. As has previously been mentioned, this is analogous to the seventh *imām*, in whom the capacity for power and the *ta'yīd* [spiritual fortification] of the seventh of the *imāms* between each of the speaking prophets is manifested. We have already discussed that you [who are listening to this discourse] are now in this period.[37]

The advent of the seventh *imām* during the cycle of Muḥammad signals the completion of the power associated with each cycle's heptad of *imāms*. This is the historical moment in which al-Nuʿmān's audience finds itself – a moment likened to the maturity of the fetus in the seventh month of gestation before the pregnant mother delivers in the ninth month.[38]

The symbolic placement of al-Nuʿmān's audience within the period between the seventh and ninth month of the child's development is telling: it is a time in which the power of *ta'yīd* is fully developed, like the fetus itself, but not entirely complete, not ready to fully emerge. Al-Nuʿmān continues:

> Some have said that a third of the seventh – which is two, the two following after [the seventh] – bring it to its completion, so he [the completion] is the ninth, just as the pregnant mother delivers [at the ninth month]; just as the Messenger of God was the final messenger. What has been transmitted from him regarding the last of the *imāms* is that he said, 'his name will be similar to my name, his *kunya* will be similar to my *kunya*, and his father's name will be similar to the name of my father.' You are familiar with these [prophetic] reports, and with the *imāms* from his progeny. So understand now the indications of *ta'wīl*, O believers! God knows you and sees you. He provides you with benefit in your knowledge. May the blessings

> of God be upon Muḥammad the Prophet, and upon the *imāms* from his pious and pure progeny, and may peace be upon them.[39]

Could this selection be pointing to the advent of the period of the second caliph-imam al-Qāʾim bi-Amr Allāh (934–46), the successor of al-Mahdī? Or is it an indication of the caliph al-Muʿizz's doctrinal reforms, in which the eschatological figure is spiritualised, and the caliph-imams become the *qāʾim*'s deputies, entrusted with the disclosure of spiritual truths until the advent of the *qāʾim* himself?[40] While the exact historical referents are unclear, it does seem clear that al-Nuʿmān is indicating prophetic fulfilment here, encouraging the community to be receptive to the *taʾwīl* of these prophetic reports.

A few pages later, al-Nuʿmān once again likens the month of Ramadan to the seal of the *imāms* and events at the end of time.

> When this *qāʾim* rises, he will reward the believers and will present each believing man and believing woman with the light by which he is guided. This is what is referred in God's word, exalted be His mention: *On the Day when you see the believers, both men and women, with their light streaming out ahead of them and to their right,* [*they will be told, 'The good news for you today is that there are Gardens graced with flowing streams where you will stay: that is truly the supreme triumph!'*] [57:12].[41]

Light that becomes a marker associated with right belief at the end of time is associated here with supporters of the *qāʾim*, who bestows his light upon true believers. The rising of this figure is also associated with a change of spiritual states for those who support him, analogous to the change in condition that accompanies death.

> Likewise, there will be movement in [spiritual] states when the final *imām* rises. Believers will rise through [successive] levels of religion, but those who are to sink down will sink down as we have previously mentioned . . . God will redeem those who call on him.[42]

The *qāʾim*'s arrival signals not only an illumination of true believers – his supporters – but also signals an elevation in their spiritual station, complete with divine protection for those who support him.

We have seen how al-Nuʿmān's *ta'wīl* links events in sacred history to the regular performance of ritual performances, resulting in a hermeneutic that recalls and embeds important moments of sacred history within communal memory; at the same time it displaces and restructures an imminent eschatology originally fused to a linear temporality. But there is a more supple quality to this *ta'wīl* that supports the view of Corbin and other scholars, that this hermeneutic is spiritual in nature.[43] As we see, al-Nuʿmān's discussion of the rites of the hajj simultaneously exemplifies a rewriting of sacred history, the displacement and creation of a new sacred centre, and the genesis of a new spiritual progression toward the *walī* of the time.

Notes

1. Walker, *Exploring an Islamic Empire*, p. 17.
2. See, for instance, the contributions in Diana Tumminia and William H. Swatos (eds), *How Prophecy Lives* (Leiden: Brill, 2011) as well as those in Stone (ed.), *Expecting Armageddon*. See also Lorne Dawson, 'When Prophecy Fails and Faith Persists: A Theoretical Overview', *Nova Religio: The Journal of Alternative and Emergent Religions* vol. 3, no. 1 (October 1999), pp. 60–82; Jon R. Stone, 'Prophecy and Dissonance: A Reassessment of Research Testing the Festinger Theory', *Nova Religio: The Journal of Alternative and Emergent Religions* vol. 12. No. 4 (May 2009), pp. 72–90; and Tumminia.
3. Brett, *Rise*, p. 112. See also the introduction, translation, and commentary on the letter in al-Mahdī bi'llāh, *Kitāb arsalahu al-Mahdī ilā nāḥiyat al-Yaman*, trans. Abbas Hamdani and François de Blois, 'A Re-Examination of Al-Mahdī's Letter to the Yemenites on the Genealogy of the Fatimid Caliphs', *Journal of the Royal Asiatic Society of Great Britain and Ireland* No. 2 (1983), pp. 173–207. For the Arabic text with commentary, see al-Mahdī bi'llāh, *Kitāb arsalahu al-Mahdī ilā nāḥiyat al-Yaman*, edited and translated by Ḥusayn b. Fayḍ Allāh Hamdānī, *On the Genealogy of Fatimid Caliphs: Statement on Mahdī's Communication to the Yemen on the Real and Esoteric Names of His Hidden Predecessors* (Cairo: American University in Cairo, 1958). See also Halm, *Empire*, pp. 156–9.
4. Brett, *Rise*, p. 113.
5. al-Mahdī bi'llāh, *Kitāb arsalahu al-Mahdī*, trans. Hamdani and de Blois,

pp. 177–8 [with minor alterations]; al-Mahdī bi'llāh, *Kitāb arsalahu al-Mahdī*, trans. Hamdānī, Arabic text, pp. 12–13.

6. For an introduction to this literature see, for instance, Cook; Ofer Livne-Kafri, 'Some Notes on the Muslim Apocalyptic Tradition', *Quaderni di Studi Arabi* vol. 17 (1999), pp. 71–94; Hayrettin Yücesoy, *Messianic Beliefs and Imperial Politics in Medieval Islam: The 'Abbāsid Caliphate in the Early Ninth Century* (Columbia: University of South Carolina Press, 2009), especially pp. 1–58.
7. Yaacov Lev also discusses some of the consequences of the caliph-imam's portrayal as the divinely mandated *mahdī* in 'From Revolutionary Violence to State Violence: The Fāṭimids (297–567/909–1171)', in *Public Violence in Islamic Societies*, ed. Christian Lange and Maribel Fierro (Edinburgh: Edinburgh University Press, 2009), pp. 73–5.
8. al-Mahdī bi'llāh, *Kitāb arsalahu al-Mahdī*, trans. Hamdani and de Blois, p. 178. Note that this selection of the text ends with a refrain similar to one that we have seen in our previous texts – that the *mahdī* is 'the end of the world'.
9. Al-Nuʿmān's vast literary output across genres is truly impressive; a complete list of these works is listed in Daftary, *Ismaili Literature*, pp. 142–6. Ismail K. H. Poonawala has worked extensively on various aspects of al-Nuʿmān's corpus. See, for instance: 'Al-Qāḍī al-Nuʿmān's Works and the Sources', *Bulletin of the School of Oriental and African Studies* 36 (1973), pp. 109–15; 'A Reconsideration of al-Qāḍī al-Nuʿmān's *Madhhab*', *Bulletin of the School of Oriental and African Studies* 37 (1974), 572–9; 'Al-Qāḍī al-Nuʿmān and Ismaʿili Jurisprudence', in Farhad Daftary (ed.), *Medieval Ismaʿili History and Thought* (New York and Cambridge: Cambridge University Press, 1996), pp. 117–43; 'The Beginning of the Ismaili *Daʿwa* and the Establishment of the Fatimid Dynasty as Commemorated by al-Qāḍī al-Nuʿmān', in Farhard Daftary and Josef W. Meri (eds), *Culture and Memory in Medieval Islam: Essays in Honor of Wilferd Madelung* (London: I. B. Tauris in association with the Institute of Ismaili Studies, 2003), pp. 338–63. See also his *Biobibliography of Ismāʿīlī Literature* (Malibu, CA: Undena Publications, 1977); and the translation of al-Nuʿmān b. Muḥammad, *Daʿāʾim al-Islām*, trans. Asaf A. A. Fyzee, completely revised and annotated by Ismail K. Poonawala, *The Pillars of Islam*: Vol. 1, *Acts of Devotion and Religious Observances* (New Delhi: Oxford University Press, 2002); and trans. Asaf A. A. Fyzee, completely revised and annotated

by Ismail K. Poonawala, *The Pillars of Islam*: Vol. 2, *Laws Pertaining to Human Intercourse* (New Delhi: Oxford University Press, 2007). See also Husain K. B. Qutbuddin, 'Fāṭimid Legal Exegesis of the Qur'an: The Interpretive Strategies Used by al-Qāḍī al-Nuʿmān (d. 363/974) in his *Daʿāʾim al-Islām*, *Journal of Qur'anic Studies* 12 (2010): pp. 109–46.

10. Sumaiya A. Hamdani, *Between Revolution and State: The Path to Fatimid Statehood*: *Qadi al-Nuʿman and the Construction of Fatimid Legitimacy* (London: I. B. Tauris in association with the Institute of Ismaili Studies, 2006), pp. 46–7.
11. Halm, 'Ismaʿili Oath', pp. 100–10.
12. The *Iftitāḥ* in one place, for instance, retains a similar mechanism of displacement and apocalyptic fulfilment as al-Mahdī's letter. One such tradition relayed by al-Nuʿmān states: 'Traditions referring to al-Manṣūr, peace be upon him, are numerous. It is related on the authority of Jaʿfar b. Muḥammad, may God's blessings be upon him, that he said, "From us is al-Mahdī and from us is al-Manṣūr." In another tradition it is reported: "Rejoice, for the days of the oppressors are about to come to an end. The restorer will come through whom God will restore the community to Muḥammad. He is al-Mahdī and then al-Manṣūr, through whom God will cause religion to triumph."' Hamid Haji (trans.), *Founding the Fatimid State* (London: I. B. Tauris in association with the Institute of Ismaili Studies, 2006), p. 21. James Lindsey has also noted parallels between the ways in which al-Nuʿmān portrays various events in the founding of the Fatimid state as parallel to events occurring during Muḥammad's lifetime. See Lindsay, pp. 39–56.
13. al-Nuʿmān b. Muḥammad, *Taʾwīl al-daʿāʾim*, ed. ʿĀrif Tāmir (Beirut: Dār al-Aḍwāʾ, 1995). References to this text read 'TAD' and the relevant volume and page number.
14. Those familiar with the corpus of al-Nuʿmān will note that a text questionably attributed to him, the *Risāla al-Mudhhiba* (ed. ʿĀrif Tāmir, in his *Khams Rasāʾil Ismāʿīliyya* [Salamiyya, Syria: Dār al-Anṣāf, 1956], pp. 27–88), discusses mahdist displacement in the context of the spiritual and terrestrial person the *qāʾim*, perhaps, as Madelung and Daftary note, consistent with the caliph al-Muʿizz's reforms on the position of the *imām* and relationship to eschatological figure at that time. See Daniel de Smet, 'The Risāla al-Mudhhiba Attributed to al-Qāḍī al-Nuʿmān: Important Evidence for the Adoption of Neoplatonism by Fatimid

Ismailism at the Time of al-Muʿizz?' in *Fortresses of the Intellect: Ismaili and other Islamic Studies in Honour of Farhad Daftary*, ed. Omar Alí-de-Unzaga (London: I. B. Tauris in association with the Institute of Ismaili Studies, 2011), pp. 309–41, esp. pp. 316–19. See also Yves Marquet, 'La pensée philosophique et religieuse du Qāḍī al-Nuʿmān à travers la 'Risāla Muḏhiba', *Bulletin d'études orientales*, t. 39/40 (1987–8), pp. 141–81.
15. See, for instance, Daftary, *The Ismāʿīlīs*, 2nd edn, pp. 164–7.
16. TAD, vol. 1, pp. 197–8.
17. TAD, vol. 1, p. 183.
18. TAD, vol. 1, p. 183.
19. TAD, vol. 1, p. 183.
20. TAD, vol. 1, p. 183.
21. TAD, vol. 1, p. 184.
22. TAD, vol. 1, p. 380.
23. TAD, vol. 1, pp. 382–3.
24. In another place in the text, al-Nuʿmān likens the *ʿishāʾ* prayer to the first hidden *daʿwa*, the *daʿwa* of the *bāṭin*. Each subsequent night prayer, he writes, is the likeness from ʿAlī to al-Mahdī. See TAD, vol. 1, p. 256.
25. TAD, vol. 1, p. 185.
26. TAD, vol. 1, p. 256.
27. TAD, vol. 1, pp. 147–8. I have reproduced the surrounding Quranic text in brackets for context.
28. TAD vol. 1, p. 335.
29. TAD, vol. 1, p. 336.
30. TAD, vol. 1, p. 336.
31. TAD, vol. 1, p. 338.
32. For more on the relationship between rituals and collective memory, see Paul Connerton, *How Societies Remember* (Cambridge: Cambridge University Press, 1989).
33. TAD, vol. 2, p. 121.
34. TAD, vol. 2, p. 121.
35. TAD, vol. 2, p. 124.
36. Cf. Q. 9:33.
37. TAD, vol. 2, p. 124.
38. It is interesting to note that al-Sijistānī, too, speaks of the development of the fetus in relation to the unfolding of history and the end of time. See Walker, *Early Philosophical Shiism*, p. 141.

39. TAD, vol. 2, pp. 124–5.
40. For more on these doctrinal reforms, see Daftary, *The Ismāʿīlīs*, 2nd edn, pp. 164–7.
41. TAD, vol. 2, p. 126.
42. TAD, vol. 2, pp. 126–7.
43. See, for instance, Henry Corbin, *The Voyage and the Messenger* (Berkeley: North Atlantic Books, 1998), p. 59, where he describes it as a 'spiritual hermeneutic'; and more broadly, his *Cyclical Time and Ismaili Gnosis* (London: Kegan Paul International in association with Islamic Publications, 1983).

6

A Spiritual Progression to a New Eschatological Centre: The *Ta'wīl al-daʿā'im* on the Hajj

Repeatedly throughout the *Ta'wīl al-daʿā'im*, the Masjid al-Ḥarām, the mosque surrounding the Kaʿba, is likened to the master of the age. This reorientation of the sacred centre should be seen in light of the rich history of alternate visions of the centre of Islam, including that of Manṣūr al-Ḥallāj (d. 922), Faḍl Allāh Astarābādī (d. 1394), and Saʿīd Qummī (d. 1691). The case of al-Nuʿmān's *Ta'wīl al-daʿā'im* is no different. Here, al-Nuʿmān writes that the true meaning of the hajj revolves around Fatimid notions of authority and sacred history.

In establishing the correspondences between different mosques and members of the *daʿwa*, al-Nuʿmān writes:

> The mosques in the *ẓāhir*, the houses in which people gather for prayer, are of different ranks and levels. The highest of them is the Masjid al-Ḥarām [the holy mosque in Mecca]. Its likeness is that of the master of the age, whether he is a prophet or an *imām*. The likeness of the command to perform the hajj and to travel to it from various regions of the earth is the likeness of the obligation on people towards the *walī* of their time, that they should come to him from every corner of the earth. The likeness of the mosque of the Prophet is the likeness of the *ḥujja*. People are similarly obligated to come to the mosque of the Prophet [in Medina], just as they are obligated to

> go to the Masjid al-Ḥarām. The likeness of the mosque of the Bayt al-Maqdis [in Jerusalem] is the likeness of his (*ḥujja*'s) gate, the greatest of the *dāʿīs* and their gates; he is called the gate of gates.[1]

Al-Nuʿmān's *taʾwīl* creates a hermeneutic in which the geographical centre of Islam is understood by possessors of true knowledge to be the master of the age. Indeed, the holy city of Mecca itself is transformed here: 'the likeness of Mecca is the likeness of the *daʿwa* of the master of the age; the first obligation of one who enters is the safeguarding of the portion of knowledge of truth that has come to him.'[2]

After once again stating that the likeness of the sanctuary is the likeness of the master of the age, al-Nuʿmān discusses the circumambulation of it.

> The likeness of circumambulating it is the likeness of the people of the *daʿwa* of truth holding fast to the *imām* of their time, their seeking his protection, their drawing near to him, and their striving for the grace of the knowledge and wisdom that he has. The likeness of the person who circumambulates the Kaʿba, who in the *ẓāhir* has completed seven circumambulations, is the likeness of the affirmation of the adherents of the *daʿwa* of truth of the seven speaker-prophets and the seven *imāms*.[3]

The centripetal pull of Mecca as a sacred centre is infused with the symbolism of the Fatimid hierarchy and its leadership: the mosque in Mecca is the master of the age; the city of Mecca is his *daʿwa*; and its circumambulation is the people of his *daʿwa* holding fast to the truth, seeking the knowledge of the master of the age.

The run between Ṣafā and Marwa that commemorates Hagar's search for water is also transformed into a kind of spiritual quest that reflects the relationship between initiate and guide. In al-Nuʿmān's *taʾwīl*, 'this run [corresponds to] the ascent of believers from one level to another of the levels of the faith';[4] this spiritual knowledge comes to them from the person who dispenses it to them (the *ḥujja* or *imām*), who, in turn, receives it from the *walī* of their time.[5]

The first rites of the hajj are performed on the eighth of the month of Dhū l-Ḥijja, also called the day of *tarwiyya*, literally the day of providing oneself with water, the day before pilgrims head to the plain of Arafat. In a remarkable passage, al-Nuʿmān discusses the relationship between this day and the imminent advent of the *qāʾim*:

> We have mentioned that the water in the *bāṭin* is like *ʿilm* [spiritual knowledge]. The day of *tarwiyya* is the eighth day of Dhū l-Ḥijja. You [listeners] are at that spiritual rank. The *walī* of the time has made the rivers of *ḥikma* [wisdom] and *ʿilm* flow copiously to you in an esoteric (*bāṭin*) manner and rivers of water [flow copiously to you] in an exoteric (*ẓāhir*) manner so that they may provide you drink in both manners, *ẓāhir* and *bāṭin*. In this way he has given you something that was not available [to those who came] before you. So praise God for His excellence in distinguishing you in this way, and draw together to accomplish His promise.[6]

The analogue of water as spiritual knowledge, coupled with al-Nuʿmān's discursive placement of his audience within the symbolic framework of the day of *tarwiyya*, allows him to create a sense of election that pinpoints this particular moment as the spiritual rank in which he and the *walī* disclose knowledge of both the *ẓāhir* and *bāṭin* to the audience – knowledge that has not been disclosed to people previously. Al-Nuʿmān states that they should praise God for this gift, as the disclosure of this knowledge is itself a sign of their election.

Al-Nuʿmān then alludes to the impending disclosure of this knowledge, which resembles the disclosure of all knowledge at the end of time.

> Its time has drawn near and its time is approaching, its characteristics will become manifest, and its signs will become visible. You will see the *bāṭin* of knowledge just as you see the water that is the *ẓāhir* of this *taʾwīl*. A long time has passed for you, and those who came before you, in earnest yearning for this [manifestation] in both the *ẓāhir* and *bāṭin*. Then God will bring you the *ẓāhir* and the *bāṭin* by way of watering and then as His wisdom has ordained and in

> accordance with His custom, [He will bring about] the showering of His blessings upon those who will be blessed by them both outwardly and inwardly. This is [the meaning] of His words: [*Do you not see how God has made what is in the heavens and on the earth useful to you,*] *and has lavished His blessings on you both outwardly and inwardly?* [*Yet some people argue about God, without knowledge or guidance or an illuminating scripture*] [31:20].[7]

He then discloses the symbolic analogues associated with the remaining days of the hajj, each of which serves to rehearse events that unfold at the end of time.

The central rite of the hajj, performed on the ninth of Dhū l-Ḥijja, is the *wuqūf* (standing) on the plain of Arafat that occurs between noon and sunset. This is a time of intense supplication; pilgrims spend the entire afternoon in prayer. Al-Nuʿmān transforms this rite into an anticipation of the *qāʾim*'s imminent arrival.

> The likeness of the day of Arafat is the likeness of he to whom the seal of the *imāms* will be born. There will be no *daʿwa* after him nor an *imām* who will call to the *daʿwa* of truth. What will come after him is only the promised day when God will gather all believers to Him. Religion will be one, and no soul [who had not believed before] will benefit, just as God has said: [*Are they waiting for the very angels to come to them, or your Lord Himself, or maybe some of His signs? But on the Day some of your Lord's signs come,*] *no soul will profit from faith if it had none before,* [*or has not already earned some good through its faith. Say, 'Wait if you wish: we too are waiting'*] [6:158].
>
> Then when the time of his manifestation has drawn near, and his time has arrived, the *imām* will move him, the *qāʾim*, in front of him. The likeness of that is the movement of the sun from its location at the middle of the day towards the direction of its setting – the sun, as has been mentioned – its likeness in *taʾwīl* is the likeness of the *imām* of the time.[8]

The *qāʾim*'s rising is associated with the finality of the end of time, concomitant with the movement of the *imām* to a position subservient to that of the *qāʾim*, and ultimately the *imām*'s disappearance, analogous to the setting of the sun. Al-Nuʿmān then writes that the likeness of the night migration from Arafat to Muzdalifa, which is performed after the *wuqūf*, corresponds to the movement of the believers' allegiance from the *imām* of their time to the *ḥujja* of the *qāʾim*.[9]

In an elegant summary of this rite, al-Nuʿmān writes:

> The likeness of the day of Arafat is the likeness of the *imām* who will precede the *qāʾim*; and the likeness of *wuqūf* [standing] in the evening on the day of Arafat until the setting of the sun is the likeness of the standing of believers waiting for the movement of this *imām* and the rising of the *qāʾim* after him.[10]

In reference to the fact that this rite is central to the fulfilment of the hajj – it is the only rite that must be fulfilled at its specified time in order for the hajj to be valid – al-Nuʿmān writes:

> In the *ẓāhir*, whoever reaches this station of the hajj has reached the completion of the *ẓāhirī* hajj. In the *bāṭin*, whoever has reached this station has fulfilled the hajj of the *bāṭin*, whose likeness in the *taʾwīl*, as we have mentioned, is the connection to the *imām* of the time, the link to the Truth, through which the works [performed by the seeker] are accepted. But the *imām* will not accept work performed by one who does not have this link with him. If he is not connected to the *imām* of this time, namely the one who is before the *qāʾim* but is connected with the *ḥujja* of the *qāʾim* whom he has established, he will surely be warned about this . . .[11]

Al-Nuʿmān then makes clear that those who did not believe in the Fatimid cause then suddenly do so after the *qāʾim*'s rising will not derive any benefit from him.

> If he was not connected to the *imām* before the rising of the *qāʾim* . . . then when the *qāʾim* rises and becomes manifest, [seeking] connection will not bring him any benefit on that day, nor will the work he performs be accepted; [this is] similar to the passing of time [for

> completing] the hajj. The *qāʾim* will not accept work from anyone who comes at this time. This is because the gate of forgiveness will at this time be closed, and the time for the acceptance of work will have passed. There will be no benefit on that day, just as God has said, *no soul will profit from faith if it had none before, or has not already earned some good* work.[12]

Just as the hajj is only valid with the performance of *wuqūf* on the plain of Arafat at a specified time, divine benefit mediated through the *qāʾim* can only take place for those who supported the true cause before the *qāʾim*'s rising.

The pilgrims then progress from Muzdalifa to Minā on the tenth of Dhū l-Ḥijja, where the rites of the next three days take place. The tenth of Dhū l-Ḥijja is the day of the *ʿīd al-aḍḥā*, the great *ʿīd,* which is likened to the *qāʾim* and his central role.

> The likeness of the day of *al-aḍḥā* is the likeness of the *qāʾim*, and the likeness of the *ṣalāt* of *al-aḍḥā* is the example of his call (*daʿwa*). His *ḥujja* will stand before him, calling to him [the *qāʾim*]. The affairs of the concealed *daʿwa* will remain as they were. Nothing about it will be unveiled until the rising of the *qāʾim*, when he becomes manifest to his enemies, and kills them as we have mentioned. The likeness of these are the sacrifices [on the day of sacrifice]. After this has happened he will manifest the *bāṭin* of *taʾwīl* and unveil it.[13]

The day on which the great *ʿīd* takes place corresponds to the *qāʾim*, and the fasting until the *ʿīd* prayer on that day is likened to secrecy, similar to the Ramadan fast. The *ʿīd* prayer is likened to the public rising of his *daʿwa*; its formerly secret state changes, and nothing emerges from it until the *qāʾim* is established and vanquishes his enemies. He will then disclose the *taʾwīl* of the *bāṭin*. The sequence is as follows:

> After the rising of *qāʾim*'s *daʿwa* and the killing of his enemies, and after food and drink, the *bāṭin* will be unveiled. This is the reason behind God's words: *On the Day when matters become unveiled they will be invited to prostrate themselves but will be prevented from doing*

> *so* [68:42] and His saying, *What are they waiting for except His ta'wīl? On the Day His ta'wīl arrives those who had previously ignored it will say, 'The messengers of our Lord had come with the truth.'* [7:53] And His saying: [*Are they waiting for the very angels to come to them, or your Lord Himself, or maybe some of His signs?*] *But on the Day some of your Lord's signs come, no soul will profit from faith if it had none before, or has not already earned some good through its faith.* [*Say, 'Wait if you wish: we too are waiting'*] [6:158].
>
> He will erase the requirement of work on that day; it will not be accepted, the *qiyāma* will be established and [people] will move to the abode of the hereafter. He will recompense the worshippers for what they had previously done whether good or evil.[14]

The rituals of the great *ʿīd* correspond to a detailed vision of eschatological triumph: the rising of the *qā'im*'s *daʿwa*; the vanquishing of his enemies; celebration with food and drink; the unveiling of the *bāṭin*; the establishment of the *qiyāma*; movement to the abode of the hereafter; and the final judgment. Here, we see a reflection of the ease with which mahdist movements create a sense of election: judgment occurs at not one, but two moments. First, terrestrially, people are judged for their support of the correct eschatological figure; believers are protected rather than vanquished by him on earth; and second, people are judged in the realm of the hereafter, in the abode of final judgment. This sense of election is also supported through a narrative that entrusts believers with the *qā'im*'s disclosure of absolute truth before the final judgment.

Al-Nuʿmān then discusses the symbolic analogues of the three days following the great *ʿīd*, the last three days of the hajj, called the *ayyām al-tashrīq*. He writes that the first of these days is likened to the *ḥujja* of the *qā'im*; the second, the *bāb* (gate) of the *ḥujja* of the *qā'im*; and the third is the caller of the *ḥujja* of the *qā'im*.[15]

> The days of *tashrīq* are named for the brilliance of the light of the *qā'im* that shines upon them. They are resplendent from his brilliance shining upon them; the believers are radiant from the light

> which has been provided to them. It is thus said of one who works by the *daʿwa* of truth that he will become radiant, that is, become resplendent by the light of the friends of God – those to whom it has been provided.[16]

The itinerary of the hajj is now complete with the *qāʾim*'s illumination of the elect, a theme we find recurring in early Shia writings[17] and reminiscent of Q. 39:67–70:

> *On the Day of Resurrection, the whole earth will be in His grip. The heavens will be rolled up in His right hand – Glory be to Him! He is far above the partners they ascribe to Him! – the Trumpet will be sounded, and everyone in the heavens and earth will fall down senseless except those God spares. It will be sounded once again and they will be on their feet, looking on. The earth will shine with the light of its Lord; the Record of Deeds will be laid open; the prophets and witnesses will be brought in. Fair judgment will be given between them: they will not be wronged and every soul will be repaid in full for what it has done. He knows best what they do.*

My examination of al-Mahdī's letter along with the *Taʾwīl al-daʿāʾim* provides a snapshot of two ways in which the Fatimids addressed the issue of imminent temporality while arguing for their divinely appointed legitimacy. These two interpretive mechanisms – among the many others not discussed here – provide us with insights into the complexity and creativity of these Fatimid exegetes, who sought to address the issue of temporality as the dynasty consolidated its authority. The caliph al-Mahdī's letter distances an immediate temporality in part by arguing that the eschatological *mahdī* will come from the line of Fatimid caliph-imams, and that Fatimid ascension before the end of time was divinely ordained.

Approximately half a century later, well into Fatimid rule, we see how Qāḍī l-Nuʿmān rewrites sacred history to locate the community between the open manifestation of the *daʿwa* of the historical caliph al-Mahdī, signaling the end of secrecy and divine trials for the community, and the advent of the awaited eschatological figure of the *qāʾim*. The result is a displacement of messianic expectation into the not-so-distant future: an expectation that is excised from linear temporality and bound to the ritual calendar of cyclical time. This reinscription of an imminent mahdism also served to reaffirm the legitimacy of the Fatimid hierarchy. Perhaps the most vivid example of this is al-Nuʿmān's *taʾwīl* of the hajj, which is likened to the centripetal, primordial pull of the *walī* of the time and the dramatic rehearsal of the *qāʾim*'s arrival.

The evolving nature of Fatimid apocalypticism is also highly suggestive of the ways in which we can understand the relationship between authority and apocalypticism more broadly. In this study I hypothesise that apocalypticism, through its discursive manipulation of temporality,[18] helps to restructure the premises of terrestrial authority through an elision of symbols associated with ultimate good or evil with actors, rituals, or objects on the terrestrial plane – a phenomenon we see in the *Kitāb al-kashf* and the *Kitāb al-rushd*, as well as in so many other examples in the history of religions. The case of Qāḍī l-Nuʿmān allows us to envision apocalyptic reinterpretation and the maintenance of authority as interrelated processes; he himself was engaged in both by virtue of his position as an ideological architect of the Fatimid state. The contents of the *Taʾwīl al-daʿāʾim*, dispensed privately in a series of *majālis* for believers, illustrates how imminent mahdist expectation was not flatly abrogated or straightforwardly reinterpreted. Rather, it was fused to regularly performed ritual practices to both displace the linearity of this expectation while also creating a new sense of sacred history: a history that believers were to internalise through the regular performance of ritual.

As al-Nuʿmān infused existing rituals with new symbolic meanings in the private sphere, he was also concerned with the ways in which rituals surrounding the *imām* would communicate the latter's sacrality in public. His *Kitāb al-himma fī ādāb atbāʿ al-aʾimma* [Code of conduct for the followers of the *imām*], for instance, details various ways in which one should interact with the *imām*, including how people should approach him, how they should make requests of him, and how believers should behave among themselves.[19] While court rituals in general can serve to order, reify, and sometimes reorder society,[20] Fatimid court ceremony, processions, and public rituals, as Paula Sanders writes, served to construct a world in which the caliph-imam was continuously constructed as centre; hierarchies existed only in relation to him.[21] As we have seen, al-Mahdī's letter modified initial conceptions of mahdism to include the progeny of al-Mahdī, and stripped it of its eschatology. At the same time, al-Mahdī's position was bolstered by claims to the role of *mahdī* – a mahdism that envisioned more than one person as *mahdī*. Not only have scholars observed the continued deployment of mahdist symbolism as associated with other Fatimid caliph-imams,[22] we also see how, in the *Ta'wīl al-da'ā'im*, the concept of *imām* as a utopian centre is retained. Perhaps, then, the utopian visions of our early texts have become instantiated and transposed onto the body of the Fatimid caliph-imams. Then rituals surrounding the caliph-imams could be seen in this light, as a means for the cultivation and public articulation of an embodied vision of utopia, created in part through apocalypticism or mahdism but stripped of an imminent eschatology. Ironically, as rituals surrounding the caliph-imams served to reify the *imām*'s position as utopian centre, al-Nuʿmān's symbolic analogues to the liturgical calendar in the *Ta'wīl al-daʿā'im* also served to distance believers' immediate eschatological expectations while reaffirming the centrality of the imamate. Here, then, we see the relationship between apocalypticism and authority laid bare: an immediate eschatology helping to install the Fatimid caliph-imams into power; a subsequent mahdism stripped of its eschatology and individual identity[23] helping them to maintain it; and public ritual serving to simultaneously reify a utopian vision on earth while also embodying the postponement of an immediate eschatology.

It is a manifestation of an immediate eschatology that we turn to next: the Nizari declaration of the end time. On 8 August 1164, the leader of the Nizari Ismaili community dramatically declared the end of the world. What was the nature of this declaration? And why was it made? The next chapter of this book addresses these questions, ultimately illustrating how this apocalyptic invocation served to solve lingering questions about the leadership of the community as well as its future trajectory.

Notes

1. TAD, vol. 1, pp. 230–1.
2. TAD, vol. 2, p. 229.
3. TAD, vol. 2, pp. 232–3.
4. TAD, vol. 2, p. 249.
5. TAD, vol. 2, pp. 247, 249.
6. TAD, vol. 2, p. 257.
7. TAD, vol. 2, p. 257.
8. TAD, vol. 2, pp. 260–1.
9. TAD, vol. 2, p. 262.
10. TAD, vol. 2, p. 293.
11. TAD, vol. 2, p. 293–4.
12. TAD, vol. 2, p. 294.
13. TAD, vol. 1, p. 338.
14. TAD, vol. 1, p. 338.
15. TAD, vol. 2, pp. 280–1.
16. TAD, vol. 2, p. 280.
17. Omid Ghaemmaghami masterfully discusses the range of tropes related to the coming of the *qāʾim* in early Shia literature in his '{And the earth will shine with the light of its Lord} (Q 39:69): Qāʾim and Qiyāma in Shīʿī Thought', in *Roads to Paradise: Eschatology and Concepts of the Hereafter in Islam*, ed. Sebastian Günther and Todd Lawson (Leiden: Brill [forthcoming]).
18. O'Leary, pp. 13, 44.
19. al-Nuʿmān b. Muḥammad, *Kitāb al-himma fī ādāb atbāʿ al-aʾimma*, abridged English translation by Jawad Muscati and Khan Bahadur A.M. Moulvi, *Selections from Qazi Noaman's Kitab-ul-Himma fi Adabi Ataba-el-aʾemma or Code of Conduct for the Followers of the Imam* (Ismailia Association [W.] Pakistan Series, no. 1. Karachi: The Ismailia Association [W.] Pakistan, 1950).
20. See, for instance, Lincoln, *Discourse*.

21. Paula Sanders, *Ritual, Politics, and the City in Fatimid Cairo* (Albany: State University of New York Press, 1994), pp. 33–7.
22. See, for instance, Daftary, *Short History*, p. 73.
23. This is a version of the argument Brett makes in his discussion of Fatimid origins. See Brett, *Rise*, p. 127.

7

Actualising the End: The Nizari Declaration of the Resurrection

It happened at the mountain fortress of Alamut, about sixty miles from present-day Tehran. At noon in the middle of Ramadan, Ḥasan *ʿalā dhikrihi al-salām*, the leader of the Nizari Ismaili community, proclaimed to his adherents that the end of the world had arrived. In accordance with Ismaili notions of sacred history, Ḥasan announced that during this period of the resurrection (*qiyāma*), the religious law (*sharīʿa*) did not apply to his believers anymore. To illustrate the community's new status at the edge of history, Ḥasan and his community celebrated the resurrection with a splendid feast – during the afternoon in the month of Ramadan.

An analysis of the context from which Ḥasan's declaration emerges shows us that his declaration cannot be dismissed as what might seem to be an aberrant manifestation of Islamic antinomianism. Rather we see here how apocalypticism emerges as a powerful solution to two particular logistical problems facing the Nizari community: the absence of a present *imām* and an inability to conquer Seljuk lands. This declaration also ruptured the Nizari reliance upon past hermeneutical methods that had become increasingly distant from the needs of the community and helped inaugurate a vision of a Shia Islam that was specifically Persianate in form.

Before we examine the case of the *qiyāma* in more detail, it is necessary to provide a brief survey of the later history of the Fatimid Empire and the historical context leading up to this declaration. I then discuss Ḥasan's declaration, focusing on both the ritualistic elements of his ceremony and on the *Haft-bāb* [Seven chapters] by Ḥasan-i Maḥmūd-i Kātib, a document written approximately forty years after the event that describes the theology behind the declaration.

The History

As we have witnessed through an examination of al-Mahdī's letter and the *Ta'wīl al-da'ā'im*, the history of the early Fatimids can be seen as an attempt to simultaneously harness utopian aspects of apocalypticism and distance its temporal imminence. Mahdism too posed a challenge for the ruling dynasty: a number of *mahdī*s arose among the Khārijīs during this time. The most serious threat to the Fatimids was the Khārajī rebel Abū Yazīd, who actually invaded the capitol city al-Mahdiyya in 332/943. Fatimid sources, including *khuṭba*s by al-Mahdī's successors al-Qā'im (d. 334/946) and al-Manṣūr (d. 341/953), depict Abū Yazīd as the *dajjāl* or the eschatological deceiver.[1] As Brett so aptly observes, both Abū Yazīd and the Fatimid caliphate deployed apocalyptic imagery to elevate the battle to the realm of cosmic history.

> At Qayrawān the Malikite jurists had consented to join with Abū Yazīd against the rule of the Mahdi-Qā'im on the strength of the Prophetic tradition that at the end of the world the Rāfiḍa or heretics, meaning in this case the Fatimids, would arise as infidels to be killed by the faithful. As for Abū Yazīd himself, the protagonist in this great struggle, the donkey on which he rode to the conquest of Qayrawān, giving him the name of Ṣāḥib al-Ḥimar or Lord of the Donkey, was the reverse of evil. The appellation was straightforwardly messianic, recalling the triumphal entry of Christ into Jerusalem, and anticipating its use as late as the twentieth century for the 'fearsome and quasi-messianic' pretender to the Moroccan throne, Bū Ḥimāra. Abū Yazīd was a *mahdī* in his own right, an emissary of God to rid the world of unbelief. His conversion by the Fatimids into the Dajjāl

> was an inversion of the identities of friend and foe proposed by the revolutionaries themselves.[2]

Abū Yazīd's apocalyptic symbolism was turned against him; he began as *mahdī* but ended up being portrayed and defeated as a *dajjāl*. The defeat of Abū Yazīd played well into the hands of Fatimid propagandists, who used the victory over Abū Yazīd to effectively inaugurate a new phase of the dynasty, signaled by the designation of al-Qā'im's successor as al-Manṣūr, the victorious.[3]

Though al-Mahdī engaged in a doctrinal shift at the beginning of his rule, specifying that he was not the awaited *mahdī* but one carrying the name '*mahdī*' from a family of *mahdī*s who would rule until the end of time,[4] the Fatimid hierarchy was not averse to the continued deployment of apocalyptic symbolism, as we have seen throughout this book, and here with the struggle against Abū Yazīd. Analogous to the regnal titles assumed by some Abbasid caliphs,[5] the Fatimid caliphs also retained titles with messianic significance.[6]

It was during the time of al-Muʿizz (953–75) – the caliph who successfully invaded Cairo and brought some of his ancestors' coffins from al-Mahdiyya to Cairo in 973 – that the caliphate once again adjusted its doctrinal stance concerning the imamate.[7] To bring the Qarmatis into the Fatimid fold, the Fatimid caliphs acknowledged that Muḥammad b. Ismāʿīl was indeed the *mahdī*. The Fatimid caliphs were deputies of this *mahdī*, carrying out his functions and they would rule until the end of time. Muḥammad b. Ismāʿīl, then, was not expected to return corporeally.[8] This was a modification of the doctrine propounded by ʿAbdallāh al-Mahdī, who denied that Muḥammad b. Ismāʿīl was the *mahdī* and claimed the position for himself.[9]

This doctrinal 'rapprochement,' Daftary writes, was only partially successful with the Qarmatis. Indeed, the Qarmatis 'persisted in parts of Persia, notably in Daylam and Azerbaiyjan, as well as in Iraq'[10] and in Bahrain. Al-Muʿizz died in Cairo in 365/975 and was succeeded by al-ʿAzīz, who reigned over a peaceful and prosperous empire until his death in 386/996. Al-Ḥākim succeeded al-ʿAzīz and it was during this time that the Fatimids faced their 'first serious internal crisis confronting the Fatimid *daʿwa* and its leadership.'[11] Perhaps unsurprisingly, this crisis was also grounded in apocalyptic symbolism.

Some *dāʿīs*, who had returned from Persia or Central Asia, began to propagate the ideas reminiscent of the Qarmatis, that the end of time had arrived, the religious laws did not need to be followed anymore, and that the caliph, al-Ḥākim (r. 386–411/996–1021) was divine. The movement was named after the *dāʿī* Muḥammad b. Ismāʿīl al-Darzī, and became quite popular in Cairo; in fact, many *dāʿīs* publicly claimed their adherence to the new doctrine.

The Persian *dāʿī* al-Kirmānī was actually brought to Cairo to refute this new doctrine and the title of the next caliph, al-Ẓāhir ('the exoteric'), illustrates just how serious this crisis became. Al-Ḥākim disappeared mysteriously in 411/1021, only heightening Druze belief in his divinity.[12]

Al-Ẓāhir (411–27/1021–36) was followed by al-Mustanṣir (r. 427–87/1036–94). It was during the reign of al-Mustanṣir that the empire began to decline. A number of reasons played a part:[13] (1) racial rivalries among the Fatimid armies, which ultimately manifested in factional fighting outside of Cairo in 454/1062; (2) famine because of low water levels in the Nile for seven years, between 1065 and 1072; (3) and the rebellion of Turkish troops. To regain order in his empire, al-Mustanṣir called on Badr al-Jamālī, an Armenian general, to quell the Turkish rebellion. In the process of restoring order, Badr al-Jamālī effectively gained control of the empire. In 487/1094 al-Mustanṣir died; he had designated his son Abū Manṣūr al-Nizār (437–88/1045–95) as his successor. The son of Badr al-Jamālī and effective ruler of the empire, al-Afḍal, supported Nizār's half brother, Abū l-Qāsim Aḥmad (467–95/1074–1101).

> The dispute over al-Mustanṣir's succession permanently split the Ismailis into two rival factions, later designated as the Nizāriyya (Nizārī) and the Mustaʿliyya (Mustaʿlī). The imamate of al-Mustaʿlī, installed to the Fatimid caliphate, was acknowledged by the official *daʿwa* establishment in Cairo, as well as the Ismaili communities of Egypt, Yaman, and western India. These Ismailis, who depended

on the Fatimid regime and later traced the imamate in al-Mustaʿlī's progeny, maintained their relations with Cairo, serving hereafter as the headquarters to the Mustaʿlī Ismaili *daʿwa*.[14]

The Fatimids had maintained the policy of expanding the *daʿwa* even during their empire; there were thus significant pockets of Fatimids in Persia and Syria. Though Cairo was facing a leadership crisis in 1094, the eastern lands were united under the leadership of Ḥasan Ṣabbāḥ, who had severed ties with Cairo and supported the imamate of Nizār.

Ḥasan Ṣabbāḥ, who had travelled for almost a decade throughout Persia as a *dāʿī* – and who before that had spent significant time in Cairo – was intent on launching an open revolt against the Seljuks. Ḥasan's revolt gathered momentum by galvanising the masses to rally against the anti-Shia policies of the Seljuks; the continued domination of Persian lands by various Turkish dynasties; and 'anarchy' caused by the constant influx of Turkish soldiers, among other causes.[15] In 1090, Ḥasan's open revolt against the Seljuks began with the capture of the mountain fortress of Alamut in northern Persia. Lewis writes about this region and its inhabitants:

> [D]uring the tenth century, under the Buyids, the Daylamis even succeeded in establishing their ascendancy over most of Persia and Iraq, and were for a while the custodians of the Caliphs themselves . . . It was among these northern peoples – predominantly Shiʿite and already strongly influenced by Ismaili propaganda – that Hasan-i Sabbah made his main effort. For the warlike and disaffected inhabitants of Daylam and Mazandaran, his militant creed had a powerful appeal.[16]

Ḥasan's populist message appealed to Nizaris and non-Nizaris as well and seemed to also appeal to the lower classes of society: 'the country's landless villagers and highlanders, as well as artisans and craftsmen, representing underprivileged social classes in Saljuk dominions,'[17] as well as those dissatisfied with foreign rule.

Persian cultural awareness seemed to play a significant role in this revolt. Daftary writes, '. . . Ḥasan's revolt was an expression of Persian 'national' sentiments, which accounts for its early popular appeal and widespread success in Persia.' In fact, Ḥasan,

> . . . as an expression of his Persian awareness and in spite of his intense Islamic piety, substituted Persian for Arabic as the religious language of the Ismailis of Persia. This was the first time that a major Muslim community had adopted Persian as its religious language. This also explains why the Persian-speaking (Nizārī) Ismaili communities of Persia, Afghanistan and Central Asia produced their literature entirely in Persian during the Alamūt period and later times.[18]

The adoption of Persian as opposed to the Arabic of Fatimid Egypt seemed to further foment the distinction between the Fatimids and the Nizaris.

The lands under the Nizaris, unlike Seljuk territory, were independently ruled, and booty was shared equally. Between 1092 and 1102, during a decade-long civil war among the Seljuks, Ḥasan improved his fortifications at Alamut and simultaneously expanded his territorial holdings, winning more converts to the cause. After the war Seljuk power became decentralised – there was no more sultan with a grand army – and Ḥasan erected a series of strongholds that served as bases for armed operations, from which he intended to take more Seljuk territory.

Ḥasan died in June 1124, having designated his lieutenant at Lamasar, Kiyā Buzurg-Ummīd, as his successor and the *dāʿī* of Daylam.[19] By this time, the Seljuks and the Nizaris were engaged in a stalemate – the Nizaris had failed to take over Seljuk lands and the Seljuks had failed to uproot the Nizaris.[20] Small skirmishes continued during the reign of Muḥammad b. Buzurg-Ummīd (1138–62). And in 1162, Muḥammad b. Buzurg-Ummīd was succeeded by his son Ḥasan, who inaugurated the end of the world.

Ushering in the End

The event occurred in the middle of Ramadan on 8 August 1164. It involved the assembly of Ḥasan's followers from various territories and the reading of a *khuṭba*, purportedly from the hidden *imām*, designed to usher the community into a new era of existence, the *qiyāma* (resurrection). Commensurate with expectations concerning the end of history, this declaration also involved the end of the practice of the *sharīʿa*. To celebrate this momentous occasion, the community celebrated this new moment in history with a feast, later an annual event in the Nizari calendar.[21]

Though the doctrine of the *qiyāma* was later abrogated, scholars have diverging opinions about its significance. The renowned Islamic historian Marshall Hodgson, who wrote extensively on the event and its surrounding history, writes that:

> The great resurrection, the end of the world, was thus understood (in a typically Ismāʿīlī manner) in a symbolic sense. It was the end of a religious era, and the beginning of a spiritual dispensation of moral, not physical, perfection . . . what mattered henceforth would be a purely spiritual life of inward states of the soul.[22]

After likening the doctrine to that of Paul the Apostle, he adds:

> More properly, it must be interpreted in Ṣūfī terms: the inner life of moral and mystical experience was the sole reality henceforth to be attended to. Those who could respond were, spiritually, already in eternal life, and those who could not were spiritually lifeless. This was the long-awaited culmination; the faithful Ismāʿīlīs who understood were to leave behind all material compromise and rise to the spiritual level which was the only true victory; that is, they were to become spiritually perfect; while the Sunnīs were defeated in the most final sense possible, in that all their further efforts were rendered spiritually meaningless. Thus was established the doctrine of the qiyāma, the Resurrection, as the new basis of Ismāʿīlī life.[23]

Henry Corbin and Christian Jambet[24] elaborate upon the spiritual nature of the declaration. Both authors believe that the resurrection should be understood in an internal sense and argue that each resurrection is symbolic of a spiritual ascent, culminating in the great resurrection, in which we achieve freedom from the law and unity with our primordial spiritual selves.[25]

Scholars have also correlated the declaration to events on the ground. On this issue, Hodgson states: 'Among the Ismāʿīlīs the qiyāma meant, along with independence from the Sunnī world and its opinion, an admission of their failure in an attempt to transform that world.'[26] Daftary echoes this opinion, adding that 'the *qiyāma* declared the outside world irrelevant. The Nizārīs envisaged themselves in spiritual Paradise, while condemning the non-Nizārīs to the Hell of spiritual non-existence.'[27] Religionist Bruce Lincoln cites the *qiyāma* as an instance of millennial antinomianism and reminds us that seemingly radical expressions such as these are not unusual in the history of religions. These expressions, after all, may provide powerful mechanisms for the assertion of a group's freedom; a renewed sense of social solidarity; and potent symbolic currency against a dominant stratum of society.[28] The *qiyāma* has thus been interpreted by various authors as an admission of the Nizari failure to take over Seljuk lands; a creative spiritual reconstruction; an inauguration of a more esoteric form of Islam; and a graphic expression of protest against those in power.

We have already seen how apocalyptic symbolism served as a potent force for the institutionalisation of the Fatimid dynasty and how the utopian dimensions of this apocalypticism were retained to help bolster Fatimid legitimacy while simultaneously distancing a sense of temporal immediacy. Building upon the work of the scholars mentioned above, my analysis of the *qiyāma* foregrounds the apocalyptic dimensions of this declaration, treating it as a manifestation of apocalypticism that was not expected or temporally distant but fully actualised in the present moment. Further, I argue that the invocation of apocalyptic symbolism in the specific form of the *qiyāma* was instrumental in mediating the transfer of authority from hidden to present *imām*. This transfer of authority helped to resolve three problems pertaining to the future of the Nizari community: (1) the continued problem of the absence of the *imām*; (2) the problem of past hermeneutical methods becoming increasingly distant from the needs of the Nizaris; and (3) the contested vision of a Shia Islam that was specifically Persianate in form.

The ceremony began when Ḥasan gathered the representatives from the major Ismaili strongholds throughout Persia. He '. . . ordered a pulpit to be constructed on an open space at the foot of Alamut in such a way that the *qibla* should be in the opposite direction to what is the custom of Islam.'[29] After demarcating his community as graphically distinct from other Islamic communities, Ḥasan then ascended the *minbar*. Daftary, based on Juwaynī,[30] reconstructs this event as follows:

> The imām of our time, Ḥasan declared, has sent you his blessings and compassion; he has called you his special chosen servants, he has relieved you of the duties and burdens of the Sharīʿa, and has brought you to the *qiyāma*, the Resurrection. Ḥasan then delivered a *khuṭba* in Arabic that was purported to be the exact words of the hidden imām. The jurist Muḥammad Bustī, who knew Arabic, had been placed at the foot of the pulpit to translate this *khuṭba* into Persian for those present. The *khuṭba* named Ḥasan not only as the imām's *dāʿī* and *ḥujja*, or proof, like Ḥasan-i Ṣabbāḥ, but also his *khalīfa*, or deputy, with plenary authority, a higher rank yet. The imām also required that his *shīʿa* must obey and follow Ḥasan in all religious and temporal matters, recognize his commands as binding, and deem his word as that of the imām's.[31]

A similar ceremony was held a few weeks later at another fortress, where Ḥasan likened his position to that of the Imām Mustanṣir.[32]

This account of Ḥasan's declaration illustrates the elegant interweaving of communal election, resurrection, and the ontology of Ḥasan's authority. The community assembled on that day was the *imām*'s elect, his 'special chosen servants.' Because of their election, his followers were brought to the realm of the resurrection, the realm in which the *sharīʿa* was rendered unnecessary. But election and resurrection were predicated more fundamentally upon the recognition of Ḥasan's newly revised position over his community. Notice that from that point Ḥasan was to be considered far more than a *dāʿī* of the *imām*; he was to be obeyed in all religious and temporal matters and his words were to be considered equal to those of the *imām*. Ḥasan thus effectively elided the *imām*'s position with his own; it was now Ḥasan who possessed ultimate authority over the community. The reification of this drastic shift in authority was mediated by Ḥasan's declaration of the end of time.

Ḥasan's declaration – perhaps commensurate with communal anticipation[33] – inaugurated the *telos* of history, a state frequently described by the Quran as one of ontological reversal and permanent reification of the way things truly are.[34] For the Fatimids and Nizaris, this was also the long-awaited state in which there is no need for *taʾwīl*, as there is no difference between the *bāṭin* and the *ẓāhir*, the hidden and the apparent, the signified and the signifier.[35] As Jambet writes, the Truth (*ḥaqīqa*) or essential reality, was rendered visible in the physical person of the Master of the Resurrection.[36] Here, invocation of apocalyptic symbolism effected and made permanent the elision of signifier (Ḥasan, the *ẓāhir*) with the signified (the hidden *imām*, the *bāṭin*).[37] *Qiyāma* symbolism allowed the entire symbolic potency of the office of imamate to be overlaid, fused and to materialise onto the person of Ḥasan. This fusion created a new and permanent *ḥaqīqa* that was disclosed to all at the grand ceremony in Alamut: the absolute leadership of the community by Ḥasan and by extension, his progeny. The disclosure of Ḥasan's true position was the content of this cosmic unveiling, this apocalypse that only became apparent in the fullness of time. Those who did not obey him were condemned to eternal oblivion.

The declaration of the *qiyāma* returns the community to the moment of primordiality, the moment, as Jambet notes, of precreation that predates the religious law.[38] Just as God makes predifferentiated creation testify to His lordship, the equivalent aspect of this theology takes place functionally on this earth, with the manifestation of Ḥasan as the present *imām*.[39] The disclosure of Ḥasan's true nature inaugurates a new societal creation that must testify to his ultimate authority over the community. Perhaps the most vivid example of this authority is Ḥasan's repeal of the religious laws, an act that fulfilled Ismaili predictions concerning a *mahdī* or *qā'im* figure who would appear and abolish the *sharī'a* at the end of history.

In the Quranic narrative, the process by which humanity came into being is predicated upon a process of initiation into God's covenant – its bearing witness, or testifying (*ashadahum*), to God's dominion over all of humanity. Similarly, participation in the ritual ceremonies of Alamut – which included the breaking of the fast and facing the direction opposite Mecca – signaled the new community's genesis in time as a new and exclusive creation. In both cases, the process of initiation not only delineated the newly created boundaries of communal identity, but also affirmed the authority of those who created these boundaries.

The declaration of the resurrection also demonstrates the way in which apocalyptic doctrines seem to easily restructure theodicy itself. The return to precreation dissolves, through the abolishment of past time, previous categories of sacred and profane and current structures of authority, including the religious law.[40] Apocalyptic rebirth in a mythic space of atemporality grafts an entirely new meaning onto the cosmos, one that equates the apex of sacredness with the extent to which one adheres to the tenets of this newly disclosed message. At this fragile moment in the community's creation, new authoritative structures were reinforced through a process of communal ritual – in this case, the breaking of the fast. In this moment, too, the boundaries between good and evil, sacred and profane, were also rigorously delineated: those who did not believe in this message were rendered simply nonexistent, bound up with the evil of the time before this disclosure. It should be noted here that this division of the cosmos into binary structures related to belief in the new message had a pragmatic function for community building as well: these structures helped ensure that this new message, and the community that bears it, will have an optimal chance for survival.

If the *qiyāma* ceremony simultaneously delineated both Nizari exclusivity and Ḥasan's authority, then it is only logical that the ceremony of the breaking of the fast remained an annual celebration until the abrogation of the doctrine. This annual commemoration becomes a (re)creation of the community according to this *apokalypsis*, a ritual that not only reaffirms communal boundaries, but also reifies social hierarchies. Put differently, performance of this ritual helps maintain the social structures created by this apocalyptic myth, the authority of the present *imām*, and the exclusivity of the Nizari community.[41] Both of these elements of the *qiyāma* are elaborated upon in the *Haft-bāb*, which further reifies this authoritative shift.

Notes

1. Paul Walker, *Orations of the Fatimid Caliphs* (New York: I. B. Tauris, 2009), pp. 72–6.
2. Brett, *Rise*, p. 171.
3. Brett, *Rise*, pp. 170–82.
4. Brett, *Rise*, p. 114; al-Mahdī bi'llāh, *Kitāb arsalahu al-Mahdī*, trans. Hamdani and de Blois, p. 177.
5. Bernard Lewis, 'The Regnal Titles of the First Abbasid Caliphs', in *Dr. Zakir Husain Presentation Volume* (New Delhi, 1968).
6. Daftary, *Short History*, p. 73.
7. See also Heinz Halm, *Die Kalifen von Kairo: Die Fatimiden in Ägypten 973–1074* (Munich: C. H. Beck, 2003).
8. Daftary, *Short History*, p. 78.
9. Daftary *The Ismā'īlīs*, 2nd edn, p. 164.
10. Daftary, *Short History*, p. 79.
11. Daftary, *Short History*, p. 100.
12. For a discussion of the *mahdism* of al-Ḥākim, see Josef van Ess, *Chiliastische Erwartungen und die Versuchung der Göttlichkeit: Der Kalif al-Ḥākim (386–411 H.)*. (Heidelberg, 1977).
13. Daftary, *Short History*, pp. 105–6.
14. Daftary, *Short History*, p. 107.
15. Daftary, *Short History*, pp. 124–5.
16. Bernard Lewis, *The Assassins: A Radical Sect in Islam* (New York: Basic Books, 1968), p. 42.
17. Daftary, *Short History*, p. 126.
18. Daftary, *Short History*, p. 125.
19. Daftary, *Short History*, p. 134.

20. Daftary, *Short History*, p. 135.
21. Daftary, *The Ismāʿīlīs*, 1st edn (1990), p. 387. Compare to M. G. S. Hodgson, 'The Ismāʿīlī State', in *The Cambridge History of Iran*, vol. 5: *The Saljuq and Mongol Periods*, ed. J. A. Boyle (Cambridge: Cambridge University Press, 1968), pp. 422–82, 458–9; and M. G. S. Hodgson, *The Secret Order of Assassins: The Struggle of the Early Nizārī Ismāʿīlīs Against the Islamic World* (Philadelphia: University of Pennsylvania Press, 2005 [1955]), pp. 148–51.
22. Hodgson, 'Ismāʿīlī State', p. 459.
23. Hodgson 'Ismāʿīlī State', pp. 459–60.
24. Christian Jambet, *La grande résurrection d'Alamût: Les formes de la liberté dans le shîʾisme ismaélien* (Paris: Verdier 1990).
25. See, for instance, Corbin, *History of Islamic Philosophy*, p. 100.
26. Hodgson, 'Ismāʿīlī State', p. 466.
27. Daftary, *The Ismāʿīlīs*, 1st edn (1990), p. 389.
28. Lincoln, *Discourse*, pp. 114–27; see also his *Holy Terrors: Thinking about Religion after September 11* (Chicago: University of Chicago Press, 2003), pp. 85–9.
29. ʿAṭā al-Dīn ʿAṭā Malik b. Muḥammad Juwaynī, *Taʾrīkh-i jahān-gushā*, trans. John Andrew Boyle, *The History of the World-Conqueror*, vol. 2 (Manchester: Manchester University Press, 1958), p. 688.
30. Juwaynī, trans. Boyle, p. 689. See also Daftary's synopsis of the relevant sources in Daftary, *The Ismāʿīlīs*, 1st edn (1990), pp. 685–6, n. 130.
31. Daftary, *The Ismāʿīlīs*, 1st edn (1990), p. 387.
32. Daftary, *The Ismāʿīlīs*, 1st edn (1990), p. 387; Hodgson, 'Ismāʿīlī State', p. 459.
33. Hodgson, 'Ismāʿīliī State', pp. 457–8.
34. Sura 99 is but one of a number of examples. For a translation and commentary on this Sura, see Sells, *Approaching*, pp. 108–9.
35. Jorrun J. Buckley, 'The Nizârî Ismâʿîlîtes' Abolishment of the Sharîʾa during the "Great Resurrection" of 1164 A.D./559 A.H', *Studia Islamica* 60 (1984): pp. 150–1. See also Jambet, p. 85.
36. '. . . la *haqîqat*, ou réalité-essentielle, se rend visible dans la personne physique du Seigneur de la Résurrection', Jambet, p. 85, n. 92.
37. The idea of Fatimid *taʾwīl* being predicated upon a system in which the signifier points to that which is signified (and unchanging) is taken from Tahera Qutbuddin's *Al-Muʾayyad al-Shīrāzī and Fatimid Daʿwa Poetry*

(Leiden: Brill, 2005), pp. 105–10, in which she discusses the *mathal* being a symbol for the immutable and normally hidden *mamthūl*.

38. Jambet, pp. 305–6.
39. Jambet writes: 'L'adhésion à l'imâm et au Résurrecteur, au dernier jour du sixième cycle, correspond exactemant à l'adhésion prééternelle à Dieu . . . Le pacte original ne fonde pas la religion légalitaire mais la resurrection spirituelle', p. 305.
40. Note the resonance between this dissolution and O'Leary's description of apocalyptic discourse: '. . . the essential topoi of apocalyptic discourse are authority, time, and evil, and that this discourse functions as a symbolic theodicy, a mythical and rhetorical solution intended to 'solve' the problem of evil through its discursive construction of temporality' (O'Leary, p. 20).
41. Bruce Lincoln writes: '. . . ritual is best understood as an authoritative mode of symbolic discourse and a powerful instrument for the evocation of those sentiments (affinity and estrangement) out of which society is constructed . . . That ritual performances can contribute powerfully to the maintenance of society . . . remains an accepted truism . . .' Lincoln, *Discourse*, p. 53. Complementing Lincoln's discussion of ritual as a powerful means of maintaining social order is Jonathan Z. Smith's assertion that '*ritual represents the creation of a controlled environment* where the variables (i.e., the accidents) of ordinary life may be displaced *precisely* because they are felt to be so overwhelmingly present and powerful . . . There is a "gnostic" dimension to ritual. It provides the means for demonstrating what ought to have been done, what ought to have taken place . . . Ritual provides an occasion for reflection and rationalization on the fact that what ought to have been done was not done, what ought to have taken place did not occur.' Jonathan Z. Smith, *Imagining Religion: From Babylon to Jonestown* (Chicago: University of Chicago Press, 1982), p. 63 (emphasis original). Smith conceives of ritual as a controlled environment engineered precisely to resolve and contemplate the incongruencies of everyday life – an incongruency here being the inability of the Nizaris to win the war on the plane of temporal history, despite their status as an elect community.

8

From Movement to Text: The *Haft-bāb*

While the declaration of the *qiyāma* served to restructure the community around Ḥasan's authority, we can view the *Haft-bāb* as an exposition of the effects of this apocalyptic event almost forty years after the initial declaration. Like many apocalyptic theologies, the disclosure of a hidden message around which an entire society is reconstructed requires the revision of existing epistemological structures. For example, conceptions of cosmology, cosmogony, spiritual leadership, the understanding of destiny, religious practice and the role of history, must be reshaped in light of this new message. The *Haft-bāb* does exactly this: it addresses fundamental questions related to the *imām*; it develops his genealogy, his relationship with the prophets, his identity as the *imām* who is the master of the resurrection; and it informs us that the full disclosure of his true identity was foreshadowed throughout history. The document also reinforces the Nizaris' status as an elect community existing exclusively with its Lord.

The *Haft-bāb* tells us that throughout time, prophets and *imāms* have attested to the presence of a man who is the locus of divinity on earth; the term for this form among the elect is Mawlānā, 'our Lord', which is also the term for the *imām*.[1] After citing suras 17:71 and 12:36, which illustrate the centrality of the *imām* to the Quranic text (17:71, for instance, states *On the day when We will call all people through their imām*), the text then cites prophetic hadith stating that salvation is predicated upon knowing the *imām*; indeed, knowing the *imām* is likened to recognising God.

The text then states that during the cycles of Adam, Noah, Abraham, Moses, Jesus, and Muḥammad, this Mawlānā figure was the locus of the truth in each cycle of history who often bestowed religious truths upon the prophets themselves,[2] though he was known by different names in each cycle of history. Each prophet and his people also attest to the return of this figure at the end time. For instance, during the cycle of Moses, we learn that the people

> . . . called Mawlâ-nâ [literally 'our Lord'] Dhû l-Qarnayn; and that the light which Ḥaḍrat Moses saw that night in that tree [or burning bush] – . . . the *ta'wîl* of the tree is a person of a man, and the light is the mercy of Union and Oneness of Mawlâ-nâ.[3]

During the time of Moses, the *Haft-bāb* states, the Lord of the time was Dhū l-Qarnayn. According to many Quranic interpreters, Dhū l-Qarnayn was Alexander the Great, who is considered Muslim.[4] In the *Haft-bāb*'s account, the burning tree is identified as that spiritual source which guided Moses, 'a person of a man, and the light is the mercy of Union and Oneness of Mawlâ-nâ.' In addition to guiding Moses during his lifetime, our author states that Moses's people believed that Dhū l-Qarnayn will return at the end of time to administer the final judgment for his people. Indeed, in each prophetic cycle, each prophet recognised this Mawlānā figure as the locus of divinity and within each cycle of history, each prophet's people point to a figure who will arrive at the end time.

After equating this figure to ʿAlī, the only individual who has the authority to 'lift the standard of the Qiyâma,'[5] Ḥasan-i Maḥmūd-i Kātib writes that, in fact, 'all the imâms are ʿAlî,'[6] and that ʿAlî 'has no end nor beginning.'[7] Thus the eternal figure who appears in each prophetic cycle, and who interacts with each prophet, is in fact ʿAlī. Our author identifies ʿAlī as every *imām*. Though these *imāms* may appear in different manifestations throughout history, their eternal essence is the same as ʿAlī's. The *qiyāma* is a unique moment in history because the true knowledge of the locus of the divinity is revealed to the elect community. But this is not all: the elect community exclusively benefits from this figure's unfettered presence – in the form of Ḥasan *ʿalā dhikrihi al-salām*. Although this figure has appeared throughout history, his true identity has been hidden until the period in which all hidden truths are manifest. He is the *qaʾīm* of the *qiyāma*, the master of the resurrection, whom Ḥasan-i Maḥmūd-i Kātib, the author of the text, also identifies as the Resurrector.

In addition to the construction of a unity of sacred history through this eschatological figure, Ḥasan-i Maḥmūd-i Kātib discusses how earlier *imāms*' predictions of historical events were always fulfilled by the actions of later *imāms*. This fulfilment points to the divine origin and mandate of the imamate, while also inscribing Ḥasan *ʿalā dhikrihi al-salām* into the office of the imamate. For instance, he writes:

> [36] Now, in a sermon [whose identity is unclear] Mawlānā ʿAlī, prostration and prayer is due upon mention of him, says: 'I will set the pulpit up in Egypt. In Damascus, I will shatter its stones into pieces, then, I will wage war against the land of Daylam and proceed further beyond, subduing its inhabitants . . . By saying so, he means that he, exalted the high, will appear in those lands, will subdue its men of power (*qawī gardanān*); and bring them into his obedience and servitude.' Then, he adds: 'from there I will wage war against India and China.'
>
> [37] In the Blessed Chapter, it is mentioned that a servant questioned our lord 'will you return to do all these things yourself?' . . . in reply [Mawlānā], exalted be his mention, said: 'One of my children will do so, it will be as if I have done it.'
>
> [38] Now he set the pulpit up in Egypt, conquered Damascus and broke the neck of the rebels: [and] that day when Mawlānā Mahdī appeared among the Kutāma tribe in the Maghreb and conquered Egypt. Or, when Mawlānā Nizār and his sons, prostration is due upon mention of them, appeared in rule and monarchy in Egypt and set the pulpit there, as he, exalted the high, has mentioned in the [above] Sermon.

> [39] The Prophet, peace upon him, says: 'On the Day of Resurrection, the sun (*chishma-yi āftāb*) will initially rise from the west, till it reaches the middle of the sky, then it will retreat and will descend in the west so that it may once again appear from the east – It should be noted that [in religious texts] whenever they mention the sun of Resurrection (*khurshīd-i qiyāmat*), they mean the *imam* – For this reason Mawlānā Mahdī appeared in the west, conquered lands close to the vicinity of Baghdad, which is the middle of earth, then returned to be hidden in the west . . .
> [41] Now, when Mawlānā 'Alī says 'I will set the pulpit up in Egypt', he did; and 'I will take Damascus', he took it; then, 'I will fight the [people of] Daylam, he did that too. There has never been a contradiction in his speech, may he be exalted and high. But, one needs insight to see him and not himself. There is not, and there has never been a contradiction in his words, all his sayings are correct.[8]

Our author cites a sermon from 'Alī, the first *imām*, which states that he, through his progeny, will conquer Egypt, defeat the Daylamis, and conquer Damascus; he writes that all of this has come true through the specific forms of *imām* al-Mahdī and the *imām* al-Nizār. Reminiscent of the Fatimid materials' association of the eschatological figure with the resurrection, the *Haft-bāb* states that the *imām* is the 'sun of Resurrection,' who, commensurate with our author's construction of the unity of the imamate, rose in the west and retreated to the west, but will rise again from the east. This knowledge – as well as this unity of sacred history – can only be seen with the 'insight' of proper perception that we discuss further below. Our author continues:

> [46] Another proof . . . all the good and pious people have pointed to the supreme proof (*ḥujjat*) of the Resurrector and have given the glad tiding about him. They have said: The position of *ḥujjat* in relation to the Resurrector is similar to that of the executors (*awṣiyā'*) to the prophets with resolution (*anbiyā'-i ulūl-i 'azm*).[9] All the good and pious people of our time also admit that Sayyidnā Ḥasan-i Ṣabbāḥ, may God sanctify his soul and bless us with his meditation (*shafā'at*),

> was the supreme proof of the *qā'im-i qiyāmat* and the Messiah of the cycle of the Resurrection and he made [his] father's work manifest (*kār-i pidar āshkārā kard*).'
>
> [47] Sayyidnā, may his soul be sanctified, says: 'When the *Qā'im* manifests himself, he will sacrifice a camel, will lift up the red banner; our lord will destroy citadels and will remove the veil of precaution (*taqiyya*). Little value will remain for the [practice] of the *sharīʿa* in the world and exoterically (*bi-ḥukm-i ẓāhir*) the *Qā'im* will have people following him.' And we witnessed all these glad tidings in our lord Ḥasan *ʿalā dhikrihi al-salām*.[10]

A unity of sacred history is also established through the relationship between Ḥasan Ṣabbāḥ, the first leader of Alamut, and Ḥasan *ʿalā dhikrihi al-salām*, inaugurator of the *qiyāma*. Ḥasan Ṣabbāḥ was the supreme 'proof' of the master of the resurrection, analogous to the *awṣiyā'* and his relationship to each prophet. Ḥasan Ṣabbāḥ conquered Alamut and established a Nizari stronghold there, preparing the way for his descendant, the *qā'im* of the *qiyāma*. Indeed, all of Ḥasan Ṣabbāḥ's predictions concerning the events of the coming of the *qā'im* of the *qiyāma* – the sacrificing of a camel, the display of the red banner, the cessation of the religious law – were fulfilled with Ḥasan II's dramatic proclamation.[11] The fulfilment of these predictions, along with the establishment of ʿAlī as all *imāms* and the *imām/imām-qā'im*, establishes a spiritual unity of the office of the imamate, while making Ḥasan *ʿalā dhikrihi al-salām* and his progeny its culmination.

A Newly Disclosed Spiritual Universe

Chapter 5 of the *Haft-bāb*, 'Illustrating the nature of the spiritual world and the attributes of people of contradiction, gradation and the people of unity,' discusses some of the features of this spiritual realm and how one can be admitted to it. Our author writes:

> [63] It must be known that sensible and spiritual worlds are complete in conjunction to each other and in isolation they are nothing. The Lord of the Resurrection *ʿalā dhikrihi al-salām*, says:

> God's unity, if comprehended with relative sight, one finds [in Him] the multiplicity of creation, and if one looks at the multiplicity of creation with real sight, one will see the unity of God Exalted the High – In brief, all opposites should be known in a similar manner. Now, anyone who looks at relative and real in their specified place, would be saved from fantasy and imagination and will rest from distress.
>
> [64] Sayyidnā, may his soul be sanctified, says: 'Whoever is in harmony with these two realms he would be saved from distress.'[12]

The true nature of the spiritual world is apparent only for those who possess proper perception, who look at the multiplicity of creation with the eye of reality; only then can seekers perceive the true nature of the divine and the spiritual world. Proper perception here becomes the key to perceiving divine unity (*tawḥīd*) and thus the exclusive means of salvation.

But what exactly is this spiritual world? Our author writes:

> [67] To sum up, it is said that the spiritual world is the realm of life (*ʿālam-i mardum*). It is in this context that [God Almighty on the tongue of] the Prophet says: *Verily the world of the Hereafter is life, if they only knew* (29:64) . . .[13]

Our text continues:

> [77] If you look carefully, you will find that in the realm of spirit (*ʿālam-i jān*), the black and white stones are also human beings; the Tablet (*lawḥ*), the Pen (*qalam*), the Throne (*ʿarsh*), the Pedestal (*kursī*), the Trusted Spirit (*rūḥ al-amīn*), the Holy Spirit (*rūḥ al-qudus*), the Intellect (*ʿaql*), the Soul (*nafs*) and all others that you may reckon, they are all human beings. Since in the Hereafter God appears in this form, then what can remain without having this form? In the Hereafter everything is specified and distinguished. One has to lift up his mind from fantasies and imaginations until he is saved from wandering in the darkness, and he arrives at the lights of the realm of religion. [78] In the same manner, in

> the Hereafter, obedience, transgression and deviation are also in human [form].[14]

In the realm of the *qiyāma*, the hereafter, all hidden truths become reified realities in the form of human beings. In the *qiyāma* the divine throne, tablet, pen, heavens, soul, intellect – all intangible objects that are normally invisible in the realm of everyday reality – appear in the form of human beings. Deviance, obedience, and transgression, too, appear in the realm of the resurrection as human beings.

Ḥasan-i Maḥmūd-i Kātib then tells us that in reality, there are three kinds of people: (1) the people of contradiction, who do not recognise themselves nor their Lord; (2) the people of gradation, who see their Lord but who are also aware of themselves; and (3) the people of unity, . . . 'a group which see Him and desire Him,' and have no desire for anything for themselves.[15]

> [81] People should try to come out of the realm of *taḍādd*, which is the realm of denial (*kufr*), enter the realm of *tarattub*, which is the realm of ascribing partners (*shirk*) and hypocrisy (*nifāq*) and try hard to reach the realm of unity (*waḥdat*) which is the realm of truth and oneness of our Lord, exalted and high, thus attaining salvation.

Notice here that the new salvific paradigm is centred around recognising the spiritual nature of the *imām* during one's lifetime. Recognition of one's true nature is inexorably linked with recognising one's Lord, the *imām*, without whom *tawḥīd* is impossible.

Ḥasan-i Maḥmūd-i Kātib writes:

> [90] The Lord of the Resurrection says: 'Reward is the proximity of God, when you are nothing; do not desire a closer proximity'. In another place, he, exalted and high, says: 'We summon people to God and divinity, not to God's recognition and worshipping.' To sum up, this is the truth, and the entirety of the Blessed Epistles confirms this meaning that mankind in this world should realise his non-existence, so that, by the rule of reality one could reach God and the Divine and be saved from denial, ascribing partners, discord and the hierarchical ascent.[16]

The *qiyāma* is the realm in which the *imāms* disclose themselves and are openly acknowledged as the exclusive summoners to God's proximity, a realm in which it is of central importance to recognise the *imāms'* true spiritual natures and seek self-annihilation.

The text's identification of what constitutes heaven and hell reflects the importance of recognising the present *imām*. It says:

> [74] Heaven and Hell are also called living entities (*mardum*). Lord Ḥasan *ʿalā dhikrihi al-salām* says:
>
>> Whoever wishes to see the person of [God's] bounty and the person of eternal Paradise must look at the man who calls people to God and divinity and restrains them from [the attractions of] the world. Whoever wants to see the person of punishment and the person of the eternal Hell should look at a person who promotes greed, prevents people from God and divinity and encourages worldly attractions . . .[17]

This symbolic elision of the identity of the *qāʾim* of the *qiyāma* with the historical person of Ḥasan, along with the materialisation of heaven and hell as human beings, is of paramount importance here. Heaven itself is not just any man; it is 'the man who calls the people to God,' the *qāʾim* of the *qiyāma* and his progeny. Improper identification and obedience to anyone else will preclude the follower from reaching the divine, since, after all, this *qāʾim* of the *qiyāma* is the true locus of divinity throughout all of history.

Ḥasan's invocation of apocalyptic symbolism and the text's redefinition of the contents of the *qiyāma* thus create a novel spiritual realm in which true reality is disclosed in the reified human embodiments of normally hidden entities. Heaven, hell, the divine tablet, the throne, obedience and disobedience become apparent here – and they are fixed and tangible. The axis around which this new realm revolves is the *imām/imām-qāʾim* figure who becomes synonymous with the terrestrial locus of heaven; those who do not believe in him are those who are condemned to eternal nonexistence.

Yet the actualisation of apocalypticism did not, of course, eliminate temporality. An analysis of the *qiyāma*'s notion of time provides us with insights into how one is one supposed to exist on this earth in a realm that is purely and seemingly permanently spiritual. How did the *qiyāma* address the paradox of temporality in this new, seemingly timeless realm?

In a remarkable theological move, this paradox of temporality is retained, yet is fused to a sense of temporal urgency concerning the necessity of proper belief in this new realm of existence. The *Haft-bāb* states:

> [81] . . . If bodily death befalls them and they are in [the realm of] *taḍādd* or *tarattub* they will perish. Meaning that instead of reaching God the Exalted, they will arrive at eternal non-existence which is the true Hell. *Nājī* [the saved one] means reaching God and Divinity which is eternal paradise and the realm of reality. [82] The Prophet, Peace upon him, says: 'After this world, there is only Paradise and Hell.' Lord Ḥasan *'alā dhikrihi al-salām* says: 'In the *Qiyāmat*, whoever reaches God attains it eternally, and whoever falls from God, remains in nothingness eternally.'[18]

There is urgency in dedicating oneself to both the recognition of the *imām* and spiritual annihilation in him, as if one dies within the realms of gradation or opposition, one cannot obtain salvation. Only those who attain the realm of unity during her or his lifetime will attain salvation. Like so many apocalyptic theologies, time itself acquires a liminality that can only be resolved through its consummation. Inherent in this liminality is a sense of urgency – this new time carries with it a new sense of responsibility and of the beliefs that must be followed – not before the world ends, but before the end of one's own existence. Yet the very idea that the fulfilment of time requires a prescriptive set of beliefs and practices is inherently paradoxical. The only way to escape this new paradox is to acquire life in the afterlife – to inhabit the spiritual realm of the master of the resurrection. The realm of this figure is redefined by the *qiyāma*'s apocalyptic disclosure. Those who do not abide by these new proscriptions will simply cease to exist – an indication of how potent apocalypticism can be in shifting the parameters of the sacred.

But what is the relationship between eschatology and the realm of the *qiyāma*? The resurrection is described as 'perpetual' in one place in the text, but it is also described as a cycle that existed before Adam.[19] In another part of the text, the author of the *Haft-bāb* writes that this declaration of the resurrection, according to the chronicles of some of the prophets and *imāms*, is the last of the cycle of resurrections of all time.

> [103] . . . it is said that every seven thousand years the Resurrector of the resurrection, peace and prostration is due upon mention of him, will rise and when it is repeated seven times, the seventh is called the Resurrection of all Resurrections (*qiyāmat-i qiyāmāt*). In our cycle, it is the manifestation of the Resurrector of all resurrections in the Resurrection of all resurrections in the fourth geographical region (*iqlīm*), which is the realm of the sun (*iqlīm-i khurshīd*), in the land of Babel, in Iran (*dīyār-i ʿajam*), among the mountains of Daylām, on the top of the mountain of Alamūt, may God protect it.[20]

Yet, the world will not end in the near future:

> [104] . . . the Prophet, Peace be upon him, says: 'In the Hereafter, the length of the day is equal to one thousand years of this world.' Thus when three hundred and sixty thousand years of this world have elapsed, it will be one year of the Hereafter.[21]

After calculations based on astrological observations, our author writes:

> [105] This world has not been created in the last few days, and the act of God does not resemble the act of children. We have said before that whatever relates to God will be eternal, beyond . . . human comprehension. Countless years have elapsed on mountains and plains and many more will elapse.[22]

There is urgency in attaining the realm of unity, yet the immediacy of eschatology is dampened by the author's insistence that the end of the world will not occur in the near future. Thus the *qiyāma* operates as an event harnessing apocalyptic symbolism while simultaneously distancing itself from an immediate eschatology – all the while reshaping the premise of terrestrial authority. Note that the result of this invocation of apocalypticism and subsequent divestment of its immediate eschatology is not terribly different from the Fatimids' revision of an immediate eschatology through the deployment of multiple *mahdīs*, or through the ritualised displacement of mahdist expectation.[23]

The Significance of the *Qiyāma*

The deployment of apocalyptic symbolism resolved three critical issues for the Nizaris. The resolution of these issues in turn provided powerful new momentum for the dynamic evolution of the community.

The first issue the *qiyāma* resolved was the absence of the leadership of the present *imām*. Since the schism with al-Mustanṣir in 1094, the community at Alamut had been without a living *imām*; since the death of Ḥasan Ṣabbāḥ in 1124, the community was embroiled in petty skirmishes with the Seljuks and were unable to realise their Shia vision of Islam in the lands around them. The *qiyāma* provided an ontological reversal – a mythic solution (to borrow a phrase from O'Leary[24]) – to both temporal problems. The Nizari community was not abandoned in its quest to return Islam to its rightful custodians. Indeed, the *qiyāma* located this community, and this community alone, as the exclusive inheritors of knowledge related to the secrets of existence. And as we have seen, the *imām* was absent no more. The effect of this transfer of authority must have been profound, for the community was now in the presence of heaven itself; it was now assured that it had won – and would perpetually win – the war on the plane of cosmic history. All others would simply be relegated to nonexistence.[25]

It is significant, too, that the *imām* installed by the *qiyāma* was Persian – a Persian intimately associated with the past leaders of Alamut. Hodgson writes that there was a certain amount of anticipation that Ḥasan II was the awaited *imām*, even before his father had died.[26] Relations with the besieged Fatimids were non-existent and the Seljuk and Abbasid versions of Islam were contrary to Ḥasan Ṣabbāḥ's vision of a Shia Islam grounded in and dominated by Persian language and culture. Installing not just a Nizari *imām* but a Persian Nizari *imām* resolved for the Nizaris once and for all their continuing drive to realise the dominance of their vision of Islam in its particularly Persian form. The installation of Ḥasan also brought Ḥasan Ṣabbāḥ's vision (and ostensibly the community's vision) to fruition. The leader that stood before the Nizaris was not just the symbolic representation of heaven itself: he was heaven itself in Persianate culture, form, and language. And this *imām*, who embodied this Persian identity, was responsible for leading his new community – from his seat in Daylam. The full implications of this transference of the imamate from Arab to Persian lands, mediated by apocalyptic symbolism, have yet to be investigated.

Finally, Corbin and others have noted the many similarities between the *qiyāma* doctrine and certain elements of Sufism. Corbin writes for instance that 'The texts of the Ismaili tradition of Alamūt show us both the way in which Imāmology fructifies in mystical experience, and how it presupposes such an experience.'[27] He goes on to say that the Ismailism of Alamut was a restoration of the similarities between Sunni modes of Sufism and Ismailism. Hodgson writes that the *qiyāma* should be '. . . interpreted in Ṣūfī terms: the inner life of moral and mystical experience was the sole reality henceforth to be attained to.'[28] The *qiyāma* allowed this restoration to take place because it redefined the relationship between text and divinely appointed exegete.

At the ceremony of the *qiyāma*, the community of Alamut was initiated into a new existence, one that admitted Ḥasan's absolute authority. This initiation was predicated upon the disclosure of hidden knowledge – the exclusive knowledge of Ḥasan's true identity. Cosmic unveiling, in the absence of the text, effaced *ta'wīl* itself – that is, *ẓāhir* and *bāṭin* became one, fused onto the person of Ḥasan and his progeny. And in the realm in which the only true reality that exists is the *imām*, Ḥasan became the totality of the culmination of secret knowledge throughout history. The *qiyāma* effectively elevated the *imām*'s position from interpreter of the text to the manifest text itself. If the *imām* became the text of Alamut, then it is no surprise that this mode of Ismailism resembles Sufism, in which *walāya* to the spiritual guide is paramount. There were no intermediaries, just the relationship between believer and his lord, who was at that point present among the community.

Dispensing with *ta'wīl*, at least temporarily, also helped free the Nizari community from relying upon the hermeneutic tools of the past. If the *imām* was now both *ẓāhir* and *bāṭin*, the trajectory of the community could be charted anew, theoretically without regard to past hermeneutic conventions. Now, the force of the text (and the history of its *ta'wīl*) was at once superseded and encompassed by the living *imām*.[29] *Ta'wīl* by authors such as al-Sijistānī (d. 975) and al-Kirmānī (d. 1020) also made the divine more and more remote and relegated its existence to the celestial pleroma.[30] The *qiyāma* at once dispensed with the constraining history of these texts and replaced them with a new living, breathing text that would chart the new Shia vision of Islam from his distinctively Persian vantage point.

Invocation of apocalyptic symbolism, here in the particular form of the *qiyāma*, thus resolved three issues facing the Nizari community: (1) the prolonged absence of a living *imām*; (2) the uncertainty regarding the future of the Nizaris' triumphalist vision in Persia; and (3) the constraints of past hermeneutical practice. Ultimately, the *qiyāma* illustrates the relative ease with which apocalyptic symbolism can instantiate a lasting transfer of authority, even after the fervor of initial apocalyptic expectation has dissipated.

Like so many apocalyptic invocations in religious history, the *qiyāma* provided an incredibly rich wellspring of symbols from which many later exegetes in Nizari Ismaili history drew. While the doctrine was subsequently repudiated by the *imām* Jalāl al-Dīn Ḥasan (r. 1210–21), allowing him to reestablish relations with neighboring Muslim communities through a reintroduction of a Sunni version of the *sharīʿa*,[31] Hodgson writes that this did not mean that the idea of the *qiyāma*, or Ḥasan *ʿalā dhikrihi al-salām*'s declaration of it, was expunged from sacred history or forgotten altogether. He writes:

> Ḥasan III and his Sunnism were not repudiated: they were explained . . . It was explained that the qiyāma, the resurrection, was not simply a final event but a condition of life which could, in principle, be withheld or granted by the imam-qā'im to mankind, or to the élite among mankind, at any time. The tacit identification between sharīʿa law and *taqiyya*, [prudent dissimulation] implied in the teaching of Ḥasan II, was confirmed, and with it, the identification of *ḥaqīqa* (spiritual reality) with qiyāma. Human life, then, alternated between times when reality was manifest and spiritual perfection could be sought directly; and times when reality was veiled . . . Ḥasan II had introduced a brief period when reality was manifest; Ḥasan III had closed that period again.[32]

Daftary summarises the situation this way: 'In sum, it was explained that in the era of Muḥammad, periods of *satr* [concealment] and *qiyāma* could alternate at the discretion of each current imam.'[33] Thus once again we see how this originally apocalyptic theology, like so many apocalyptic theologies in the history of religions, was infused with new interpretations having lasting legacies. One legacy retained the idea of the *qiyāma* as an accessible spiritual realm while emphasising that this realm must alternate in certain circumstances with its concealment – a reinterpretation of the urgency associated with the original doctrine's conception of salvation.

The idea of the resurrection was developed – eschatologically and in non-eschatological ways – by the famous theologian (and perhaps collaborator of the author of the *Haft-bāb*)[34] Naṣīr al-Dīn Ṭūsī (d. 1274) in his *Rawḍa-yi taslīm*, completed in 1243. A study of the text's various conceptions of the resurrection could be a book in its own right; here I briefly discuss how the author elaborates upon some of the themes of the resurrection we see in the *qiyāma*.

Playing upon some of the synonyms of the *qiyāma*, particularly the *ḥashr* (gathering), and the *ākhira* (the afterlife), Ṭūsī states that various developments in the natural, bodily, and spiritual world may constitute resurrections (*ḥashr*) and thereby indicate attainment to different natural, corporeal, or spiritual levels.[35] In addition to the *ḥashr*s within the various aspects of celestial, spiritual, and earthly existence, our own world is the realm of the *dunyā*. This is,

> . . . the realm of similitudes (*kawn-i mushābahat*), where the followers of truth and of falsehood, the true and the false, correct and incorrect, the veracious person and the liar, good and evil, the wicked and good, all seem to be the same. [It is] a state in which all contradictory things are similar to each other, in which man is so bewildered and veiled from the truth that he cannot distinguish between any of these things.[36]

This realm of similitudes is diametrically opposed to the realm of the hereafter (the *ākhira*), which is

> . . . a state in which all things deceptively similar to each other are clearly distinguished, where right from wrong and the righteous from the wrongdoers are made distinct and clearly apparent by the grace of divine gnosis (*maʿrifat-i ilāhī*).[37]

Upon entering earthly existence, we live in the *dunyā*, where the truth of things is 'confused and ambiguous.'[38] Humanity's goal is to come to the knowledge of true meaning. It is the divine intermediary, here the manifestation of the First Intellect, who is the exclusive gate to the truth; this is the *imām*.[39]

As the unique manifestation of the First Intellect, the *imām* is also the divinely appointed standard of ethical behavior for all humanity. To truly distinguish oneself from others – to enter into the world of the resurrection – the seeker must engage in specific ethical practices that are tied to the practice of truthful thoughts, speech, and good deeds. 'All three must be linked to the command of the Imam of the time – may salutations ensue upon mention of him.'[40] Thus the exhortation to ascend in the spiritual ranks toward a true knowledge of the *imām*'s spiritual self as described in the *Haft-bāb* is given specific structure here. It becomes a detailed paradigm of ethical behavior inexorably linked to spiritual ascent.

The text discusses, for instance, pragmatic guidance on how to improve one's character; this guidance is based upon the *imām*'s words, which are to be contemplated in certain situations. One situation concerns social conduct with others. Ṭūsī writes that the individual should contemplate the following saying of the *imām*; part of the text reads: 'O God, bless Muḥammad and his Household, and point me straight to confront him who is dishonest toward me with good counsel, repay him who separates from me with gentleness, reward him who deprives me with free giving . . .'[41] This guidance is to be coupled with the numerous other sayings of the *imām* – sayings relating to wealth and to fear of God, in addition to specific teachings regarding how to keep one's sexual desire and anger in check. The implementation of these teachings results in the refinement of character and directly translates into admission into the realm of spiritual reality, a spiritual ascent through the various gradations of existence we normally cannot see.

Thus these selections of the *Rawḍa-yi taslīm* reinterpret the *qiyāma* in a multiplicity of ways. The text attenuates the original doctrine's sense of urgency while still admitting a final resurrection. Temporality, as in the case of the early Fatimids, is divested of an urgent eschatology. Images associated with the afterlife, shorn of their eschatological valences, are deployed to explain not only the composition of the material world but also how to live in it. One of the main consequences of this deployment is a detailed construction of a pragmatic programme for moral and ethical development. Following these ethical teachings becomes a modality of spiritual ascent to the realm of true understanding, defined in part through the imagery of the resurrection. And at the apex of this ethical universe is the *imām*, a unique manifestation of the First Intellect, the possessor of the knowledge of things as they truly are – the master of the resurrection. Once again, we see how potent this apocalyptic imagery can be in its initial invocation and attenuation: here it has reconstructed authority, consolidated authority, and provided an ethical and spiritual framework for humanity's ascent.

Notes

1. Many thanks to Professor Jalal Badakhchani of the Institute of Ismaili Studies for providing me with a Persian edition of the *Haft-bāb* and a preliminary translation of it, used with his permission here (with minor alterations), soon to be published by the Institute of Ismaili Studies; Ḥasan-i Maḥmūd-i Kātib, *Haft-bāb*, edited and translated by Jalal Badakhchani (London: I. B. Tauris, forthcoming), paras 8–12. With a few exceptions, Badakhchani's translation is used throughout this chapter, cited by paragraph number, and the corresponding endnote reference is to Hodgson's translation of the *Haft-bāb* that appears in his *Order of Assassins*; here, pp. 284–9.
2. Wilfred Madelung, 'Ismāʿīliyya', *Encyclopaedia of Islam*, second edition, ed. P. Bearman, et al. (Leiden: Brill, 1960–2005), vol. 4, pp. 198–206.
3. Hodgson, *Order of Assassins*, p. 287.
4. W. Montgomery Watt, 'Al-Iskandar', *Encyclopaedia of Islam*, second edition, ed. P. Bearman, et al. (Leiden: Brill, 1960–2005), vol. 4, p. 127.
5. Hodgson, *Order of Assassins*, p. 295.
6. Hodgson, *Order of Assassins*, p. 296.
7. Hodgson, *Order of Assassins*, p. 295.
8. Ḥasan-i Maḥmūd-i Kātib, *Haft-bāb*, ed. and trans. Badakhchani, paras 36–9, 41; Hodgson, *Order of Assassins*, pp. 295–6.
9. Hodgson defines this as the six great prophets, presumably Adam, Noah, Abraham, Moses, Jesus, and Muḥammad.
10. Ḥasan-i Maḥmūd-i Kātib, *Haft-bāb*, ed. and trans. Badakhchani, paras 46–7; Hodgson, *Order of Assassins*, pp. 301–2.
11. Note here the striking parallels in the construction of authority and sacred history via the fulfilment of apocalyptic prophecy between this case and the case of al-Mahdī's letter, as well as the portrayal of al-Manṣūr's defeat of the '*dajjāl*' Abū Yazīd. See the discussion in Brett, Rise, pp. 170–82.
12. Ḥasan-i Maḥmūd-i Kātib, *Haft-bāb*, ed. and trans. Badakhchani, paras 63–4; Hodgson, *Order of Assassins*, p. 312.
13. Ḥasan-i Maḥmūd-i Kātib, *Haft-bāb*, ed. and trans. Badakhchani, para. 67; Hodgson, *Order of Assassins*, pp. 312–13.
14. Ḥasan-i Maḥmūd-i Kātib, *Haft-bāb*, ed. and trans. Badakhchani, para. 77; Hodgson, *Order of Assassins*, p. 315.

15. Hodgson, *Order of Assassins*, pp. 315–16.
16. Ḥasan-i Maḥmūd-i Kātib, *Haft-bāb*, ed. and trans. Badakhchani, para. 90; Hodgson, *Order of Assassins*, p. 318.
17. Ḥasan-i Maḥmūd-i Kātib, *Haft-bāb*, ed. and trans. Badakhchani, para. 74; Hodgson, *Order of Assassins*, p. 314.
18. Ḥasan-i Maḥmūd-i Kātib, *Haft-bāb*, ed. and trans. Badakhchani, para. 81; Hodgson, *Order of Assassins*, p. 316.
19. Ḥasan-i Maḥmūd-i Kātib, *Haft-bāb*, ed. and trans. Badakhchani, para. 46; Hodgson, *Order of Assassins*, p. 301.
20. Ḥasan-i Maḥmūd-i Kātib, *Haft-bāb*, ed. and trans. Badakhchani, para. 103; Hodgson, *Order of Assassins*, p. 322.
21. Ḥasan-i Maḥmūd-i Kātib, *Haft-bāb*, ed. and trans. Badakhchani, para 104. This text does not appear in Hodgson's translation.
22. Ḥasan-i Maḥmūd-i Kātib, *Haft-bāb*, ed. and trans. Badakhchani, para. 105. This text does not appear in Hodgson's translation.
23. Jambet has, in fact, made the argument that the claim more generally that Ḥasan's *qiyāma* revived the mahdīst spirit of early Shiism, particularly in its Qarmatian iteration. See Jambet, p. pp. 17–18.
24. O'Leary, p. 6.
25. He writes: 'But the imām's appearance had led, still less than in the early Fāṭimid period, to a visible triumph over the Sunnī world. The Resurrection was the moment when Hell and Paradise were no longer distant possibilities but immediate actualities . . . and in the Sunnīs' refusal they had *ipso facto* been judged and condemned to a spiritual non-existence . . .' Hodgson, 'Ismāʿīlī State', p. 462.
26. Hodgson, 'Ismāʿīlī State', pp. 457–8.
27. Corbin, *History of Islamic Philosophy*, p. 102.
28. Hodgson, 'Ismāʿīlī State', p. 459. For a masterful discussion of the gradual interiorization of Sufi visions of heaven and hell, see Christian Lange, *Paradise and Hell in Islamic Traditions* (Cambridge: Cambridge University Press, 2016), pp. 236–44.
29. See also the discussion in Jambet, pp. 91–3.
30. Though, interestingly, Jambet points out that the three-fold division of humanity into the people of unity, order, and opposition corresponds with the Neoplatonic scheme used by some Fatimid authors to designate the divine pleroma–the One, the Intellect, and the Soul. See Jambet, pp. 358–60.

31. Hodgson, 'Ismāʿīlī State', pp. 469–72.
32. Hodgson, 'Ismāʿīlī State', p. 473.
33. Daftary, *The Ismāʿīlīs*, 2nd ed., p. 381.
34. Hermann Landolt, 'Introduction', in *The Paradise of Submission: A Medieval Treatise on Ismaili Thought*, trans. S. J. Badakhchani (London: I. B. Tauris in association with the Institute of Ismaili Studies, 2005), pp. xv–xvi.
35. al-Ṭūsī, *Rawḍa-yi taslīm*, trans. Badakhchani, *Paradise*, paras 257–64, English pp. 90–2.
36. al-Ṭūsī, *Rawḍa-yi taslīm*, trans. Badakhchani, *Paradise*, para. 247, English p. 88.
37. al-Ṭūsī, *Rawḍa-yi taslīm*, trans. Badakhchani, *Paradise*, paras 248, English p. 88.
38. al-Ṭūsī, *Rawḍa-yi taslīm*, trans. Badakhchani, *Paradise*, para. 249, English p. 88.
39. al-Ṭūsī, *Rawḍa-yi taslīm*, trans. Badakhchani, *Paradise*, para. 254, English p. 89.
40. al-Ṭūsī, *Rawḍa-yi taslīm*, trans. Badakhchani, *Paradise*, para. 267, English p. 94.
41. al-Ṭūsī, *Rawḍa-yi taslīm*, trans. Badakhchani, *Paradise*, para. 276, English p. 96.

Conclusion

In this book I have traced an evolutionary trajectory of various iterations and manifestations of Fatimid apocalyptic myth. It first illustrated how social structures such as oath-taking, tithing, and centres of the *daʿwa* terrestrially instantiated a vision for the establishment of utopia on earth, a utopia to be inaugurated imminently by the *mahdī*. To be part of this cause, intiates pledged an oath of allegiance that provided them the keys to understanding some of the mysteries of the universe. Initiation also bestowed upon them an exalted lineage, a lineage shared by prophets and *imāms* that emplotted all oath takers as the true inheritors of righteousness throughout Quranic history. Textual evidence from the *Kitāb al-kashf* illustrates in detail how, at the level of *taʾwīl*, the Quranic text was interpreted to argue for this cause. Specifically, we find that the re-signification of Quranic visions of the end of time as the *mahdī* reoriented the tenets of salvation around belief and support for his cause, while *walāya* operated to specify and distinguish those on the right and wrong sides of history. The *Kitāb al-rushd* picks up these themes too, adding a sense of mahdist anticipation through a numerological hermeneutic.

In both the social structures of the revolutionary Fatimids and the early texts that are analysed here we find the theme of emplotment, the inscription of human actors in a cosmic drama that will unfold according to a scripted plan and result in the complete terrestrial vindication of true believers. The *mahdī*'s arrival and relationship to his believers is, for instance, rehearsed in the *Kitāb al-kashf*, while portions of both texts also make the organisational structure of the *daʿwa* integral to the cosmic order. This emplotment is not unusual in the sociology of millenarian movements; in fact, the sociologist Michael Barkun writes that:

> . . . millenarian movements lay claim to a total, all-encompassing truth and make concomitantly broad demands upon their members. Membership is neither nominal nor clearly demarcated from other areas of life and thus differs from traditional conceptions of, say, political party membership or interest-group affiliation. The movement enfolds its members in a belief system that provides meaning and explanation for virtually all problems and in a round of activities that allays feelings of personal insecurity and builds a new and strong sense of identity.[1]

Committing to the cause of the *mahdī* required, as we have seen, broad demands, and may have oriented followers to a new, scripted, cosmic destiny that ensured their victory. Through a shared symbolic universe they not only joined the elect throughout history, they were also initiated into a new religious community. Some of the earliest Fatimid coins' marginal inscriptions also pointed to this vision of eschatological triumph.

This vision of eschatological triumph at the edges of history was a major source for community building among the earliest Muslims as well, as recent scholarship has shown.[2] This triumph was in part mediated through the Quran's sense of election. Indeed, the Quran repeatedly insists that the majority of people remained and continue to remain ignorant of the true divine message (*but most people do not understand*, 28:12, or *This is God's promise: God never breaks His promise, but most people do not know*, 30:6). This duality is inexorably linked to the Quran's presentation of Muḥammad's community, as his prophetic consciousness and the evolution of the early Islamic community are patterned after past prophets and their rightly guided followers:

> . . . the Qur'an does tell the story of the Prophet's mission and the story of the nascent Islamic community indirectly, through typology. Earlier prophets are discussed in the text not merely as historical figures but as models for the Prophet Muhammad; their acts and experiences are directly relevant to his . . . In Q. 54, explicit parallels are drawn between those in the Prophet's audience who reject his message and the peoples of earlier prophets – the people of Noah, ʿAd, Thamud, the people of Lot, and Pharaoh and the Egyptians – who rejected their messages.[3]

The nascent Muslim community, its Prophet, and its history are fashioned in the image of – and indeed become the culmination of – past prophetic history which in the Quran is nothing other than cycles of rightly guided prophets leading small numbers of their followers to correct belief and eternal salvation.

It is perhaps this sense of election – this sense of living true *tawḥīd* – that was heightened for the first believers by the notion that the end of the world was just around the corner, or had already begun.

Donner writes:

> For the early Believers, then, the terrifying expectation of a Judgment soon to come made them intent on constructing a community of the saved, dedicated to the righteous observance of God's law as revealed to His prophets. It was a community that followed closely the leadership of the latest prophet, Muhammad; they believed that his guidance, more than any other thing, would ensure their individual and collective salvation when the End suddenly came . . . It seems just as likely, however, that the early Believers were convinced that, by establishing their community in Medina, they were ushering in the beginning of a new era of righteousness, and hence that they were actually witnessing the first events of the End itself. It is possible, then, to conjecture that they thought that the events leading to the Last Judgment were actually beginning to unfold before their very eyes . . .

> As a result of this process, the Believers would literally inherit the earth from the sinful, just as the followers of earlier prophets had done . . . For those Believers who fully accepted Muhammad's mission, this complex of ideas, which combined the displacement of unbelieving opponents from their property with God's plan for the End of Days, must have been a powerful motivator to engage in positive action – military if necessary – to vanquish unbelief in the world and to establish what they saw as a God-guided, righteous order on Earth.[4]

Muḥammad's mission, then, was inexorably intertwined with the culmination of history and prophecy. The establishment of a utopian settlement at Medina was predicated upon the believers being exclusive upholders of the uncorrupted divine message; through the tangible establishment of a community grounded in the primordial Quranic principle of *tawḥīd* they were the defenders of the boundaries of true belief. To be sure, the Quran not only places them within the liminality of realised eschatology, but also – through its revelations placed in dialogue with historical events – it illustrates how God can guarantee earthly victory, and thus presumably eternal salvation, for the elect. The divine would entrust the world to the true upholders of *tawḥīd*; the world which is for true believers, now and in the City of the Prophet. He would guarantee their salvation, too, in the life to come – certainly a profound motivation for implementing the Quranic ethos on the terrestrial plane before the end of the world.

But part of the Quran's rhetorical potency lies not just in asserting the certainty of the resurrection, but also in asserting that the resurrection is tied to an eschatology that is left temporally unspecified. Its *knowledge is only with God* (7:187, 31:34, 33:63), *it is certain to come* (15:85, 40:59), and is described as in the process of arriving (20:15). *Yet most people do not know about it* (40:59); and it could be distant, but *perhaps it is near* (33:63, 42:17). It will come upon people *suddenly* (7:187), *like the blink of an eye or quicker* (16:77). The Quran's vision of potentially multiple eschatological temporalities makes the argument for the resurrection all the more forceful, as the prelude to the resurrection could come at any moment.

We have seen how our texts have harnessed the persuasive force of the Quran's apocalyptic architecture while re-signifying its details. Election, the certainty of the resurrection, and the indeterminacy of the end of time are all retained in the *Kitāb al-kashf* and the *Kitāb al-rushd*, but are re-signified to reconstitute society with a sense of imminence around the *mahdī*. The process of this re-signification, this dual hermeneutic process of uncovering hidden meaning and crafting a new narrative based upon divine disclosures, is a process shared by the interpretive modalities of *ta'wīl* and apocalypticism. What might some of their differences be? And what is it about apocalypticism itself that allows for the premise of the sacred to shift with relative ease?

One theory offered here is that mahdist or apocalyptic expectation involves a distinct notion of temporality. Time becomes short because it is rushing to its end. This shift in temporal perception allows the process of re-signification to acquire a flexibility and permanence that is distinct from normal temporal modalities. In apocalyptically mediated disclosures, the locus of the sacred seamlessly shifts and is redefined; the Day of Judgment becomes the awaited *mahdī* himself. In the *qiyāma*, heaven is the master of the resurrection. On the purely symbolic plane, then, divine disclosures, mediated through apocalyptic situations, allow symbols themselves to be redefined. Thus the Fatimid *mahdī* is not simply Muḥammad b. Ismāʿīl. The very concept – the very symbol – of the *mahdī* is transformed and acquires certain characteristics (for instance, the Day of Judgment *is* the *mahdī*) through the process of divine disclosure. It is myth redefined.

Apocalyptic disclosures then elide these newly redefined symbols with historical events or actors, which in the Fatimid context is the historical figure of the Mahdī (Muḥammad b. Ismāʿīl) himself. The elision of refashioned symbol with historical actor or situation results in a reconstruction of authority. Apocalypticism, then, at once engineers a new symbolic vision of utopia while transposing that vision onto the plane of history, and in the process relocates the premise of the sacred. Apocalyptic disclosures act as potent forces for societal transformations in part because these disclosures are mediated within a framework of re-signified dualities; all those who do not believe in these new visions of heaven will be left behind. Apocalyptic temporality – the urgency of the imminent end – only serves to ensure that individuals will make the 'correct' decision to believe in this newly disclosed transcript, lest they suffer the permanent consequences of having followed the wrong path.

Both apocalypticism and *ta'wīl* serve as powerful modalities for uncovering 'Truth.' But whereas *ta'wīl* is dynamic – a process of the unveiling of things according to individual spiritual states – apocalypticism provides what might be described as a more fixed, more focused framework for the instantiation of a communal uncovering of things as they truly are. This should not be taken to mean that *ta'wīl* is not communal, and that the apocalypse is not spiritual: al-Nuʿmān's *Ta'wīl al-daʿā'im* was, after all, preached communally to the elect, and the *qiyāma* created novel realms for spiritual ascent. But the *qiyāma* did away with *ta'wīl* for a period by permanently equating symbol with symbolised, representing a temporary end to the process of re-signification. Ultimately, though, the idea of the *qiyāma* itself became re-signified through the reintroduction of symbolic interpretation.

In this book I have also illustrated some of the interpretive modalities deployed by the Fatimids to maintain their role as custodians of an expected utopia while simultaneously distancing its arrival. The Mahdī's letter displaces an immediate expectation onto multiple members of the Fatimid ruling dynasty, and ensures that all of the progenitors of the caliph al-Mahdī are in some sense *mahdī*s until the eschatological *mahdī*, who will come from the line of the Fatimids. For al-Nuʿmān, the ritual calendar was invested with symbolic correlates that placed the community within a certain temporal framework – between the advent of the caliph al-Mahdī and the advent of the *qā'im*. In both cases, the notion of the *mahdī* is retained and re-worked. The arrival of the caliph al-Mahdī, in fact, became proof for the fact that at least part of this utopian expectation had been achieved, and in turn it provided important insights into the ways in which apocalypticism could be reinterpreted to correlate with the consolidation of authority.

The advent of the *qiyāma*, too, signals the ways in which apocalypticism can be deployed to not only inaugurate a sense of utopia, but also to reify a new authoritative structure – here the transfer of authority from hidden to present *imām*. While the *qiyāma* presented a theological solution to some of the Nizaris' problems on the ground, it, too, had to be reinterpreted: as a theology of ongoing utopian existence it proved difficult to sustain. Thus one interpretation of this doctrine was that *qiyāma* was a certain modality of existence that coincided with times in which spiritual truths could be disclosed openly.

Throughout this book we have seen the variegated textures of Fatimid and Nizari apocalypticism, as well as their concomitant effects on social organisation and the consolidation of authority. We have seen that apocalypticism, whether expressed in the Quran or in Fatimid and Nizari materials, seems to construct for its audiences a sense of election, placing them at the *telos* of history, inscribing them in a geneaology that leads to a special moment in history, a moment in which they must choose to adhere to this divine disclosure, or to ignore it. The consequences of this choice are not just dramatic but also have eternal ramifications: by ignoring it or disobeying it they risk punishment in this world as well as in the hereafter. It is not surprising, then, that the potency of apocalyptic symbolism and its persuasive force are ubiquitous even today. The Mayan apocalypse, the apocalypse of Harold Camping, and the rhetoric of candidate Barack Obama in 2008, all presented various visions of a utopia that seem imminently attainable on earth, so often in language that grafts the cosmic onto the historic to present a new vision for the future.

The American presidential election of 2008 is a case in point. Candidate Barack Obama used the phrase 'We are the ones we have been waiting for', thus framing his campaign as a unique point in history, and his future inauguration as ushering in a utopian America that would finally transcend divisions in race, politics, and class. Among those who supported Obama were people who equated him with the messiah, the long-awaited cosmic figure who in this situation could unleash the healing potential latent in a fractured America to redress so many long-standing inequalities. Throughout the campaign, detractors, too, used apocalyptic symbolism, and compared Obama to the Antichrist or the harbinger of the Antichrist; the McCain campaign, in fact, issued a television ad called 'The One' hinting that Obama may actually be a cosmic deceiver, questioning not only his character but his legitimacy to be inscribed in the genealogy of presidential history. This deployment of myth and counter-myth reflects competing narratives of the nature of utopia and methods of its instantiation. It is the apocalypse and its associated symbols that have, over the course of human history, so often provided an expression to these utopian visions, and will continue to do so until the world finally does come to an end.

Notes

1. Michael Barkun, *Disaster and the Millennium* (New Haven, CT: Yale University Press, 1974), p. 19.
2. Shoemaker; Donner; Nerina Rustomji, *The Garden and the Fire: Heaven and Hell in Islamic Culture* (New York: Columbia University Press, 2009).
3. Devin Stewart, 'Prophecy', in *Key Themes for the Study of Islam*, ed. Jamal Elias (New York: Oneworld, 2010), p. 288.
4. Donner, pp. 80–2.

Bibliography

Primary Sources

Columbus, Christopher. *The Book of Prophecies, Edited by Christopher Columbus*. Edited by Roberto Rusconi, translated by Blair Sullivan. Berkeley: University of California Press, 1997.

Ḥasan-i Maḥmūd-i Kātib. *Haft-bāb*. Edited and translated by Jalal Badakhchani. London: I. B. Tauris, forthcoming.

Ibn Ḥawshab Manṣūr al-Yaman, Abū l-Qāsim al-Ḥasan b. Faraḥ (Faraj). *Kitāb al-rushd wa-l-hidāya*. Edited by Muḥammad Kāmil Ḥusayn [Silsilat makhṭūṭāt al-Fāṭimiyyīn, 2], in W. Ivanow (ed.), *Collectanea*: Vol. 1, pp. 185–213. Leiden: Brill, 1948.

——. *Kitāb al-rushd wa-l-hidāya*. Translated by W. Ivanow as 'The book of righteousness and true guidance', in *Studies in Early Persian Ismailism*, pp. 51–83 (1st ed.), pp. 29–59 (2nd ed.). Leiden: Brill, 1948.

Ibn al-Haytham, Abū ʿAbdallāh Jaʿfar b. Aḥmad al-Aswad. *Kitāb al-Munāẓarāt*. Edited and translated by Wilferd Madelung and Paul E. Walker as *The Advent of the Fatimids: A Contemporary Shiʿi Witness*. London: I. B. Tauris in association with the Institute of Ismaili Studies, 2000.

Jaʿfar b. Manṣūr al-Yaman, Abū l-Qāsim. *Kitāb al-ʿālim wa-l-ghulām*. Edited and translated by James W. Morris as *The Master and the Disciple: An Early Islamic Spiritual Dialogue*, Arabic edition and English translation of Jaʿfar b. Manṣūr al-Yaman's *Kitāb al-ʿālim wa-l-ghulām*. London: I. B. Tauris in association with the Institute of Ismaili Studies, 2002.

——. *Kitāb al-kashf.* Edited by Muṣṭafā Ghālib. Beirut: Dār al-Andalus, 1984.

——. *Kitāb al-kashf.* Edited by Rudolf Strothmann. Published for the Islamic Research Association by Geoffrey Cumberlege. London: Oxford University Press, 1952.

Juwaynī, ʿAlāʾ al-Dīn ʿAṭā-Malik b. Muḥammad. *Taʾrīkh-i jahān-gushā*, trans. as *The History of the World-Conqueror* by John Andrew Boyle. Manchester: Manchester University Press, 1958.

Khams rasāʾil Ismāʿīliyya. Edited by ʿĀrif Tāmir. Salamiyya, Syria: Dār al-Anṣāf, 1956.

al-Mahdī biʾllāh, Abū Muḥammad ʿAbdallāh, *Kitāb arsalahu al-Mahdī ilā nāḥiyat al-Yaman,* in *Kitāb al-farāʾiḍ wa-ḥudūd al-dīn* by Jaʿfar b. Manṣūr al-Yaman, edited and translated by Ḥusayn b. Fayḍ Allāh Hamdānī as *On the Genealogy of Fatimid Caliphs: Statement on Mahdī's Communication to the Yemen on the Real and Esoteric Names of His Hidden Predecessors.* Occasional paper no. 1. Cairo: American University at Cairo, 1958.

——. *Kitāb arsalahu al-Mahdī ilā nāḥiyat al-Yaman,* in *Kitāb al-farāʾiḍ wa-ḥudūd al-dīn* by Jaʿfar b. Manṣūr al-Yaman. Translation by Abbas Hamdani and François de Blois as 'A Re-Examination of Al-Mahdī's Letter to the Yemenites on the Genealogy of the Fatimid Caliphs'. *Journal of the Royal Asiatic Society of Great Britain and Ireland,* no. 2 (1983): 173–207.

al-Nuʿmān b. Muḥammad, al-Qāḍī Abū Ḥanīfa. *Kitāb Asās al-taʾwīl.* Edited by ʿĀrif Tāmir. Beirut: Dār al-Thaqāfa, 1960.

——. *Iftitāḥ al-daʿwa.* Edited by Wadād al-Qāḍī. Beirut: Dār al-Thaqāfa, 1970. Trans. by Hamid Haji as *Founding the Faṭimid State.* London: I. B. Tauris in association with the Institute of Ismaili Studies, 2006.

——. *Kitāb al-himma fī ādāb atbāʿ al-aʾimma.* Abridged English translation: Jawad Muscati and Khan Bahadur A.M. Moulvi, *Selections from Qazi Noaman's Kitab-ul-Himma fi Adabi Ataba-el-a'emma or Code of Conduct for the Followers of the Imam.* Ismailia Association [W.] Pakistan Series, no. 1. Karachi: The Ismailia Association [W.] Pakistan, 1950.

——. *Taʾwīl al-daʿāʾim.* Edited by ʿĀrif Tāmir. 2 vols. Beirut: Dār al-Aḍwāʾ, 1995.

——. *Daʿāʾim al-Islām.* Trans. Asaf A. A. Fyzee, completely revised and annotated by Ismail K. Poonawala as *The Pillars of Islam*: Vol. 1, *Acts of Devotion and Religious Observances*. New Delhi: Oxford University Press, 2002; and *The Pillars of Islam*: Vol. 2, *Laws Pertaining to Human Intercourse*. New Delhi: Oxford University Press, 2007.

al-Ṭūsī, Naṣīr al-Dīn Abū Jaʿfar Muḥammad b. Muḥammad. *Rawḍa-yi taslīm*. Edited and translated by S. J. Badakhchani as *Paradise of Submission: A Medieval Treatise on Ismaili Thought*. London: I. B. Tauris in association with the Institute of Ismaili Studies, 2005.

Secondary Sources

Agamben, Georgio. *The Sacrament of Language*. Translated by Adam Kotsko. Redwood City, CA: Stanford University Press, 2010.

Alexandrin, Elizabeth. 'The Sphere of Walāya: Ismāʿīlī Taʾwīl in Practice according to al-Muʾayyad (d. ca. 1078 C.E.)'. PhD diss., McGill University, 2006.

Allison, Dale. *Jesus of Nazareth: Millenarian Prophet*. Minneapolis, MN: Augsburg Press, 1998.

Amir-Moezzi, Mohammad Ali. *The Divine Guide in Early Shiism: The Sources of Esotericism in Islam*. Translated by David Streight. Albany: State University of New York Press, 1994.

——. 'Notes à Propos de la Walāya Imamite'. *Journal of the American Oriental Society* 122 (2002): 722–41.

Ankersmit, Frank R. 'Why Realism? Auerbach on the Representation of Reality'. *Poetics Today* 20 (1999): 53–75.

Anwar, Sherif and Jere L. Bacharach. 'Shiʿism and the Early Dinars of the Fāṭimid Imam-caliph al-Muʿizz li-dīn Allāh (341–365/952–975): An Analytic Overview'. *Al-Masāq* 22, no. 3 (December 2010): 259–78.

Ayoub, Mahmoud. 'The Speaking Qurʾān and the Silent Qurʾān: A Study of Imāmī Shīʿī *tafsīr*', in *Approaches to the History of the Interpretation of the Qurʾān*, edited by Andrew Rippin. New York: Oxford University Press, 1988, 177–98.

Bacharach, Jere L. *Islamic History through Coins*: *An Analysis and Catalogue of Tenth-Century Ikhshidid Coinage*. Cairo and New York: American University in Cairo Press, 2006.

Bar-Asher, Meir M. *Scripture and Exegesis in Early Imāmī Shiism*. Leiden: Brill, 1999.

Barkun, Michael. *Disaster and the Millennium*. New Haven, CT: Yale University Press, 1974.

Bashir, Shahzad. *Fazlallah Astarabadi and the Hurufis*. New York: Oneworld, 2005.

——. *Messianic Hopes and Mystical Visions*. Columbia: University of South Carolina Press, 2003.

Bierman, Irene A. *Writing Signs: The Fatimid Public Text*. Berkeley: University of California Press, 1998.

Bloom, Jonathan M. *Arts of the City Victorious: Islamic Art and Architecture in Fatimid North Africa and Egypt*. New Haven, CT, and London: Yale University Press in association with the Institute of Ismaili Studies, 2007.

Boyer, Paul. *When Time Shall be No More*. Cambridge, MA, and London: Belknap Press, 1992.

Brett, Michael. 'The Mīm, the ʿAyn, and the Making of Ismāʿīlīsm'. *Bulletin of the School of Oriental and African Studies* 57 (1994): 25–39.

——. *The Rise of the Fatimids*. Leiden: Brill, 2001.

Buckley, Jorrun J. 'The Nizârî Ismâ'îlîtes' Abolishment of the Sharî'a during the 'Great Resurrection' of 1164 A.D./559 A.H.'. *Studia Islamica* 60 (1984): 137–65.

Collins, John J. *The Apocalyptic Imagination: An Introduction to Jewish Apocalyptic Literature*, 2nd edn. Grand Rapids, MI: Wm. B. Eerdmans Publishing Co., 1998.

——, Bernard McGinn, and Stephen J. Stein (eds). *The Encyclopedia of Apocalypticism*. 3 volumes. New York: Continuum, 2000.

Connerton, Paul. *How Societies Remember*. Cambridge: Cambridge University Press, 1989.

Cook, David. *Studies in Muslim Apocalyptic*. Princeton, NJ: Darwin Press, 2002.

Corbin, Henry. *Cyclical Time and Ismaili Gnosis*. London: Kegan Paul International in association with Islamic Publications, 1983.

——. *History of Islamic Philosophy*. Translated by Liadain Sherrard and Philip Sherrard. London: Kegan Paul International in association with Islamic Publications, 1993.

——. 'Sabian Temple and Ismailism', in *Temple and Contemplation*, translated by Philip Sherrard and Liadain Sherrard. London: Kegan Paul International in association with Islamic Publications, 1983, pp. 132–82.

——. *Trilogie ismaélienne*. Paris: Verdier, 1994.

——. *The Voyage and the Messenger*. Berkeley: North Atlantic Books, 1998.

Daftary, Farhad (ed.). *Intellectual Traditions in Islam*. London and New York: I. B. Tauris in association with the Institute of Ismaili Studies, 2000.

——. 'The Ismaili *Daʿwa* outside the Fatimid *dawla*', in *L'Égypte Fatimide: Son Art et Son Histoire*, edited by Marianne Barrucand. Paris: Presses de l'Université de Paris-Sorbonne, 1999, pp. 29–43.

——. *Ismaili Literature: A Bibliography of Sources and Studies*. London: I. B. Tauris, 2004.

——. *The Ismāʿīlīs*. 2nd edn. Cambridge: Cambridge University Press, 2007. First published in 1990.

——. *A Short History of the Ismailis*. Edinburgh: Edinburgh University Press, 1998.

Dakake, Maria Massi. *The Charismatic Community: Shiʿite Identity in Early Islam*. Albany: State University of New York Press, 2007.

——. 'Hiding in Plain Sight: The Practical and Doctrinal Significance of Secrecy in Shiʿite Islam'. *Journal of the American Academy of Religion* 74.2 (2006): 324–55.

Dawson, Lorne. 'When Prophecy Fails and Faith Persists: A Theoretical Overview'. *Nova Religio: Journal of Alternative and Emergent Religions* 3, no. 1 (October 1999): 60–82.

Delaney, Carol. *Columbus and the Quest for Jersualem*. New York: Free Press, 2012.

De Smet, Daniel. 'The Risāla al-Mudhhiba Attributed to al-Qāḍī al-Nuʿmān: Important Evidence for the Adoption of Neoplatonism by Fatimid Ismailism at the Time of al-Muʿizz?', in *Fortresses of the Intellect: Ismaili and Other Islamic Studies in Honour of Farhad Daftary*, edited by Omar Alí-de-Unzaga. London: I. B. Tauris in association with the Institute of Ismaili Studies, 2011, pp. 309–41.

Donner, Fred M. *Muhammad and the Believers*. Cambridge, MA: Harvard University Press, 2010.

Ebstein, Michael. 'Secrecy in Ismāʿīlī Tradition and in the Mystical Thought of Ibn al-ʿArabī'. *Journal Asiatique* 298.2 (2010): 303–43.

Eliade, Mircea. *The Quest: History and Meaning in Religion*. Chicago: University of Chicago Press, 1969.

Ernst, Carl W. *Following Muhammad*. Chapel Hill: University of North Carolina Press, 2003.

—— and Richard C. Martin. *Rethinking Islamic Studies: From Orientalism to Cosmopolitanism*. Columbia: University of South Carolina Press, 2010.

Ess, Josef van. *Chiliastische Erwartungen und die Versuchung der Göttlichkeit: Der Kalif al-Ḥākim (386–411 H.)*. Abhandlungen der Heidelberger

Akademie der Wissenschaften. Philosophisch-historische Klasse. Heidelberg, 1977.

Fahd, T. 'Ḥurūf'. *Encyclopaedia of Islam*, second edition. Edited by P. Bearman, Th. Bianquis, C. E. Bosworth, E. van Donzel, and W. P. Heinrichs, vol. 5, pp. 595–6. Leiden: Brill, 1960–2005.

Festinger, Leon, Henry Riecken, and Stanley Schacter. *When Prophecy Fails.* Minneapolis: University of Minnesota Press, 1956.

Filiu, Jean-Pierre. *Apocalypse in Islam.* Translated by M. B. DeBevoise. Berkeley: University of California Press, 2011.

Fromherz, Allen. *The Almohads, the Rise of an Islamic Empire.* London and New York: I. B. Tauris, 2010.

García-Arenal, Mercedes (ed.). *Mahdism et millénarisme en Islam, Revue des Mondes musulmanes et de la Méditerranée.* Aix-en-Provence: Éditions Édisud, 2000.

—— (ed.). *Messianism and Puritanical Reform: Mahdis of the Muslim West.* Leiden: Brill, 2006.

Ghaemmaghami, Omid. '{And the earth will shine with the light of its Lord} (Q 39:69): Qā'im and Qiyāma in Shīʿī Thought', in *Roads to Paradise: Eschatology and Concepts of the Hereafter in Islam*, edited by Sebastian Günther and Todd Lawson. Leiden: Brill, forthcoming.

Gunkel, Hermann. *Creation and Chaos in the Primeval Era and the Eschaton.* Translated by K. William Whitney Jr. Grand Rapids, MI: Wm. B. Eerdmans, 2006. Originally published in German in 1895.

Hall, John R. *Apocalypse.* Malden, MA: Polity Press, 2009.

Halm, Heinz. *The Empire of the Mahdī: The Rise of the Fatimids.* Translated by Michael Bonner. Leiden: Brill, 1996.

——. 'The Ismaʿili Oath of Allegiance (*ʿahd*) and the 'Sessions of Wisdom' (*majālis al-ḥikma*) in Fatimid Times', in *Mediaeval Ismaʿili History and Thought*, edited by Farhad Daftary. New York: Cambridge University Press, 1996, pp. 91–116.

——. *Die Kalifen von Kairo: Die Fatimiden in Ägypten 973–1074.* Munich: C. H. Beck, 2003.

Hamdani, Sumaiya A. *Between Revolution and State: The Path to Fatimid Statehood: Qadi al-Nuʿman and the Construction of Fatimid Legitimacy.* London: I. B. Tauris in association with the Institute of Ismaili Studies, 2006.

Hodgson, M.G.S. 'The Ismāʿīlī State', in *The Cambridge History of Iran*, Volume

5: *The Saljuq and Mongol Periods*, edited by J. A. Boyle. Cambridge: Cambridge University Press, 1968, pp. 422–82.

——. *The Secret Order of Assassins: The Struggle of the Early Nizārī Ismāʿīlīs Against the Islamic World*. Philadelphia: University of Pennsylvania Press, 2005 (1955).

Hollenberg, David. 'Disrobing Judges with Veiled Truths: An Early Ismāʿīlī Torah Interpretation (*taʾwīl*) in Service of the Fāṭimid Mission'. *Religion* 33 (2003): 127–45.

——. 'Interpretation after the End of Days: The Fāṭimid-Ismāʿīlī tāʾwīl (interpretation) of Jaʿfar ibn Manṣūr al-Yaman (d. ca. 960)'. PhD diss., University of Pennsylvania, 2006.

Horsely, Richard, and Scott Hanson. *Bandits, Prophets, and Messiahs: Popular Movements in the Time of Jesus*. Minneapolis, MN: Seabury, 1985.

Idleman Smith, Jane and Yvonne Yazbeck Haddad. *The Islamic Understanding of Death and Resurrection*. Albany: State University of New York Press, 1981.

Izutsu, Toshihiku. *Ethico-Religious Concepts in the Qur'ān*. Montreal: McGill-Queen's University Press, 2002 (1966).

Jambet, Christian. *La grande résurrection d'Alamût: Les formes de la liberté dans le shî'isme ismaélien*. Paris: Verdier, 1990.

Johnson, Nels. 'Religious Paradigms of the Sudanese Mahdīyah'. *Ethnohistory* 25, no. 2 (Spring 1978): 159–78.

Juergensmeyer, Mark. *Terror in the Mind of God*. Berkeley and Los Angeles: University of California Press, 2000 (2003).

Kitts, Margo. *Sanctified Violence in Homeric Society*. New York: Oxford University Press, 2012.

Landes, Richard. *Heaven on Earth*. New York: Oxford University Press, 2011.

Landolt, Hermann. 'Introduction', in *The Paradise of Submission: A Medieval Treatise on Ismaili Thought*, trans. S. J. Badakhchani. London: I. B. Tauris in association with the Institute of Ismaili Studies, 2005.

——. '*Walāyah*', in *The Encyclopedia of Religion*, edited by Mircea Eliade. New York: Macmillan, 1987, pp. 316–23.

Lane, Edward William. *An Arabic-English Lexicon*. Cambridge: Islamic Texts Society, 1984.

Lange, Christian. *Paradise and Hell in Islamic Traditions*. Cambridge: Cambridge University Press, 2016.

——. 'Where on earth is hell? State punishment and eschatology in the

Islamic middle period', in *Public Violence in Islamic Societies*, edited by Christian Lange and Maribel Fierro. Edinburgh: Edinburgh University Press, 2009, pp. 156–78.

Lawson, Todd. 'Duality, Opposition and Typology in the Qurʾan: The Apocalyptic Substrate'. *Journal of Qurʾanic Studies* 10 (2008): 23–49.

Lev, Yaacov. 'From revolutionary violence to state violence: The Fāṭimids (297–567/909–1171)', in *Public Violence in Islamic Societies*, edited by Christian Lange and Maribel Fierro. Edinburgh: Edinburgh University Press, 2009, pp. 67–86.

——. *State and Society in Fatimid Egypt*. Leiden: Brill, 1991.

Lewis, Bernard. *The Assassins: A Radical Sect in Islam*. New York: Basic Books, 1968.

——. 'The Regnal Titles of the First Abbasid Caliphs', in *Dr. Zakir Husain Presentation Volume*. New Delhi, 1968, pp. 13–22.

Lincoln, Bruce. *Discourse and the Construction of Society*. New York: Oxford University Press, 1989.

——. *Holy Terrors: Thinking about Religion after September 11*. Chicago: University of Chicago Press, 2003.

Lindsay, James E. 'Prophetic Parallels in Abu 'Abd Allah al-Shiʿi's Mission among the Kutama Berbers, 893–910'. *International Journal of Middle East Studies* 24 (1992): 39–56.

Livne-Kafri, Ofer. 'Some Notes on the Muslim Apocalyptic Tradition'. *Quaderni di Studi Arabi* 17 (1999): 71–94

Madelung, Wilferd. 'al-Mahdī', in *Encyclopaedia of Islam*, second edition, edited by P. Bearman, Th. Bianquis, C. E. Bosworth, E. van Donzel, and W. P. Heinrichs. Leiden: Brill, 1960–2005.

——. 'Das Imamat in der frühen ismailitischen Lehre'. *Der Islam* 37 (1961): 43–135.

——. 'Ismāʿīlīsm: The Old and the New Daʿwa', in *Columbia Lectures on Iranian Studies 4: Religious Trends in Early Islamic Iran*, edited by Ehsan Yarshaten. New York: Persian Heritage Foundation, 1988, pp. 93–105.

——. 'Ismāʿīliyya', in *Encyclopaedia of Islam*, second edition, edited by P. Bearman, Th. Bianquis, C. E. Bosworth, E. van Donzel, and W. P. Heinrichs. Leiden: Brill, 1960–2005, vol. 4, pp. 198–206.

——, and Paul E. Walker (eds and trans). *The Advent of the Fatimids: A Contemporary Shiʿi Witness*. New York: I. B. Tauris, 2000.

Marquet, Yves. 'La pensée philosophique et religieuse du Qāḍī al-Nuʿmān à travers la "Risāla Muḍhiba".' *Bulletin d'études orientales* 39/40 (1987–8): 141–81.

Marsham, Andrew. *Rituals of Islamic Monarchy*. Edinburgh: Edinburgh University Press, 2009.

Martin, Richard (ed.). *Approaches to Islam in Religious Studies*. Tucson: University of Arizona Press, 1985.

McGinn, Bernard, John J. Collins and Stephen J. Stein (eds). *Encyclopedia of Apocalypticism*. New York: Continuum, 1998.

Melton, J. Gordon. 'Spiritualization and Reaffirmation: What Really Happens when Prophecy Fails', in *Expecting Armageddon, Essential Readings in Failed Prophecy*, edited by Jon R. Stone. New York: Routledge, 2000, pp. 145–57.

Merchant, Alnoor Jehangir. 'Qur'anic Inscriptions on Fatimid Coinage', in *Word of God, Art of Man: The Qur'an and its Creative Expressions*, edited by Fahmida Suleman. New York: Oxford University Press in association with the Institute of Ismaili Studies, 2007, pp. 105–21.

Mottahedeh, Roy. *Loyalty and Leadership in an Early Islamic Society*. London, New York: I. B. Tauris, 2001. First published by Princeton University Press, 1980.

Nanji, Azim. 'Shīʿī Ismāʿīlī Interpretations of the Qurʾan', in *Proceedings from the International Congress for the Study of the Qurʾān*, 2nd edn. Canberra: Australian National University, 1980, pp. 39–49.

Nicol, Norman D. *A Corpus of Fāṭimid Coins*. Trieste: G. Bernardi, 2006.

Nomoto, Shin. 'Early Ismāʿīlī Thought on Prophecy According to the Kitāb al-Islāh by Abū Ḥātim al-Rāzī (d. ca. 322/934–5)'. PhD diss., McGill University, 1999.

Olaf-Blitchfield, Jane. *Early Mahdism: Politics and Religion in the Formative Period of Islam*. Leiden: Brill, 1985.

O'Leary, Stephen D. *Arguing the Apocalypse*. New York: Oxford University Press, 1994.

Poonawala, Ismail K. H. 'The Beginning of the Ismaili *Daʿwa* and the Establishment of the Fatimid Dynasty as Commemorated by al-Qāḍī al-Nuʿmān', in *Culture and Memory in Medieval Islam: Essays in Honor of Wilferd Madelung*, edited by Farhard Daftary and Josef W. Meri. London: I. B. Tauris, 2003, pp. 338–63.

——. *Biobibliography of Ismāʿīlī Literature*. Malibu, CA: Undena Publications, 1977.

——. 'Ismāʿīlī *taʾwīl* of the Qur'ān', in *Approaches to the History of the Interpretation of the Qurʾan*, edited by Andrew Rippin. New York: Oxford University Press, 1988, pp. 199–222.

——. 'Al-Qāḍī al-Nuʿmān and Ismaʿili Jurisprudence', in *Medieval Ismaʿili History and Thought*, edited by Farhad Daftary. New York and Cambridge: Cambridge University Press, 1996, pp. 117–43.

——. 'Al-Qāḍī al-Nuʿmān's Works and the Sources'. *Bulletin of the School of Oriental and African Studies* 36 (1973): 109–15.

——. 'A Reconsideration of al-Qāḍī al-Nuʿmān's *Madhhab*'. *Bulletin of the School of Oriental and African Studies* 37 (1974): 572–9.

Qutbuddin, Husain K. B. 'Fāṭimid Legal Exegesis of the Qurʾan: The Interpretive Strategies Used by al-Qāḍī al-Nuʿmān (d. 363/974) in his *Daʿāʾim al-Islām*'. *Journal of Qurʾanic Studies* 12 (2010): 109–46.

Qutbuddin, Tahera. *Al-Muʾayyad al-Shīrāzī and Fatimid Daʿwa Poetry*. Leiden: Brill, 2005.

Redles, David. *Hitler's Millennial Reich*. New York: New York University Press, 2005.

Russell, D. S. *Divine Disclosure*. Minneapolis, MN: Fortress Press, 2007 (1992).

Rustomji, Nerina. *The Garden and the Fire: Heaven and Hell in Islamic Culture*. New York: Columbia University Press, 2009.

Sachedina, Abdulaziz. *Islamic Messianism: The Idea of the Mahdi in Twelver Shiism*. Albany: State University of New York Press, 1981.

Sanders, Paula. *Ritual, Politics, and the City in Fatimid Cairo*. Albany: State University of New York Press, 1994.

Sells, Michael A. *Approaching the Qur'ān*. Ashland, OR: Whitecloud Press, 1999 (2007).

——. 'Armageddon in Christian, Sunni and Shia Traditions', in *Oxford Handbook of Religion and Violence*, edited by Michael Jerryson, Mark Juergensmeyer and Margo Kitts. New York: Oxford, 2013, pp. 467–95.

Shakir, M. H. (trans.). *The Qurʾan*. Elmhurst, NY: Tahrike Tarsile Qurʾan, 1989.

Shoemaker, Stephen J. *The Death of a Prophet*. Philadelphia: University of Pennsylvania Press, 2012.

Smith, Jonathan Z., *Imagining Religion: From Babylon to Jonestown*. Chicago: University of Chicago Press, 1982.

——. 'Religion, Religions, Religious', in *Critical Terms for Religious Studies*, edited by Mark C. Taylor. Chicago: University of Chicago Press, 1998, pp. 269–84.

Stewart, Devin. 'Prophecy', in *Key Themes for the Study of Islam*, edited by Jamal J. Elias. New York: Oneworld, 2010, pp. 281–303.

Stone, Jon R. (ed.). *Expecting Armageddon: Essential Readings in Failed Prophecy*. New York: Routledge, 2000.

——. 'Prophecy and Dissonance: A Reassessment of Research Testing the Festinger Theory'. *Nova Religio: The Journal of Alternative and Emergent Religions* 12, no. 4 (May 2009): 72–90.

Sweet, Leonard I. 'Christopher Columbus and the Millennial Vision of the New World'. *Catholic Historical Review* 72, no. 3 (July 1986): 369–82.

Tumminia, Diana. *When Prophecy Never Fails: Myth and Reality in a Flying-Saucer Group*. New York: Oxford University Press, 2005.

——. and William H. Swatos (eds). *How Prophecy Lives*. Leiden: Brill, 2011.

Tweed, Thomas. *Crossing and Dwelling*. Cambridge, MA: Harvard University Press, 2006.

Van der Leeuw, G. 'Primordial Time and Final Time', in *Man and Time: Papers from the Eranos Yearbooks*, Bollingen Series 30, vol. 3, edited by Joseph Campbell. Princeton, NJ: Princeton University Press, 1957.

Velji, Jamel A. 'Apocalyptic Religion and Violence'. *Oxford Handbook of Religion and Violence*. New York: Oxford University Press, 2013, pp. 250–59.

——. 'Apocalyptic Rhetoric and the Construction of Authority in Medieval Ismaʿilism', in *Roads to Paradise: Eschatology and Concepts of the Hereafter in Islam*, edited by Sebastian Günther and Todd Lawson. Leiden: Brill, forthcoming.

Voll, John O. 'The Mahdī's Concept and Use of 'Hijrah'.' *Islamic Studies* 26:1 (1987): 31–42.

Walker, Paul E. *Early Philosophical Shiism*. New York: Cambridge University Press, 1993.

——. *Exploring an Islamic Empire: Fatimid History and Its Sources*. London: I. B. Tauris, 2002.

—— (ed. and trans.). *Orations of the Fatimid Caliphs*. New York: I. B. Tauris, 2009.

Walls, Jerry L. (ed.). *Oxford Handbook of Millennialism*. New York: Oxford University Press, 2010.

Watt, Montgomery. 'Al-Iskandar'. *Encyclopaedia of Islam*, second edition. Edited by P. Bearman, Th. Bianquis, C. E. Bosworth, E. van Donzel, and W. P. Heinrichs, vol. 4, p. 127. Leiden: Brill, 1960–2005.

Wessinger, Catherine. *How the Millennium Comes Violently*. New York: Seven Bridges Press, 2000.

Yücesoy, Hayrettin. *Messianic Beliefs and Imperial Politics in Medieval Islam: The ʿAbbāsid Caliphate in the Early Ninth Century*. Columbia: University of South Carolina Press, 2009.

Index of Names

Aaron, 16
Abbasids, 37, 46, 77, 111
ʿAbdān, 35
Abraham, 16, 25–6, 86, 88, 124
Abū ʿAbdallāh al-Shīʿī, 71–2
Abū Bakr [al-Ṣiddiq], 54
Abū Manṣūr al-Nizār (437–88/1045–95), 112
Abū l-Qāsim Aḥmad (467–95/1074–1101), 112
Abū Yazīd, 110–11
  rebellion of, 5
ʿAd, 144
Adam, 16, 19, 33, 85–6, 132
  cycles of, 124
  descendants of, 26–7
Afghanistan, 114
Aghlabids, 75
Alamut, 9, 109, 113–14, 117, 127, 132–3, 135
  ceremonies in, 118–19
Alexander the Great, 124
ʿAlī b. Abī Ṭālib, 16, 18, 50–3, 75, 83–4, 86, 124–6
  descendants of, 17
  as every *imām*, 124
  name [i.e., ʿ-l-ī], 81
  time of, 87
  walāya of, 50–1
Antichrist, 3, 149
Arafat, 99–102
Astarābādī, Faḍl Allāh (d. 1394), 97
Azerbaiyjan, 111
al-ʿAzīz (caliph, d. 386/996), 111

Badr al-Jamālī, 112
Baghdad, 126
Bahrain, 37, 111
Barkun, Michael, 143
Bayt al-Maqdis, 98
Brett, Michael, 42, 58, 72, 76, 110
Bū Ḥimāra, 110
Buyids, 113

Cairo, 2, 111–12
Camping, Harold, 3
Central Asia, 112, 114
China, 125
Christ, 110; *see also* Jesus
Christianity/Christian(s), 1, 6, 25–6
  apocalypticism, 10n
  communities, 45
Columbus, Christopher, 10n
Corbin, Henry, 8, 92, 115, 134

Daftary, Farhad, 36, 58, 111, 114, 116, 136
Dakake, Maria, 46
Damascus, 125, 126
Daylam, 111, 113, 125–6, 132, 134
Donner, Fred, 37, 144, 149
Druze, 5, 112

Ebstein, Michael, 30–1
Egypt/Egyptians, 125–6, 144

Fatimids, 3–4, 7, 71–2, 101, 111, 114, 118, 138, 142, 146–7
  advent of, 42, 78
  apocalypticism, 6–10, 14, 21n, 105, 116, 142, 148
  authority, 8, 21, 81, 97
  caliph-imams, 8, 104, 106
  coins, 72, 143
  court ceremonies, 106
  da'wa, 63, 112
  dynasty, 111, 116
  Empire (909–1171), 2, 4, 18–19, 76, 110–13
  and esoteric interpretation (*ta'wīl*), 43
  exegesis/exegetes, 3, 104
  hierarchy, 4, 22, 46, 58, 61, 63, 67–9, 71, 98, 105, 111
  legitimacy of, 79–80, 116
  materials/texts, 7, 32, 67, 69
  political theology, 76
  revolution, 4, 20n, 38
  rule/rulers, 75, 79, 104
  theology of, 8, 73n

Hagar, 98
al-Ḥākim (r. 386–411/996–1021), 5, 111–12
Halm, Heinz, 19, 23, 35, 36
Hamdani, 93n
Ḥamdān Qarmaṭ, 35
Ḥasan II (= Ḥasan *'alā dhikrihi al-salām*), 9, 109, 125, 127, 130–1, 134–6
  authority of, 119, 123
  declaration of, 109–10, 117–19
Ḥasan III = Jalāl al-Dīn Ḥasan (r. 1210–21), 135–6
Ḥasan-i Maḥmūd-i Kātib, 110, 124–5, 129
  Haft-bāb, 9, 110, 123–4, 126, 131, 137
Ḥasan Ṣabbāḥ (d. 1124), 113–14, 126–7, 133–4
Hodgson, Marshall, 115–16, 133, 135
Ḥusayn, 51, 77

Ibn Ḥawshab (d. 914), 4, 76
  Kitāb al-rushd wa-l-hidāya, 4, 8, 32, 38, 46, 61, 66, 80, 105, 142, 146
Ibn Rizām, 35, 36
Ifrīqiya, 72, 76
India, 112, 125
Iran (*dīyār-i 'ajam*), 132
Iraq, 35, 111, 113
Ishmael, 16
Ismaili(s)/Ismailism, 2, 7, 17, 19, 58, 75, 115–16, 134–5
  faith, 30
  history, 9
  jurisprudence/law, 80
  Persianate phase of, 10
  propaganda, 113
Israel, Children/tribe of, 25–6
Ivanow, Wladimir, 61, 69
Izutsu, Toshihiko, 43

Ja'far b. Manṣūr al-Yaman (d. ca. 957), 4, 46, 76
  Kitāb al-'ālim wa-l-ghulām, 23, 69
  Kitāb al-kashf, 4, 8, 16, 27, 30, 46, 49–52, 54, 56, 58, 62, 71, 80, 105, 142–3, 146
Ja'far al-Ṣādiq (d. 765), sixth *imām*, 16, 19, 29, 58, 77, 79
Jalāl al-Dīn Ḥasan (r. 1210–21), 135
Jambet, Christian, 115, 118
Jerusalem, 98
Jesus, 16, 25–6, 77, 86, 124
Jewish, 45
Juwaynī, 117

Khārijīs, 110
al-Kirmānī (d. 1020), 112, 135
Kitts, Margo, 31, 32
Kiyā Buzurg-Ummīd, 114
Kufa, Iraq, 19, 36
Kutāma tribe, 125

Landolt, Hermann, 16, 17, 49
Lewis, Bernard, 113
Lincoln, Bruce, 6, 116
Lot, 144

Madelung, Wilferd, 46
Maghrib, 71, 125
al-Mahdī, 'Abdallāh, 72, 75–80, 83–9, 105, 111, 147
  letter of, 9, 76, 79, 84, 94n, 104, 106, 110, 139n, 147
al-Mahdī Muḥammad b. Ismā'īl, 16, 19, 36, 146
al-Mahdiyya [capital city], 5, 110–11
al-Manṣūr (caliph, d. 341/953), 79, 80, 110, 111, 139n
Manṣūr al-Ḥallāj (d. 922), 97
Marwa, 98
Masjid al-Ḥarām, 97
Mazandaran, 113
Mecca, 37, 97–8, 119
Medina, 37, 97, 144–5
Melton, Gordon, 73n
Minā, 102
Morocco, 2
Moses, 16, 25–6, 86–7, 124

Muḥammad (Prophet), 15–18, 25, 33, 35, 37, 50–2, 62–6, 81, 83, 86, 88, 90–1, 124, 143–5
  daʿwa of, 87–8
  progeny/family of, 77–8, 82, 89
Muḥammad b. Buzurg-Ummīd (1138–62), 114
Muḥammad b. Ismāʿīl al-Darzī, 112
Muḥammad Bustī, 117
al-Muʿizz (caliph-imam, r. 952–75), 71, 80, 91, 94n, 111
Mustaʿliyya (Mustaʿlī), 112, 113
al-Mustanṣir (r. 427–87/1036–94), 112, 117, 133
Muzdalifa, 101, 102

Naṣīr al-Dīn Ṭūsī (d. 1274), 136, 138
  Rawḍa-yi taslīm, 136, 138
al-Nizār, *imām*, 125–6
Nizaris/Nizariyya, 112, 114, 116–18, 133–4
  apocalypticism, 10, 148
  calendar, 115
  and declaration of *qiyāma* (resurrection), 5
  Ismaili communities, 5, 9, 114, 120
  materials, 7
Noah, 16, 25–6, 86, 124, 144
North Africa, 2, 9, 37, 75; *see also* Maghrib
al-Nuʿmān, 82–3, 85, 89–90, 147
  ta'wīl of, 86, 92, 98, 105

Obama, Barack, 3, 149
O'Leary, Stephen, 6, 133

Persia/Persian, 111–14, 117, 134–5
Persian Gulf, 19
Persianate culture, 10, 109, 117, 134
Persian language, 114, 117, 133–4
Pharaoh, 88, 144

Qāḍī l-Nuʿmān (d. 974), 4, 72, 79–81, 104
  Daʿā'im al-Islām, 79–80
  Iftitāḥ al-daʿwa, 80
  Kitāb al-himma fī ādāb atbāʿ al-a'imma, 105
  Sharḥ al-akhbār, 80
  Ta'wīl al-daʿā'im, 4, 9, 79–80, 105, 110, 147
Qā'im, 19, 127
  Muḥammad b. Ismāʿīl, 58
al-Qā'im bi-Amr Allāh (caliph-imam, r. 934–46), 91, 110–11
Qarmatis/Qarmatian, 36, 111–12, 140n
Qayrawān, 110

Rappaport, Roy, 31
Rayy, Iran, 19

Ṣafā, 98
Ṣāḥib al-Ḥimar (Lord of the Donkey), 110
Saʿīd Qummī (d. 1691), 97
Salamiyya, Syria, 19
Sanders, Paula, 106
Seljuk(s), 9, 109, 113, 133
  lands/territory, 114, 116
Sells, Michael, 43
Seth, 16
Shem, 16
Shoemaker, Stephen, 149
Sicily, 75
al-Sijistānī (d. 975), 135
Simon Peter, 16
Smith, Jonathan Z., 7
Syria, 113

Thamud, 144
Tunisia, 2
Turkish dynasties, 113
Tweed, Thomas, 7

Umayyads, 51, 77
United States, 10–11n

Walker, Paul, 75

Yemen (Yaman), 19, 37, 76, 112

al-Ẓāhir (411–27/1021–36), 112

Subject Index

adversaries (*al-aḍdād*), 30
afterlife (*ākhira*), 53, 131, 136, 138; *see also* hereafter
ʿahd see covenant
ahl al-bayt, 67; *see also Index of Names*: Muḥammad (Prophet)
ahl al-ḥaqq (people of the truth), 36
allegiance, 25, 29, 33, 101
allowed, *vs* forbidden, 23
ʿamal (deeds), 77; *see also* deeds
amāna (trust), 27–8
amīr al-muʾminīn, 50
angels, 40, 53–4, 86, 100, 103
antinomianism, 9, 109, 116
apocalypse/apocalyptic, 6, 32, 59n, 71–2, 80, 119, 149
  disclosures, 131, 146–7
  events, 5, 123
  expectation, 2, 9, 42, 79, 135, 146
  fulfilment, 37, 78–9, 94n
  imagery, 2, 34, 38, 43, 47, 58, 110, 138
  imminent, 3, 42, 72
  Mayan, 3, 148
  movements, 2, 7–9
  myths, 22, 120, 142
  narratives, 6, 56
  prophecy, 6, 10n, 76, 79, 139n
  punishments, 48, 53
  rhetoric, 2, 6–8, 64, 78–9, 122n
  symbolism, 43, 79, 111–12, 116, 118, 130, 133–5, 148–9
  temporality, 147
  theology(s), 123, 131, 136
apocalypticism, 22, 43, 76, 79, 105–6, 109–10, 132–3, 146–8
  actualisation of, 130
  definition of, 5–6
  Fatimid, 6–10, 14, 21n, 105, 116, 142, 148
  nature of, 1–2
apokalypsis, 120
Arabic, 114, 117
  root h-d-y, 78
  root w-l-y, 16
atemporality, 119
authority, 1, 3–4, 6–7, 10, 31, 139n, 146
  apocalypticism and, 79, 105–6, 122n
  consolidation of, 76–7, 104, 138, 148
  Fatimid, 8, 21, 81, 97
  of God, 72
  of Ḥasan, 117–19, 123–4, 134
  of the Mahdī/dynasty, 78, 84
  of the present *imām*, 120
  of the *qāʾim*, 54
  temporal, 48
  terrestrial, 105, 133
  transfer of, 116, 133, 135, 148

bāb/*bābs* (gates; pl. *abwāb*), 17, 28, 47–8, 103
basmala, 62
bāṭin (hidden, esoteric), 14–16, 18, 23–4, 67–8, 70–1, 88, 99, 101, 118, 134–5; *see also ẓāhir* (apparent)
  commentaries, 57

bāṭin (hidden, esoteric) (*cont.*)
and the *daʿwa*, 70, 81–3, 95n
as night, 82
and prayers, 81, 83, 85
unveiling of, 102–3
belief, 29, 44, 71, 119, 143
in end of time/resurrection, 32, 42–3, 68, 131
in *imāms*, 30, 53, 130
in the *mahdī*, 48–9, 58, 65
true/correct, 23, 65, 71, 87, 91, 144–5
believers, 25–6, 35, 46–7, 67–9, 77–9, 90–1, 98, 100–1, 103, 105–6, 135, 142
and application of sharia, 109
commander of [ʿAlī], 52
early, of Medina, 37, 144–5
obligations of/oaths, 23–4, 42
trials of, 84–6, 88
true, 20, 30, 48, 52–3, 55, 57, 68, 70, 91, 143, 145
booty, 35, 114

calendar, 89, 105–6, 115, 147
Islamic, 37
caliph-imams, 8, 71, 80, 91, 93n, 104, 106
ceremony(s)
of Fatimid court, 106
of Ḥasan, in Alamut, 110, 117–19, 134
charismata (*karāmāt*), 20n
circumambulations, 74n, 98
class, 113, 148
coinage, 71; *see also* numismatic (evidence/material)
commander, of the believers/faithful, 49–52, 54–7, 87
communal
anticipation, 118
authority, 18
boundaries, 6, 8, 31, 35–6, 120
election, 117
identity, 24, 35, 119
memory, 3, 92
structure/restructuring, 10, 15, 38
community(ies), 9, 25–6, 28–9, 35, 55, 80, 85–9, 91, 143
elect, 62, 122n, 123, 125
Ismaili, 37, 94n, 104–5, 112, 147
Muslim, 2–4, 35, 37, 41n, 114, 117, 135, 143–5
Nizari Ismaili, 5, 9, 106, 109, 114–20, 123, 133–5
Shia, 7, 46, 52
Companions of the Right, 34, 69–70
concealment (*kitmān, satr*), 30, 83–5, 87–9, 136
converts/conversion, 30, 35, 45, 70, 114
cosmogony/cosmology, 123
cosmos, 119
covenant (*ʿahd, mīthāq*), 23–8, 32–3, 38
people of, 70
primordial, 26, 39n
creation, 24, 28, 31–2, 34–5, 68–9, 92, 118–19
best of, 28, 45–6
elect of, 38
multiplicity of, 128
worst of, 45
cycles, 15–16, 82, 90, 127, 132
of history, 15, 124
of prayer(s) (*ṣalāt*), 81, 86, 89
of prophets, 124, 144
of time, 105

dāʿīs (callers, summoners), 17, 19, 23, 32, 34–6, 55, 67–71, 82, 98, 112–13, 117–18
of Daylam, 114
of the Yemen, 76
dajjāl (eschatological deceiver), 110–11, 139n
damnation, 45–6; *see also* hell/hellfire
damned, *vs* saved, 1, 49, 71; *see also* saved
dār al-hijra(s) (abode(s) of migration), 34, 36–7, 42
daʿwa (call, mission), 34–8, 42, 54–5, 67, 70, 81–4, 87–9, 97–8, 100, 102–5, 112–13, 142
concealed, 83, 88, 102
on earthly plane, 86, 142
as hierarchy, 17, 19, 63
of al-Mahdī, 84–5
members of, 71, 97
organisational structure of, 19, 58, 87, 143
ranks of, 24, 30, 48
secrecy of/secret, 47–8, 54, 89
spread of, 19, 21n
death, 91, 131
deeds, 49–50, 52, 70, 77, 137
Record of, 104
denier, *vs* believers, 47, 53, 70
destiny, 123, 143
dhimma (protection), 34, 70
Dhū l-Qarnayn, 124
dīn
al-ḥaqq (religion of the truth), 36
as reckoning, 43
as religion, 53, 65
disbelief/disbelievers, 29–30, 49, 51, 53–5, 71

disclosure(s), 17, 38, 48, 84–5, 89, 91, 99, 103, 118–19, 123, 131, 134
divine, 9, 29, 146–8
disobedience, 45, 130
dissimulation (*taqiyya*), 83, 136
divinity, 112, 129–31
locus of, 123–5
duʿā, 28
duality, 44, 46, 59n, 143

earth/earthly, 22, 24, 27, 30, 32, 36, 52–4, 56–7, 66–9, 86, 97, 100, 103–4, 106, 118, 123, 126, 131, 142, 145, 148
existence, 137
mountains, 27, 48, 50, 132
elect, 3, 16, 19–20, 24, 28–9, 34, 36, 38, 51, 67, 104, 143, 145, 147
community, 29, 62, 122n, 123, 125
of God, 15, 69
of the *imām*, 117
election, 46, 99, 146
communal, 117
sense of, 34, 103, 143–4, 148
elite, 22, 30, 136
empire, 9, 14, 18–19, 76, 111–12
emplotment, 142–3
end, of the world, 5, 77, 93n, 109–10, 114–15, 132–3, 144–5
end of time, 8–9, 22, 31–2, 36–7, 48, 60n, 65–6, 76–7, 84, 89, 91, 95n, 99–100, 104, 111–12, 118, 142, 144, 146
events of, 47–8, 100, 124
imminence of, 2–3, 43
Quranic descriptions of, 47–9, 62
re-signification of, 47, 58, 61, 142
era(s)
ʿaṣr, 57–8
of Muḥammad, 136
new, 78, 115, 144
of Prophet (Muḥammad), 18, 37, 75
utopian, 19
eschatology/eschatological, 44, 49–50, 52, 54–5, 76, 87, 106, 132–3, 145
figure, 4–6, 29, 42, 54, 62, 72, 78, 82, 88–9, 91, 94n, 103, 110, 125–6
imagery, 38, 43, 58
imminent/immediate, 22, 57, 92, 106, 133, 138
mahdī, 5, 9, 16, 78–9, 84, 104, 147
al-qāʾim, 16, 80, 82, 105
re-signification, 47
symbols, 79
triumph/success (*thawāb*), 53, 103, 143
esoteric (*bāṭin*), 99
commentaries, 18, 46, 57
form of Islam, 116
interpretation of scripture (*taʾwīl*), 2–3, 8, 15, 18, 43
knowledge, 38, 47, 67–8
truths, 16
ethics/ethical
behaviour/practices, 137–8
boundaries, 46
code/Quranic, 43–4
imperatives, 34, 39n
evil, 6, 53, 103, 105, 119, 122n, 137
evildoers, 33, 50, 52–3
executors (*awṣiyāʾ*), 28, 126–7
exegesis/exegetes, 8, 15, 17–18, 43, 51, 76, 134–5
Fatimid, 3, 104
exile (*al-hijra*), 35
exoteric (*ẓāhir*), 17, 99

faith/faithful, 24, 86, 100, 102–3, 110
bond of (*ʿuqdat al-īmān*), 57
denial of, 45
Ismaili, 30
profession of (*tashahhud*), 83–4
false
idols/*imāms*, 50–3
vs true, 137
falsehood, 23, 47, 71–2, 76
famine, 112
fast/fasting, 5, 87–9, 102, 119
feast, 109, 115
at Alamut, 119
fire, 26, 34, 45, 50, 52, 55–6, 64–5, 70; *see also* hell/hellfire
fiṭra, 27–8
payment of, 35
forbidden, 23, 27
forgiveness, gate of, 102
Friday congregational prayer (*al-jumʿa*) *see* prayer(s)
friends, of God (*awliyāʾ*), 28, 54, 68–9, 104

gardens, 33–4, 45, 69–70, 91
genealogy, 24, 123
gnosis, divine (*maʿrifat-i ilāhī*), 137
God, 14–16, 23–30, 43, 45, 47–53, 69, 138, 143–4
and covenant, 119
judgment of, 63–4
oath (*ʿahd*), 27, 32–3
obedience to, 17, 33
One/unity of, 19, 44, 56, 65, 128
proximity of, 129–30
good, 55, 86, 100, 102–3, 126
vs evil/bad, 44–5, 103, 105, 119, 137
news, 67, 77–8, 84, 88, 91
Gospels, 25

guidance, 17–18, 23, 35, 42, 50–1, 72, 78–9, 100, 138, 144
guide, 98, 135
  hādī, 77–8
  murshid, 15

hadith, 124
hajj, 9, 69, 81, 87, 97
  rites of, 92, 99–104
  taʾwīl of, 105
  wuqūf (standing), 100–2
ḥashr (gathering; resurrection), 136–7; *see also* resurrection (*qiyāma*)
heaven(s), 1, 6, 27, 34, 38, 47–8, 52, 66–9, 100, 104, 129–30, 133–4, 146–7
hell/hellfire, 1, 6, 30, 34, 38, 51, 56, 64, 70, 116, 130–1, 140n
  defined, 54–5
  people of, 34, 46, 69
helpers
  anṣār, 54
  walī naṣīr, 16, 20n
hereafter, 103, 128–9, 132, 137, 148; *see also* afterlife
heretics, 26, 110
hermeneutics/hermeneutical, 2–4, 6, 9, 14, 22, 61–2, 64, 76, 80, 87, 92, 98, 135, 142
  Ismaili, 18
  methods/processes, 14, 47, 109, 116, 146
  Shia, 8, 15
  of unveiling, 46
hierarchy(s), 35–6, 46, 89, 106
  Fatimid, 4, 17, 46, 58, 61–3, 67–9, 71, 98, 105, 111
  formal/official, 19, 29
  religious, 2, 58
  social, 120
hijra (emigration), 35, 37, 41n
ḥikma (wisdom), 99
history, 4, 7–8, 16, 19–20, 37, 80, 97, 118, 123, 130, 135, 144–6
  cosmic, 110, 133
  cyclical structure of, 15, 124
  end of, 71, 78, 115, 119; *see also* end, of the world
  linear, 80
  Quranic, 32, 34, 38, 142
  of religions, 89, 105, 116, 136
  sacred, 5, 9, 22, 27, 50, 62–3, 76–7, 82, 85–9, 92, 97, 104–5, 109, 125–7, 136, 139n
  telos of, 118, 148
  temporal, 122n
Hour, 64–6, 77, 79
ḥujjas/*ḥujjat* (proofs), 17, 48, 53–4, 57–8, 59n, 62–3, 66–9, 71, 74n, 82–3, 85, 89, 97–8, 101–3, 117, 126
humanity/human beings, 15, 27–8, 39n, 47, 119, 128–30, 136–8, 140n, 143
hypocrisy (*nifāq*), 129

Iblis, 33
ʿīd, 87, 89
  al-aḍḥā (the great *ʿīd*), 87–9, 102–3
  al-fiṭr (breaking of Ramadan fast), 87
identity, 7, 53, 76, 106, 123, 125, 130, 134, 143
  communal, 24, 35, 119
idolaters, 45, 72
ignorance, 67–8, 83
  divine, 45
imāma/imamate, 51, 53, 58, 68–9, 106, 111–13, 118, 125–7, 134
imām-qāʾim, 127, 130, 136
imāms, 4, 9, 15, 18, 24, 29, 30, 48, 50, 51, 53, 56, 57, 62, 63, 66, 67, 79, 82, 85, 91, 98, 106, 123, 124, 126, 130, 137, 142
  completer (*mutimm*), 63
  concealment of, 84, 85, 87, 88, 89
  counter-*imāms*, 51
  devotion to, 17
  disappearance, 101
  false, 50–2
  gates of, 57
  hidden, 87, 115–17
  living, 135
  present, 109, 118, 120, 133
  recognition of, 9, 17, 57, 83, 117, 129–31
  sayings of, 138
  seal of, 90, 100
  seven, 82
  seventh, 16
  spiritual nature of, 129
  of their time, 101
  twelfth, 2
infidels, 110
initiates/initiation, 3, 17, 19, 22–4, 26–8, 30, 32, 35, 38, 70, 80, 83, 85, 98, 119, 134, 142–3
inscriptions, 71–2, 143
instantiation, 32, 147, 149
intellect, 128–9, 140n
  First, 137–8
intercession, 26, 52
iqlīm (geographical regions), 132
Islam/Islamic, 15, 17–19, 28–9, 71–2, 97–8, 116, 134, 143–4
  government/empire, 75
  history, 2, 8, 16, 37, 72

law of, 16, 19
Shia, 109, 117, 133–5
studies, 2–3
true, 4, 28, 54
islands (*jazīra*, pl. *jazāʾir*), 34, 37, 42, 62
twelve, 37, 69, 83

Jahannam, 45; *see also* hell/hellfire
jinn, 33
judgment, divine/final, 27, 37, 44, 54–6, 63–4, 103–4, 124, 144
day of, 34, 47, 50, 57, 70, 146
justice, 36, 72, 78

Kaʿba, 97–8
khalīfa (deputy), 117
khums (fifth), 35
khuṭbas, 110, 115, 117
kitmān (concealment; secret), 84, 88–9
knowledge, 26, 32, 34, 48, 57, 77, 89–90, 98–100, 125–6, 135, 137–8, 145
esoteric, 38, 47
hidden/secret, 4, 17–18, 23–4, 28–9, 47–8, 51, 80, 133–4
ʿilm, 67–8, 77, 99
of the *imāms*, 47–8, 51, 67, 137
spiritual, 98–9
those firmly rooted in, 14–15

Last Day, 48–9
law, religious (*sharīʿa*), 16, 109, 118
abrogation/cessation of, 87, 127
leadership/leaders, 4–5, 51, 78, 89, 98, 106–7, 109, 112–13, 118, 123, 127, 133–4, 144
hudā, 77
Shia, 2, 52
twelve, 25, 63, 69, 83
letters, science of, 51, 62–3, 73n, 81–2
light, 103–4, 124, 128
vs darkness, 85
daylight, 81
of guidance, 91
lineage/genealogy, 78–9, 123, 142
sacred, 23–4
living beings/entities (*mardum*), 33, 39, 130; *see also* creation; humanity

*mahdī*s, 2, 20, 23, 34–5, 37–8, 42, 53, 58, 77, 110–11, 119, 142, 146
advent of, 22, 53, 61–2, 64–5, 71–2, 78
anticipation of, 4, 65, 77
Arabic root h-d-y, 78
arrival of, 16, 19, 36, 43, 46, 48, 52, 62–3, 66, 143
cause of, 46–7, 71, 143
as end of time, 47–9, 61–2, 93n, 146
eschatological, 5, 9, 78–9, 84, 104, 147
identity of, 16, 46, 62, 66, 93n
multiple, 77–8, 106, 110–11, 133, 147
and salvation, 4, 43, 47, 65, 142
support of, 32, 34, 38, 46, 49, 58, 65, 70–2
mahdism/mahdist, 6, 78–9, 81, 94n, 106, 110, 140n
expectation/anticipation, 8, 48, 57–8, 61, 77, 79–80, 89, 105, 133, 142, 146
imminent, 73n, 105
movements, 37, 73n, 103
majālis (sessions), 80, 105
master of the age, 49, 54, 97–8
messenger(s), 27–8, 56, 63–4, 72, 81, 84, 90, 103
-prophet (*rasūl*), 58
stations of the, 68–9
messiah, 3, 61, 127, 148
messianic
expectation, 89, 105
figure(s), 5, 19, 110
rhetoric, 2
metanarrative, 65, 89
millenarian movements, 36, 143
mīthāq see covenant
moral
categories/conduct, 43–4; *see also* ethics/ethical
experience, 115, 134
mosques, 97–8
muḥrim, 69, 71
murīd (committed one), 15, 18
murshid (guide), 15, 18
mutammims, 63–5
myth, 6–7, 22, 120, 142, 146, 149
and counter-myth, 149

naqībs, 62
nāṭiqs (speaker), 15–16, 47, 51, 54, 57–8, 62–6, 68, 82
seventh (the *mahdī*), 61, 64–6, 70
night, 81–2, 84–5; *see also* time
and day, alternation of, 87
nonexistence, 130–1, 133
nujabāʾ, 28
numerology/numerological
correspondence, 61–3, 65
hermeneutic, 142
numismatic (evidence/material), 3, 6, 71–2
nuqabāʾ, 28, 68–9, 83

oath(s) (*ʿahd*), 27–9, 30–5, 39–40n
of allegiance, 22–3, 32, 46, 142
-taking, 8, 24, 27, 30–4, 38, 46, 142
obedience, 4, 17, 28, 33, 47, 51, 57, 67–8, 125, 129–30
obligation, 23, 27, 32–4, 38, 42, 48, 63, 68, 81–2, 84, 97–8
occultation (*ghayba*), 19
ontology/ontological, 63
of Ḥasan's authority, 117
reversal, 48, 118, 133
opposition, 59n, 131, 140n
order, 31–2, 112, 140n

paradise, 23–5, 35, 57–8, 116, 130–1, 140n; *see also* heaven(s)
pedestal (*kursī*), 128
pen (*qalam*), 128–9
people of the book, 45
pilgrims, 69, 74n, 99–100, 102
pledge, 23, 25–6, 29, 33, 38, 46, 70, 142
polytheists (*mūshrikūn*), 27, 45; *see also* unbelief/unbelievers
prayer(s) (*ṣalāt*), 44–5, 51, 70, 81–3, 85, 87, 125
of *al-aḍḥā*, 102
cycle, daily, 81, 86, 89
fajr, 85–6
Friday congregational prayer (*al-jumʿa*), 5, 80, 87–8
ʿishāʾ, 83
maghrib, 85
supplicatory (*qunūt*), 83
witr, 83–5
ẓuhr (or noon) prayer, 81–2
precreation, 118–19
primordial
concept of *amāna*, 28
covenant, 26–7, 39
events, 30–1
time/moment, 22, 31, 35, 118
processions, 106
property, 35–6, 38, 145
prophecy, 6, 10n, 16, 73n, 76, 79, 139n, 145
prophet(s), 15–16, 25, 27–30, 33–4, 57–8, 66–7, 88, 97, 104, 123–4, 126–7, 132, 139n, 142, 144–5; *see also* Index of Names, Muḥammad
speaker-, 62, 66, 86, 89–90, 98
prostrations, 33, 85, 102, 125, 132
punishment, 29–30, 33, 48, 52–5, 70, 130, 148

qāʾim, 16, 27, 46, 54–5, 80, 82, 88–9, 94n, 101, 103–4, 119, 136
advent/rising of, 52, 54–7, 82, 86–7, 91, 99–103, 105, 107n, 147
al-qiyāma, 86, 125, 127, 130
qibla, 74n, 117, 119
qiyāma (resurrection), 51, 64, 82, 86, 88, 90, 103, 109, 117–18, 120, 124–5, 127, 130–1, 133–6, 138, 146–8
ceremony of, 119, 134
declaration of, 5, 9, 118, 123, 132
doctrine, 115–16, 134
realm of, 129–30, 132, 136
Quran/Quranic, 8, 16, 18, 25, 29, 43–6, 143–5, 148
apocalyptic imagery, 43, 47, 53, 58
apocalyptic narrative of, 43, 46, 48, 53, 55–6, 64, 145–6
correspondences of, 61–3
dualities of, 44, 47, 49
equivocal verses of, 14–15
ethics, 43–4
exegesis/commentary of, 43, 46, 68–9, 124
inscriptions, 72
narrative, 4, 28, 45–6, 48, 52–3, 56, 118–19
and oaths, 22, 27, 32, 34, 142
and resurrection/end of time, 43, 47, 49, 59n, 62, 64–5, 71, 142
sense of election, 143, 148
symbolic meanings of, 51
terms, 8, 61, 88
verses, 48–50, 62–5, 68, 72, 87, 123

Ramadan, 5, 87–91, 102, 109
realm(s)
of the *dunyā*, 137
of life (*ʿālam-i mardum*), 128
natural, 48
of reality, 129–31, 134
of resurrection, 117, 129, 131–2
of similitudes (*kawn-i mushābahat*), 137
of spirit (*ʿālam-i jān*), 128
spiritual, 127–8, 130–1, 136, 138, 147
of the sun (*iqlīm-i khurshīd*), 132
symbolic, 15, 18, 24
temporal, 53
terrestrial, 67, 79, 86, 105, 145
of unseen, 3, 51
reckoning, 43–4, 71, 77
religionists, 7
religion(s)/religious, 7, 22–4, 28, 33–4, 45, 82, 84, 89–91, 94n, 100, 105, 116, 123–4, 128, 136
apocalyptic, 71–2

authority, 4, 117–18
community, 46, 143
and covenants/oaths, 25–6, 32
dīn, 43, 53, 65
hierarchy, 2, 58
identity, 35
inward and outward, 82, 84–5
knowledge *ʿilm*, 67–8, 77, 99
laws, 15–16, 18, 87, 109, 112, 118–19, 127
movements, 9, 36
perfection of, 60n, 65, 86–7
renewal of, 84, 86
scholars (*ʿālim*), 67
sociology of, 76
studies, field of, 3, 6–7
true, 19–20, 28–9, 36–7, 42, 68–9, 72, 86, 124
religiosity, 1, 5, 8, 29
repentence, 77
re-signification, 46–53, 55, 57–8, 61, 64, 142, 146–7
resurrection (*qiyāma*), 43, 46–7, 51–2, 64–5, 68, 77, 109, 115–16, 126–7, 132, 136–7, 145–6
declaration of, 5, 9, 119, 132
imagery of, 138
Lord of the, 127, 129
master of, 118, 123, 125, 127, 131, 138, 146
realm of, 117, 129, 137
Resurrection, Day of, 27, 47, 52, 104, 126
Resurrector, 125–6, 132
Revelation, Book of, 6
revelation(s), 15–18, 145
reward, 25, 33, 53, 91, 129
rituals, 5, 6, 8, 31–2, 89, 105–6, 120; *see also* ceremony(s)
performance, 92, 122n
rūḥ al-qudus (Holy Spirit), 128

sacred, 132, 146
centre, 92, 97–8
lineage/genealogy, 23–4
months/calendar, 68–9, 74n, 89
vs profane, 119
text(s), 17–18
saints, 20n, 24; *see also* friends, of God
ṣalāt see prayer(s)
salvation, 4, 17, 30, 43, 47, 49, 52, 65, 82, 124, 128–9, 131, 136, 142, 144–5
satr (concealment), 58, 84–5, 88–9, 136
saved, 1, 49, 53, 71, 128–9, 131, 144
secrecy/secret(s), 8, 17, 23, 28–31, 38, 42, 46–8, 54, 83, 84–5, 88–9, 102, 105
daʿwa, 47–8, 89
knowledge, 4, 24, 28–9, 80, 135
sects, 25
sermons, 6, 125–6
sharīʿa, 81–2, 86, 115, 117, 127, 135–6
abolition of, 19, 109, 115, 117, 119
Shia/Shiism, 2, 7, 16–17, 30, 42, 46, 48–9, 77–9, 113, 140n
hermeneutics, 8, 14–15
imāms, 2, 4, 19, 52, 78
Ithnā ʿAsharīyah (Twelvers), 17
Persianate, 109, 117
vision of, 109, 133–5
writings/works of, 3, 104, 107n
shirk (ascribing partners), 129
signs (*āyāt*), 52–3, 86–7, 99–100, 103
social
order, 122n
solidarity, 116
structures, 22, 42, 120, 142, 148
transformations, 1
sociology
of millenarian movements, 143
of religion, 76
soul(s) (*nafs*), 18, 25, 57, 69–70, 86, 100, 102–4, 115, 128–9, 140n
sources, 2, 7–8, 43, 76, 110
speaker-prophets, 62, 66, 86, 89, 98; *see also nāṭiqs*
spiritual
ascent, 18, 92, 98, 115, 137–8, 147
reality, 18, 136, 138
states/ranks, 88, 91, 99, 137, 147
success (*falāḥ, thawab*), 53
Sufism/Sufi, 16, 134–5
terms, 115, 134
works, 3
sunna, 24, 66, 68, 84
Sunnis/Sunnism, 14, 17, 115–16, 134–6, 140n
symbolism/symbolic, 15, 35, 37–8, 42–3, 45, 49, 58, 72, 87–8, 90, 98–9, 106, 111–12, 115–16, 118, 122n, 130, 133–5, 143, 146–7, 148–9
analogues/correspondences, 79–82, 85–6, 89, 100, 103, 106
apocalyptic, 43, 79, 111–12, 116, 118, 130, 133–5, 148–9
interpretation, 3, 9, 80, 147
meanings, 17, 51, 80, 87, 105
realm, 15, 18, 24
referents, 8, 47, 62, 68
symbols, 19, 49, 59n, 68, 79, 88, 105, 122n, 135, 146

tablet (*lawḥ*), 128–30
tafsīr (exegesis), 15, 18, 71

tanzil (revelation of scripture), 15, 18
taqiyya (dissimulation, precaution), 83–4, 127, 136
taslīm (salutation [on the Prophet]), 83–4
tawḥīd (divine unity, monotheism), 17, 65, 128–9, 144–5
ta'wīl (esoteric interpretation), 2–5, 8–9, 14–15, 17–20, 24, 27, 30, 34, 43, 53–8, 61–2, 66–9, 89–92, 98, 100, 103, 124, 142, 146–7
  and *bāṭin/ẓāhir*, 71, 85, 99, 101–2, 118, 134–5
  of the prayer, 81, 85–6
  and symbolic referents, 47, 49, 80–1
taxes, 34–5, 46
  bulgha, 35
  fifth (*khums*), 35
telos, 47, 86–7
  of history, 118, 148
temporality(ies), 6, 12n, 57, 69, 122n, 131, 138, 145–6
  imminent, 104
  linear, 9, 92, 105
  plane of, 54
terrestrial
  authority, 105, 133
  locus of heaven, 130
  mission, 20, 34, 36
  plane/realm, 67, 79, 86, 105, 145
  salvation, 52
  utopia, 22–3, 36, 42, 142
test/trial (*miḥna*), 84, 88
theodicy, 12n, 119, 122n
theology/theological, 4–5, 7–9, 30, 51, 73n, 76, 110, 118, 148
  apocalyptic, 123, 131, 136
  Ismaili, 17
  texts, 3, 6
throne (*'arsh*), 128–30
time, 1, 6, 36–7, 119, 122n, 131, 146
  appointed, 47, 56, 64
  cyclical, 105, 132
  days of the week, 86
  months, 69
  of prayers, 82, 85
  primordial, 22, 31, 35, 118
tithes/tithing, 8, 34, 38, 46, 142; *see also* taxes
Torah, 25
trial (*balā'*), 88, 105
trust (*amāna*), 27–8
Trusted Spirit (*rūḥ al-amīn*), 128
truth/true, 29, 38, 65, 67, 70, 75, 77, 91, 98, 100–1, 103–4, 124, 143, 147–8
  esoteric, hidden, 16, 18, 48, 125, 129
  vs false, 23, 47, 71–2, 137
  ḥaqīqa, 15, 18, 36, 118
typologies, 44, 49–50, 59n, 144

unbelief/unbelievers, 49, 110, 145
unity, 116
  divine (*tawḥīd*), 17, 26, 65, 128–9, 144–5
  people of, 127, 129, 140n
  realm of, 129, 131–2
unseen, 18, 50, 56
  world/realm of, 3, 51
unveiling, 23–4, 46, 51, 83, 89, 102–3, 118, 134, 147
utopia, 4, 8, 19–20, 38, 80, 142, 149
  expectations of, 22, 36, 80–1, 147–8
  terrestrial, 22–3, 36, 42, 76, 106, 142
  vision of, 36, 106, 146, 149

walāya, 4, 16–17, 20n, 23–4, 26, 28, 42, 47, 49–50, 52, 55, 58, 60n, 135, 142
  Arabic root w-l-y, 16
  of the commander of the faithful, 50–1
  counter-*walāya*, 50–1, 60n
  of the wrongdoers, 55
walīs (helpers), 16–17, 20n, 81
  of the time, 92, 97–9, 105
waṣī/waṣiyya (legatee), 16, 67–9, 84
  'Alī, 27, 51, 84, 89
water, 45, 67, 98–9
wealth, 25, 138
world, spiritual, 127–8, 130–1, 136
worship, 19, 25–6, 45, 52

ẓāhir (apparent, literal), 14, 16, 18, 67–8, 71, 81–3, 85, 97–9, 101, 118, 134–5

EU representative:
Easy Access System Europe
Mustamäe tee 50, 10621 Tallinn, Estonia
Gpsr.requests@easproject.com

www.ingramcontent.com/pod-product-compliance
Lightning Source LLC
Chambersburg PA
CBHW051118230426
43667CB00014B/2633
9781474432207